The Thrill of
the Chase

The Thrill of the Chase

WOMEN AND THEIR NORTH AMERICAN BIG-GAME TROPHIES

by

Kathy Etling

&

Susan Campbell Reneau

SAFARI PRESS

The trademark Safari Press ® is registered with the U.S. Patent and Trademark Office and in other countries.

Etling, Kathy
Reneau, Susan Campbell

First edition

Safari Press Inc.

2004, Long Beach, California

ISBN 1-57157-180-9

Library of Congress Catalog Card Number: 2003109078

10 9 8 7 6 5 4 3 2 1

Printed in USA

Readers wishing to receive the Safari Press catalog, featuring many fine books on big-game hunting, wingshooting, and sporting firearms, should write to Safari Press Inc., P.O. Box 3095, Long Beach, CA 90803, USA. Tel: (714) 894-9080 or visit our Web site at www.safaripress.com.

Christmas '03

To My Darling Daughter

Enjoy

your proud & loving

Dad

TABLE OF CONTENTS

FOREWORD

For too many years, hunting has been considered a male activity. No one knows that better than I, since I was raised in an Italian-American family where only the men hunted. That scenario wasn't limited only to my family, for I never saw a woman in the woods from the days I began hunting in the early 1950s through the next couple of decades. There were exceptions, of course, but hunting has largely been dominated by men.

That all changed during the so-called feminist revolution when women tossed away bras, learned how to drive bulldozers and eighteen-wheelers, and taught themselves how to shoot. This movement wasn't cheerfully embraced by all, especially a certain segment of America's menfolk, though some indeed welcomed women into the hunting fraternity. Today, the sight of a female hunter no longer raises eyebrows, though there is the occasional man who is still uncomfortable with women afield. That's becoming the exception rather than the rule, and happily, more and more women are showing up wearing camo, hunting boots, and bug spray.

I was guilty of being one of those males who was initially complacent, if not completely disinterested, in woman hunters. I have a son and three daughters, and it was Dan who received all my attention when it came to hunting and shooting, even though he is my second oldest child. When he was eight, I bought him a BB gun; a .22 when he was 10; a .243 when he was 12, and so on. He sat on my shoulders when he was in diapers as I worked my bird dog in the pheasant fields. He accompanied me on many of my hunts before he was old enough to get a hunting license, and occasionally Janette, my oldest child, went along as well. Janette was shy and quiet, and read books in hunting camp while Dan tagged along with me.

Janette came home from college one day and told me her boyfriend hadn't invited her on the annual deer hunt with him and his dad and brothers.

"I'd like to hunt too, Dad," she said, "but no one ever asks me to go."

I was shocked, and when Janette admitted that she had been disappointed when I had taken only Dan and ignored her, I was dismayed. I never knew she wanted to hunt, but, then again, I had never bothered to ask. I immediately taught her to shoot my .30-06, and a month later she shot a forked-horn muley buck. That little deer will always rank high as a grand trophy in my memory.

I didn't make the same mistake with my other daughters. Judi and Angela learned how to shoot when they were very young, and when each got their hunting licenses, they easily took limits of cottontail rabbits with scope-sighted .22s. From there they graduated to deer and elk, and I enjoyed teaching them about the woods, animal behavior, and hunting strategies.

My own experiences were mirrored in what I read in this book. I not only found it interesting to learn how other females entered the hunting world, but I also enjoyed reading tales of their hunts. Kathy Etling, one of the coauthors, is an old hunting pal of mine. I can recall times when she and her husband, Bob, and I hiked into remote woods with heavy backpacks to hunt elk. Kathy is one of the best hunters I know, and I never once considered her gender to be a disadvantage. I've also known coauthor Susan Reneau for years, and am familiar with the work she's done compiling data for the many hunting books she's edited. Susan recently took to the woods with a rifle and is now an accomplished hunter as well.

One of the most interesting aspects of the thirty-one women who share their hunting memories in this book is the fact that they're *passionate* about hunting. They aren't out to prove themselves because they're women; they truly love the outdoors. That feeling comes through clearly with every chapter.

I hunted caribou in the Arctic with Madleine Kay, one of the contributors, when she was the only other woman in camp with fifteen hunters and ten Inuit guides. Although it was a tough hunt, she never complained when we took our canoes across eighty miles of the Arctic Ocean; in fact, it was Madleine who shot the biggest bull, which came as no surprise to anyone. And then there's my Canadian friend Erna Fillatre, another of the contributors who has, amazingly, taken nine bull elk on her own with no help from anyone. Erna is a petite woman who has always welcomed the profound challenge of finding an elk, shooting it, and somehow transporting it to her pickup truck by herself. I'm acquainted with a number of the other contributors as well, and all can easily hold their own with male hunters.

A recent study funded by the National Shooting Sports Foundation revealed that the number of women entering the hunting fraternity is growing by leaps and bounds. For years I've been an instructor for BOW workshops conducted by SCI at their Wyoming ranch, and I find it extremely gratifying to introduce a woman to shooting and then watch her graduate from a .22 to a magnum caliber.

Each woman who shares her hunting experiences with us in *The Thrill of the Chase* has a story to tell. I've enjoyed reading each story, and I'm sure you will, too. The book inspires confidence, dedication, enthusiasm, and above all, a sincere love of the outdoors. It's must reading, not only for experienced male and female hunters, but for everyone who hesitates to take that first big step in the woods. All of us can learn from the wonderful stories related within these pages.

Jim Zumbo, Hunting Editor
OUTDOOR LIFE

INTRODUCTION

When I first became a hunter, few people could believe a woman would want to hunt just for the sheer joy of it. Men thought I went hunting so my boyfriend—now my husband—could shoot more game, using my tag, of course. Women thought I'd become a hunter so I could meet more men. Neither notion was true.

The first time I went deer hunting, another deer hunter actually accused me of letting my boyfriend shoot my deer earlier in the day. That evening, while several deer hunters were out 'coon hunting, this fellow challenged me to knock Bre'r Coon out of the treetops with one shot from the communal .22. Never one to back down, I did just that, surprising even myself in the process. Mr. Sour-Grapes packed his bag and went home, muttering as he left something about "a woman's place. . . ."

A woman's place. How often have I heard that phrase? Surprisingly, not very. How often have other female hunters heard it? Well, back when I started hunting nearly forty years ago, I'm sure most of my sister hunters heard it fairly often. Of course, back then not many women were hunters, and most of those who did hunt resided in places like Alaska, Wyoming, Idaho, and Montana, where the frontier was reality, not memory, and hunting was the traditional way to put meat on the table.

When I started hunting, I'd attract a milling check-station crowd whenever I brought in a white-tailed deer or wild turkey I'd bagged myself. Today, my daughter and I often meet other successful females at the same check stations. It's been almost forty years coming, but I've lived long enough to see the results of stubborn perseverance, a gut realization that hunting is not only great fun for the entire family and a source of healthy, organically grown meat, but a sport that is morally right. Women of all ages can find the same sense of joy and fulfillment that has served me and other women so well by merely deciding to give hunting a chance. Luckily for all hunters and for the future of the sport, they have and continue to do so—and the face of hunting will never again be the same.

I, for one, look forward to a new hunting tradition: introducing my granddaughter, Shelby Ply, to the sport. Maybe, someday, if I'm lucky, there will be a grandson to school in the ways of the wilderness as well.

Hunting and bowhunting are both sports that rely not so much on brute strength but on stealthiness, intellect, woodsmanship, perseverance, and sheer physical endurance. To hunt truly wild animals in their native habitats and to do it legally, morally, and ethically requires not only a love of wildlife and wilderness, but a lot of gumption, too. Hunters are tested—all the time—by the plethora of videos they watch and by a certain segment of the hunting world that is impressed by results only. But the sport is called "hunting," not "killing." Anyone can take a junket to the nearest so-called "game farm" and kill an animal. That is not hunting, not by any stretch of the imagination.

A true hunter, a person who is a hunter in her mind and soul as well as in her heart, would never equate game-farm killing with hunting the way it is supposed to be done. The two activities are as different as night is from day and should never be confused.

Hunting, the pursuit of our magnificent big-game animals on their own turf, stands on its own merits, and will forever. Hunting! There's nothing like it in the world! And for that I thank God every day.

Kathy Etling
Osage Beach, Missouri
August 2003

INTRODUCTION

When Kathy Etling and I decided to write a book about women who love to hunt big game, we knew this would be a unique project. We both love to hunt and spend as much time in the field as we can during various seasons to fill our tags for such favorites as mule and white-tailed deer, elk, and pronghorn.

My passion for hunting was ignited only recently, in 1998, when I finally mustered enough courage to load a rifle, fire it, and attend hunter-safety classes with twelve-year-olds. Unlike Kathy, who has hunted her entire teen and adult life, I was a true novice to hunting, even though I had written about the topic for years and lived with a husband and three sons who all urged me to hunt with them. I can identify with women who tell me they would never hunt because they don't like to get cold and wet and don't like the sight of something being killed. I was in their shoes just a few years ago.

For me, hunting is not about killing but about absorbing the total experience of nature. When I hunt, I become one with the world and the ebb and flow of life and death. To write a book that highlights some of the more astounding women hunters in North America, I knew, would give me more confidence and inspire me to do the same. Too, I thought these stories would make a fabulous book for anyone who loves to hunt or would like to begin.

The Thrill of the Chase was born in 2000 when Kathy and I exchanged our experiences in the field and I shared with her how I had discovered the wonders of hunting. I was on deadline for another book, *Colorado's Biggest Bucks and Bulls*, second edition, which features twenty-two women and hundreds of men who took Boone and Crockett, Pope and Young, and Longhunter Muzzleloader big-game trophies in Colorado from 1850 to the present. She was impressed that I was raised in a family that never hunted and was influenced by a mother who would be termed modestly antihunting.

My father was an avid deep-sea and fly fisherman who served as a U.S. Marine Corps officer. My time with my father was limited because of his many assignments in Asia during the Korean and Vietnam Wars, so fishing with my dad was a welcome change from my normal childhood experiences. I was responsible for gutting the fish, my favorite part of fishing, and for carrying the string of fish back to our station wagon. Fishing was my only chance to explore the outdoors, and it gave me time to get to know my father.

When I wasn't fishing with my dad, I was collecting grasshoppers and fireflies in mayonnaise jars, picking up jellyfish and snails, and keeping garter snakes as pets for a day. Throughout all these outdoor experiences, however, I never hunted.

A conference held in August 1990 at the University of Wisconsin-Stevens Point was among the first to foster frank discussions about why women do not hunt. The results were startling to me because they reflected so much of what had happened in my own life. The top two reasons offered by women interviewed at this conference who did not hunt were the images portrayed by the antihunting movement and the expense and shortage of suitable equipment. Another factor was social pressures against hunting from parents, friends, and other family members because it was a "man's sport." In my case, hunting was never discussed or offered as an option as I grew up, and I knew no women who hunted. The people attending the conference echoed my experience, saying that few women role models existed. Just as significant, most conference participants said they grew up in anti- or nonhunting families or families that enjoyed fishing over hunting. That certainly was my family.

The 1990 conference motivated dozens of women to call the event's organizers to beg for training and field experiences, and the first workshops of Becoming an Outdoors-Woman were created to meet the need. A separate chapter in this book features BOW and other outstanding organizations that motivate women to enjoy the outdoors.

Contrary to the image of hunters portrayed in the media and by antihunting groups, women who hunt and shoot are more educated, more politically active, more outspoken, and wealthier than the general female population. These findings are among the results of a series of surveys conducted by the National Rifle Association in 2002 to determine the makeup of the women who join the NRA. NRA women members were almost twice as likely as the average woman to write a public official, and also voted more often in local, state, and federal elections. They also were more likely to be active in a church, business, or service organizations. An NRA woman member is more likely to have attended college and to have a higher median household income.

The women featured in *The Thrill of the Chase* are dynamic, involved, courageous, intelligent, and independent. Every one of the women I interviewed for the book hunts alone or with a male friend or family member and seldom sees a female hunter in the field. Certainly, that has been my experience when I hunt in the West. I have seen only three women in the field, and they were with their husbands. I hope our book will motivate more men to take their daughters and wives afield so the hunting tradition can be shared with a new generation. And I hope this book will motivate more girls and women to go outside and hunt. If anyone will inspire them, it will be the women featured in these pages.

Susan Campbell Reneau
Missoula, Montana, and Pueblo, Colorado
August 2003

ACKNOWLEDGMENTS

I'd like to acknowledge all the women who cooperated in the writing of this book and who unselfishly loaned us their precious photos for our use. I'd also like to thank the various personnel at the record-keeping organizations who helped us gather information while we were writing this book.

I'd also like to thank my good friend, hunting buddy, and mentor, Jim Zumbo, and also the NRA's John Zent, editor of *American Hunter*, and his assistant Linda Faulk, *Trophy Hunter* magazine's Rusty Hall, Guy Sagi, Don Burgess of the Rocky Mountain Elk Foundation, and Rich LaRocco. Thanks also go out to Russell Thornberry, Darren Thornberry, Linda O'Connor, and Jackie Bushman, all of the fine Buckmasters organization, as well as T. J. Schwanky, Michael Hamrick, Bob Bergquist, Larry Heathington, Michael Hamrick, Don Kisky, and Dick Johndrow.
—Kathy Etling

I'd like to extend my thanks to the women and their family members who provided photographs and detailed hunting stories for this book. Thanks also to the staff of the Boone and Crockett Club, Becoming an Outdoors-Woman, Safari Club International, National Wild Turkey Federation, National Rifle Association, National Muzzleloading Rifle Association, and Pope and Young Club for providing us with information about their organizations and about various big-game records.
—Susan Campbell Reneau

Four major national programs exist in which the primary objective is to educate and encourage women to hunt, shoot, fish, as well as take part more fully in other traditionally male-oriented forms of outdoors recreational activities. These four programs and their sponsoring organizations are: Safari Club International's Foundation Sables, the National Wild Turkey Federation's Women in the Outdoors (WITO), the National Rifle Association's Women on Target, and the Becoming an Outdoors-Woman (BOW) program, first sponsored by the University of Wisconsin. Each program is discussed in the following paragraphs, starting with the oldest program and ending with the most recent.

Safari Club International's Foundation Sables

In 1984, women working or affiliated with Safari Club International (SCI) decided to organize as a new group: a foundation within SCI dedicated to the promotion and propagation of SCI's many fine conservation, educational, and humanitarian programs.

The Safari Club International Sables annually raises thousands of dollars for SCI programs and activities, including the American Wilderness Leadership School and the International Wildlife Museum. Here, students learn about wildlife at the museum.

This group, originally called the Safari Club Lionesses, is now known as the Sables.[1]

The two major beneficiaries of the Sables' volunteerism and fund-raising activities are the American Wilderness Leadership School and the International Wildlife Museum. Each year at SCI's international convention, the Sables host an auction where guests can bid on diamond jewelry, original artwork, luxurious furs, limited-edition firearms, and exotic trips throughout the world. The proceeds from the various fund-raisers benefit the school and museum, as well as a variety of conservation projects. Many projects directly benefit wildlife, such as providing funding for much-needed mineral supplements for the bighorn lambs of Wyoming's well-known Whiskey Mountain herd. These supplemental minerals have helped wildlife biologists working with the herd's lambs alleviate or eliminate rough coats, swollen eyes, respiratory ailments, nasal secretions, retarded growth rates, slumped shoulders, and stiff legs.

At the time when the Sables were still calling themselves the Safari Club Lionesses, the members organized a Save Our School campaign to retire a large mortgage held on SCI's educational facility, the Granite Ranch in Jackson, Wyoming. The mortgage was paid off quickly, but SCI's leadership no sooner had taken full control of the title when a fire totally destroyed the ranch's cook cabin, which had served as classroom, dining hall, and sitting room. The Sables met this challenge, too, retiring this new mortgage in 1985. Women who want to experience adventure and learn more about the great outdoors travel from all over the world to attend SCI's American Wilderness Leadership School, formerly known as the Granite Ranch, thanks to the selfless and ceaseless efforts of the Sables. Courses taught there include hands-on instruction in shooting, camping, fishing, whitewater rafting, and wilderness survival, to name just a few.

Tucson, Arizona's International Wildlife Museum also benefits from the efforts of SCI and the Sables. There visitors can view more than four hundred species of mammals, birds, reptiles, and insects on display in realistic dioramas depicting the natural world. The museum was conceived and designed with children in mind, and

---

[1]*SCI also recognizes top female hunters. Each year the group bestows their Diana Award upon an outstanding female hunter in recognition of her hunting abilities, as well as her service to conservation. This award, named for the mythical goddess of the forests and the hunt, focuses not only on a woman's hunting accomplishments, including the variety and quality of the world's big-game animal species she's taken, but upon her dedication to wildlife conservation and education as well as her overall involvement in SCI activities. The Diana Award is an eagerly awaited honor that is presented at SCI's final banquet each year.*

young visitors are encouraged to handle artifacts, view live animals, and explore dioramas. Interactive computers, as well as wildlife films, motivate students to investigate the natural world and its many wonders further. The Sables ever provided the museum with interest-free loans to help finance projects as varied as an oasis entrance for the building and a projection room.

SCI's educational efforts continue to receive substantial support from the Sables. Members give generously of both time and money. The Sables financially supports regional and national 4-H shooting programs, as well as Becoming an Outdoors-Woman programs. In addition, the group helps to introduce inner city children to nature and all her wonders through their sponsorship of the Sensory Safari program.

Another innovative example of the Sables' work is Safari in a Box. Sables' volunteers pack large boxes with animal bones, skulls, skins, and other wildlife- and nature-related objects. These boxes are then shipped to classrooms throughout the United States. The Sables' version of Safari in a Box was based upon a similar program created by the Pennsylvania Game Commission. Sables members will also visit local schools to teach children firsthand about wildlife and conservation using the hands-on teaching aids to be found in their clever Safari in a Box learning kits.

Each year at SCI's international convention, a lively auction by the Sables raises money for a variety of projects. Members of the 2001 Sables governing board included, left to right: Ellen Thomas, Jeannie Epley, Wilma Kim, Audrey Murtland, Chrissie Jackson, Mary Parker, Barbara Strawberry, Janet Nyce, Dee Ridley, Kathy Middleton, and Marty Paulin.

To learn more about Safari Club International's Foundation Sables, log on to the organization's Web site at http://www.firstforhunters.org/content/website/midpanel/sciwoman/, or call national headquarters in Tucson, Arizona, at 520-620-1220.

Becoming an Outdoors-Woman

A conference entitled "Breaking Down Barriers to Participation of Women in Angling and Hunting" turned out to be groundbreaking on its own merits. Meetings to discuss problems confronting women in the outdoors were held at the University of Wisconsin (UW) – Stevens Point on 25 August 1990. A workshop focus group identified twenty-one barriers preventing girls and women from fully enjoying outdoors activities. Chief among them was what many attendees regarded as the primary obstacle: Girls were neither taught outdoors skills as children, nor were they included in outdoors activities while they were growing up. With no basis in the outdoors to build upon, women failed to participate in outdoors recreation as adults. Thanks to that 1990 conference, the first BOW workshop was conducted in 1991.

Faculty from the UW College of Natural Resources, led by Associate Dean Christine L. Thomas, joined members of the Wisconsin Coon Hunters Association, the Wisconsin Bear Hunters Association, Badger Fly Fishers, Wisconsin Wildlife Federation, Wisconsin Hunter Education Association, Safari Club International, and the National Rifle Association in organizing and teaching that first workshop's courses. Personnel from a number of state fish and game agencies attended as well. At the program's conclusion, Dr. Thomas was gratified to receive requests for workshop information and guidance from twenty additional wildlife agencies.

"As media coverage intensified, I also began to receive phone calls and letters from women who wanted to learn how to hunt and fish, and who thought that we might be teaching these things at our workshop," wrote Christine Thomas. "We could see that there was an obvious need that could be addressed by clinics like ours."

BOW workshops have grown until each year they now reach many tens of thousands of women who hail from forty-four states and seven Canadian provinces. Many workshops are held in some states several times annually to prepare new participants for various hunting and fishing seasons. Waiting lists fill up quickly for courses designed to introduce participants to hunting, shooting, and fishing in an enjoyable, nonthreatening atmosphere. A three-day BOW program will usually offer courses in firearms safety, basic fishing, camping, shotgun and rifle shooting, camp cookery, canoeing, orienteering, and plant and wildlife identification.

Archery skills are learned at BOW workshops. (Photograph courtesy of Becoming an Outdoors-Woman)

Beyond Bow programs offer advanced education to women who want to take their outdoors education to another level. Beyond Bow participants might sign up for an all-day canoe trip, a day-long pheasant hunt, or a weekend backpacking trip into the high country, to name just a few of the adventures that await them.

BOW workshops are usually held at a camp or resort. Meals and equipment are generally provided for one flat rate that sometimes includes lodging as well. Days are filled with hands-on lessons in various outdoors skills. Women eighteen years or older are eligible to attend BOW workshops and participate in Beyond Bow advanced outdoors training courses and events.

To find a BOW workshop near you, log on to www.uwsp.edu/cnr/bow/ or contact your local, state, or provincial game and fish or wildlife agency. Or you can call BOW's international headquarters at 877-269-6626.

National Wild Turkey Federation's Women in the Outdoors

Turkey hunters as well as nonhunters sign up for the myriad courses offered by the National Wild Turkey Federation's

Learning to shoot is one aspect of Becoming an Outdoors-Woman program. (Photograph by Jack Reneau)

offshoot, Women in the Outdoors (WITO). Hundreds of events have been sponsored around the United States and Canada since the program's inception in 1997. In late 2001, membership received a boost when members of the Women's Shooting Sports Foundation (WSSF) merged with WITO to create a single entity.

NWTF regional staff members today coordinate with local North American NWTF and WITO chapter leaders to produce events geared toward introducing women to traditional outdoors pursuits. WITO even publishes its own glossy, four-color quarterly magazine, *Women in the Outdoors.* Articles run the gamut from wilderness hunting adventures to wild game recipes, from health tips to WITO news and views. WITO's volunteers and staff are skilled at encouraging girls and women to enjoy the outdoors and to do all the fascinating things that men have enjoyed for centuries.

The WITO program was officially founded not only to provide women with enjoyable outdoors activities and educational support, but also to help conserve wild turkeys and to preserve the hunting tradition. In 1998, membership was a mere 1,300. By the early 2000s, that number had increased almost forty-fold, with additional members joining each day.

For details about the WITO and other NWTF programs, call national headquarters at 803-637-3105 or visit their Web site at www.nwtf.org.

National Rifle Association's Women on Target

Women have been involved with the National Rifle Association since the organization's birth in 1871. Throughout the group's history, the NRA has created and designed programs especially for women. December 1999, however, marked the beginning of a new era. Women on Target was formed by the group with the specific goal of encouraging women to become involved with hunting and shooting in a friendly, noncompetitive environment. Each year, members and guests participate in a variety of activities, including organized hunting trips, shooting clinics, and charity shooting events.

Recent surveys conducted by the National Sporting Goods Association reveal that approximately two million women in the United States hunt, while four million target shoot. Women on Target provides these experienced female hunters and shooters with the opportunity to mentor beginning members in real-life situations, as well as in educational classes. Recent hunting trips taken by Women on Target members include an early fall Wyoming pronghorn expedition, a Pennsylvania whitetail hunt, and a duck hunt held in California's wetlands.

"Women on Target creates many opportunities for women shooters to hone their shooting and hunting skills," said Stephanie Henson, manager of NRA's Women's Programs. As the twentieth century came to a close, the NRA was being increasingly bombarded with calls from women who wanted to learn how to hunt and shoot. Women on Target was created to fill an obvious and ever-increasing need. The group's events emphasize shooting, firearms safety, and firearms maintenance and inspection. Also taught are the basics of firearms accuracy for each category of firearms—rifles, shotguns, and pistols, as well as black-powder versions of these three types of firearms. "Women on Target differs from other outdoors programs geared toward women in that our focus is solely upon hunting and shooting," Stephanie explained. "It's the next step upward once another organization's introductory programs have been completed; moreover, our group gives women the chance to apply what they've learned elsewhere."

Women on Target's instructional video, entitled *Hunting with the Women of the NRA*, was awarded top honors at the Outdoor Writers Association of America's 2002 gathering. This award, as well as others like it, serves to illustrate the importance that groups dedicated to fostering the environment and preserving the outdoors traditions of hunting, shooting, and angling place upon the recruitment of women, and, by extension, their children into their ranks.

The NRA's Women's Programs department also coordinates that organization's popular Refuse to Be a Victim seminars and instructor workshops that focus on personal awareness as a means of preventing criminal confrontations. Special emphasis is given to security considerations within the home, vehicle, while traveling, and even while using the Internet. Refuse to Be a Victim programs are conducted for groups consisting of both men and women, although women-only seminars are still offered in most locations.

The NRA in 1995 also established the Sybil Ludington's Women's Freedom Award to be bestowed annually upon a female leader dedicated to the defense of Second Amendment freedoms, or for her tireless efforts on behalf of hunting or shooting. Recipients to date include Marion P. Hammer, first female NRA president, Suzanna Gratia Hupp, a tireless Texan who has spent years speaking out in favor of Right to Carry laws, and Sue King, first president of the Women's Shooting Sports Foundation as well as one of the subjects of this book.

The NRA's new monthly journal, *Woman's Outlook*, ties it all together for its women members with articles of interest to any women who likes to hunt or shoot or who supports the Second Amendment to our nation's Constitution.

To learn more about the NRA and its programs, visit the organization's Web site at www.nrahq.org. Information related to women's programs and activities may be found at www.nrahq.org/women/. Or you may call the NRA's Women's Programs Department at 800-861-1166 or 703-267-1413.

RECORD-KEEPING PROGRAMS FOR BIG GAME

Three organizations, the Boone and Crockett Club (B&C), the Pope and Young Club (P&Y), and the National Muzzle Loading Rifle Association's (NMLRA) Longhunter Program collect and maintain the records of North American big-game animals using the measuring system created in 1950 by the Boone and Crockett Club. Boone and Crockett, which was founded in 1887, accepts for listing in their record book only North American big-game animals that belong to thirty-eight separate species or subspecies taken in legal, fair chase. Record-class animals are recognized whether antlers, horns, tusks, or skulls have been picked up or whether animals were killed by hunters. All methods of taking game—modern firearms, black powder, archery, pickup—are included within Boone and Crockett's pages in a celebration of the very finest North American big-game animals known to have walked the continent. The Boone and Crockett record book, first published in 1932, is a testament to the success of modern biological methods of wildlife management and fair-chase principles.

The Pope and Young Club was established in 1961 to recognize North American big-game animals taken with archery equipment. Minimum qualifying scores for each species recognized by Pope and Young are significantly lower than for Boone and Crockett simply because it is so much more difficult for a bow hunter to kill a large, trophy-class animal than for someone using a firearm.

The National Muzzle Loading Rifle Association founded the Longhunter Muzzleloading Big-Game Records Program for North American big game in 1988. Minimum qualifying scores for each recognized North American species or subspecies again are lower to reflect the difficulties involved in getting close enough to a mature big-game animal to kill it using one of these primitive—and often undependable—firearms.

Two other organizations also maintain records of big-game animals. Unlike the preceding three organizations, neither Buckmasters Trophy Record System (BTR) nor Safari Club International (SCI) focuses on perfect symmetry of horn or antler. These latter groups qualify an animal based upon the total amount of antler or horn mass acquired at the time it is killed. Such systems are termed 'hunter-friendly' because lack of symmetry deductions do not apply toward the total score. In other words, these latter two systems appropriately reward an animal for all the tremendous variations naturally found in its headgear.

Our last group, Safari Club International (SCI), had come into its own by the end of 1971. The organization's minimum big-game qualifying scores are, as noted previously, much lower than Boone and Crockett's. The advantages to this system include the fact that many more hunters are recognized for their accomplishments, which keeps record-book listings high.

SCI recognizes not only North American big-game animals, but animals from all over the world. It is possible for a hunter to take trophy-caliber animals anywhere, and then later be rewarded by being listed in one of SCI's many record books. SCI also recognizes hunters who have taken various 'slams' of animals, such as the world's sheep, goats, big cats, boars, bears, etc. Another level of recognition is awarded to those who participate in SCI's World Hunting Awards Program. Hunters receive Copper, Silver, Gold, or Diamond levels of recognition depending on how many different species of a particular category of animal the hunter has harvested.

The major downside to SCI, in the authors' opinions, is that the organization also recognizes big-game animals taken within high-fenced areas where "fair chase" often does not exist. The authors do not believe in hunting any high-fenced areas, which we believe exist as a travesty to an otherwise noble pursuit, and so we have done our best to ensure that no high-fenced animals are represented within the pages of this book.

The Buckmasters Trophy Record (BTR) scoring system formerly was known as the Alberta Trophy Scoring System. BTR does not penalize for lack of balance or symmetry in antlers. The system is used only for scoring whitetail and Coues deer at the present, although it could also be used on mule deer antlers. All Buckmasters trophies must be taken through methods of fair chase. Antler 'pick-ups' and 'sheds' are also recognized.

Under BTR antlers are classified as perfect, typical, semi-irregular, and irregular. Boone and Crockett, Pope and Young, and the Longhunters classify them as either typical or nontypical.

BTR further breaks down classifications to reflect hunting methods: centerfire rifle, shotgun, blackpowder, centerfire pistol, compound bow, recurve bow, longbow, or crossbow. Categories also exist for antlers that have been picked up after the bucks bearing them have died of natural causes, and also for shed antlers. BTR's system provides an excellent frame of records-keeping reference so that harvest difficulty is factored into each category. In other words, bucks killed with a longbow are listed with other longbow-taken bucks so that readers will not be comparing apples with oranges, so to speak.

All record-keeping associations add together various measurements of the respective sets of antlers or horns to arrive at a total "score." These measurements for antlers will usually include the length of each antler's main beam, the length of each of the rack's tines, and the circumferential measurements of the main beam at four different designated spots.

The horns of big-game animals are measured in a manner similar to that of antlered big game, while predators such as bears and cougars are scored by adding together the length and width measurements of their dried skulls.

Scores reported within this book may mean nothing to a reader who is unacquainted with the various record-keeping programs, but will reveal reams of information to anyone who is now a hunter or who has hunted in the past. Rest assured, dear reader, that as you make your way through the following chapters that the scores and scoring systems will become easier to understand.

Remember, too, that neither author hunts for a "score," but rather for the love of wilderness and wildlife, the beauty to be found in nature while fully engaged in the hunt, and the thrill of the chase, which is a thrill beyond all reckoning.

A CALCULATED APPROACH
MARY K. ANDERSON
Muskox, Mountain Caribou

Mary K. Anderson is one cool customer, and has been for many years. Mary recently traveled with husband, Tom Lovas, to Alaska's Kodiak Island, where she bagged a long-haired blond Kodiak bear with gorgeous dark chocolate legs and markings. It was not the ten-footer for which Mary had been hoping, but with spring weather late in arriving and only a few bears around, Mary was thrilled to get him. "Especially since his pelt was so beautiful," she said.

Mary has lived in Alaska for many years, so hunting the state's wilderness is easier for her than it would be for a nonresident. But making a trip from her suburban home to Kodiak, not far from the state's western shoreline, still requires a great deal of logistical savvy, which Mary seems to come by naturally. "Anyone who has ever been to Kodiak in the spring knows that the weather will be miserable," she said. "We'd planned to take our large tent and camp just off the beach.

"To prepare for a trip like this involves a lot of work," Mary continued. "In Alaska there's no such thing as going hunting for a weekend. Every trip becomes an expedition. You must first decide on the best time to go, then plan what to take and how to get there. We shipped our gear to Kodiak the week before we were due to arrive. We flew commercial jet to Kodiak on a Friday so that we'd be able to check in prior to our hunt, as required by law, with local officials of the Alaska Department of Fish and Game. Then we chartered a float plane to transport us to a beach on the island's south shore. Kodiak weather is especially unpredictable, so hunters must realize that they will be able to fly back out again only when the weather is good enough. Luckily, most Alaskan employers understand that their employees can't control the weather."

Mary Anderson may not be able to control weather, but judging from her resume, she seems to have all else well in hand. She graduated from Washington State University in Pullman with a bachelor's degree in business and an emphasis in finance and economics. After a long career as an accountant, she came to the belated realization that no matter how good her accounting capabilities may have been, proper respect would not be forthcoming unless she earned a CPA. School was but a dim memory when Mary enrolled in CPA review classes. Several years later she passed the difficult examination, and her certificate now hangs on her office

Mary Anderson's big muskox missed qualifying for Boone and Crockett by a mere 1½ points.

wall. "I'd told people for years that I was a good accountant," she stated. "Now I have the proof for everyone to see."

Mary's approach to everything in life is similarly high-powered. She is the assistant controller of a multifaceted Alaska company that deals primarily in construction materials and is listed on the New York Stock Exchange. She shoots skeet at a local U.S. Army base in the Arctic Warriors league, which as its name suggests is made up of retired and ex-military shooters. "The members are terrific coaches and mentors, as well as great shooters," she said. "I shoot for fun, but also for the chance to complain that I can't see those birds under the lights whenever we must shoot during a snowstorm. It's pretty frigid out there. but I don't get colder than anyone else. Everyone is just happy to finish a few rounds and go back inside to warm up."

Mary and Tom, both avid hunters, realized soon after moving to Alaska that they'd need wings to hunt the state's very best wildlife locales. Both enrolled in flight school and became pilots. "When I earned my pilot's license in 1982, it carried a single-engine land rating," Mary said. "In 1992 I joined the Civil Air Patrol, where I earned both search-and-rescue and transport qualifications, as well as a high performance rating. In 1997 I earned my seaplane rating." The couple owns a Cessna 182 with wheels as well as a 50-percent share in a Citabria 7GCBC floatplane. "I've worked on my instrument flight rating, too," Mary said. "To complete it, though, I should spend less time at work and more time flying."

The Civil Air Patrol, a volunteer organization, is comprised of units scattered across the state. Given Alaska's vast amounts of wilderness, the group's pilots must be ready, willing, and able to be in the air almost at a moment's notice. Towns are located a great distance from each other, requiring many Alaskans to know how to fly. Private planes and air taxis go down at a rate that would be alarming in the Lower 48. Almost-daily disasters require the attention of an agency like the Civil Air Patrol. "We not only search for downed aircraft but also snow-machiners, skiers, hikers, floaters, and sometimes hunters," Mary said. "If someone doesn't return on time, we go looking for them. Thankfully, we recover most people alive. When we must return a body, that, too, has untold value for the grieving family."

Mary also has helped law-enforcement officials on a few occasions by flying counter-narcotics missions. "The CAP sometimes will ask for volunteers to fly reconnaissance to aid the DEA and local law enforcement with their searches."

Mary has never had a qualm about the morality of hunting. "Never, even for a moment, has it ever crossed my mind that hunting might be wrong," she said. "Hunting is food, and always has been."

Mary grew up on a small Montana cattle ranch. "As a child I remember hunters coming to our ranch each fall," she said. "Some were family members—uncles, aunts, and cousins—but once they arrived, everyone went hunting. Ten or twelve people would cram into two vehicles. When I was a youngster during the 1950s and 1960s, only the grown men would shoot deer. I never saw a woman hunt.

"Many years afterward, my mother admitted that when she married my father she was the better shot," Mary continued. "When they really needed meat and didn't have much ammunition, it was

Mary Anderson's mountain caribou bull scored 378 Boone and Crockett points.

my mother who would take the rifle to go hunting. Both parents knew that mother would produce more meat with less ammo. Yet I never saw my mother fire a gun.

"My brother, who's three and a half years older than I, killed his first deer when he was ten. My mother seemed very excited about his deer hunt. My brother, God bless him, taught me to shoot his .22. Being male, he was given a gun. I wasn't."

Mary met her husband-to-be when they shared a classroom during their undergraduate days in Pullman, but not until several years after graduation did they start dating. "We ran into one another one day and started discussing what mutual friends had been doing," Mary said. "I had become interested in backpacking, and as we talked I learned that Tom enjoyed backpack hunting. When I expressed an interest, he invited me to go along with him. That inspired a shopping trip where I bought my first pair of Danner boots. I paid $110 for them and thought, *This guy is costing me a lot of money*.

"Hunting isn't cheap," she said. "It's cost me a lot of money ever since."

That first year of backpacking with her not-yet-fiancé resulted in several wilderness expeditions to catch fish or hunt bears. "We both took average black bears in Idaho," Mary said. "Both pelts had good fur and no rubbed spots."

Those early bear hunts were probably the most economical treks Tom and Mary have ever made. Since their marriage, they have hunted in many of the western Lower 48 states and in Canada, and made numerous African safaris.

In North America Mary so far has killed black bear, Kodiak brown bear, mule deer, white-tailed deer, pronghorn antelope, bobcat, several Dall sheep, mountain caribou, barren-ground caribou, muskox, mountain lion, and an aoudad. The mountain caribou scored 378 Boone and Crockett points, and the muskox scored 103⅜, or just 1½ points less than the minimum qualifying score for Boone and Crockett's all-time record book. Mary's largest mule deer, with its rack's excellent mass, long main beams, and deep back forks, would also score extremely well, although it is difficult to say with certainty whether it would crack B&C's magic 190-point minimum. It's safe to say, however, that every one of Mary's animals would rank extremely high in SCI's record book.

In Africa Mary has scored on many impala, two leopards, a civet cat, two serval cats, both black-backed and striped jackals, eland, zebra, greater kudu, waterbuck, two genets, a lioness, lion, sable, grysbok, and two African wildcats. Her sable is nothing short of spectacular with its curving, scimitarlike horns that measure more than 42 inches in length.

Mary prefers shooting a Remington Model 700 Classic chambered for the .270 Winchester. For dangerous African game, she owns a Whitworth Express chambered for .375 H&H Magnum, which has had two inches taken off the barrel. "It's really a sweet-shooting gun," Mary commented.

"My goal is to take a good, mature, representative animal of whichever species I'm hunting," Mary explained. "My barren-ground caribou, for example, would have booked in Boone and Crockett had I not briefly lost track of it. As the caribou were traveling away over a series of small hills, I shot the last one in the group.

"After the bull had fallen, Tom said, 'Why did you shoot that one?'

"I replied, 'It was the big one.'

"He said, 'No, the big one was in the lead.'

"He was right, but by the time I realized it the caribou were gone."

Nevertheless, people who know a lot about caribou instantly spot the rack at Mary's home and always comment on its size.

"The fact that I'd made such an error in judgment bothered me for ages, even though my bull's rack dwarfed the others at the flight station as we returned home. As time passes, though, it's become easier to discuss."

Mary has had many close calls involving hunting. "In 1985 I drew a Montana mountain goat tag," she recalled. "I planned to borrow two of my brother's horses so Tom and I could hunt goats out of a high-country camp. One of the horses, Tina, I thought was well broke, so we trailered her up to where we then lived. The second horse was a green-broke three-year-old.

"Since I was the more experienced rider, I decided to ride the green-broke horse while Tom rode Tina. One evening, as we rode in preparation for our hunt, Tina bolted, raced toward a barbed-wire fence, thought better of it, and swerved at the last second. Tom made an ungraceful dismount as the mare went one way and he went the other. I rode up to ask if he was all right. He said he'd just had the wind knocked out of him."

A neighbor saw Tom's wreck, so he rode out and gave Tom a ride back to the house. Mary, meanwhile, put the horses away and checked them over to be certain they were all right.

"When I got home I found Tom lying in the recliner, sweating profusely," she said. "He wasn't visibly bleeding, and insisted he was fine. I told him I was taking him to the hospital for an x-ray. As I turned off the freeway at the hospital's exit ramp, Tom began gasping for breath. Luckily, two attendants were waiting outside with a wheelchair. Tom couldn't even get out of the car, so the attendants jerked him out, placed him in the chair, and disappeared inside.

"Soon a doctor came to tell me that he'd summoned a surgeon to stop Tom's internal bleeding. In the emergency room I found Tom shaking violently as he went into shock. They rolled him away, and I nearly passed out. Nurses brought me back around with smelling salts.

"It took the doctor more than four hours to repair Tom's injuries. His lung was punctured, his spleen torn, and a rib broken. When they finally allowed me to see him, tubes had been placed in his nose, mouth, and chest, and a machine was pumping blood from his lungs. Tom was confined to intensive care for three days and remained in the hospital two additional days for observation. When he finally walked out, gripping his stomach, he complained that his guts felt like they were ready to fall out of his body."

Tom's injuries had been serious, but six weeks later the two of them were glassing into Hell's Canyon. "We called it that," Mary said, "because when I saw the sheer cliffs lining the canyon I said, 'There's no way in hell I'm going in there.' With Tom in such marginal shape, I knew hunting time would be at a premium. I called a local wildlife biologist, and he gave us some good information. One Friday night we loaded our camper with gear and our dogs and headed out.

"The next morning we slept in until Tom felt well enough to accompany me." The couple spotted a lone billy and decided that its horns were fairly good. They returned to their truck and navigated logging roads until they could go no farther. After a long climb, the couple decided it was too late in the day to risk going farther, so they hiked back to their truck and spent the night there.

The next morning, Mary and Tom left while it was still dark. A heavy frost covered the earth, slicking the log they used to cross an icy stream fed by mountain snowmelt. As the couple halted for a break, Tom again spotted the billy, which bedded down as the pair watched him. After another strenuous climb, Mary and Tom settled down to share a candy bar. They could see that the goat was still bedded. But the next time they looked, the tuft of goat hair they'd been checking was gone. Mary said, "I thought I'd lost my goat for three bites of a candy bar. I stared in disbelief at the mountain for several seconds, and then the goat suddenly stepped forward to peer over the edge of the shelf on which it had been bedded. A goat's face showing over a ledge isn't a very substantial target, but there was no time to debate the shot. I picked a spot and squeezed the trigger. The goat leaped off that ledge and onto another. I fired again but missed, and now the goat hurled himself off that ledge and disappeared."

Mary headed up the slope to check on her goat while Tom remained behind as a lookout. "It took forty-five minutes to climb to where I could see the goat," Mary said. "He was dead, but on that treacherous slope it took me another half-hour to reach him."

The couple now had to field-dress and cape out the animal, then renegotiate the perilous terrain back to the truck, crossing numerous streams running high from snow that had melted off the peaks during the warm daylight hours. Mary and Tom, their backpacks filled with meat, gear, cape, and horns, carefully picked their way through the rocks until they reached a game trail they recognized as one they'd followed earlier in the day. But then Tom stumbled and fell, screaming out with pain. "I thought this time I'd killed him for sure," Mary said.

But Tom toughed it out, and both hunters continued down the trail. Their ordeal lasted until 4 A.M., when the last of the meat had been placed inside the refrigerator. "I was so stiff and my feet were so sore I had trouble sleeping," Mary said. "But getting up for work a couple hours later wasn't all that bad."

Mary with her huge 42-inch sable bull.

When Tom returned the next week for his post-surgery checkup, the doctor asked how his exercise program was going. "We just returned from a successful goat hunt," Tom said. The doctor replied, "Well, I guess you don't need to come here anymore."

Alaska, Land of the Midnight Sun, is starkly beautiful, but it can be dangerous. Mary once found herself sharing a bed—sort of—with a male friend on a rough, rocky slope after an aborted stalk on a group of Dall rams. "We'd gone as far as possible, but then realized we'd better turn back," Mary said. "We started back to camp, where Tom was waiting, but soon discovered we'd covered more country than either Lynn, our friend, or I had thought. On the way back it became very dark. We remembered an extremely steep bank in this one area, and worried that one of us might step off it and fall directly into an icy, boulder-strewn stream. So we found a level spot, pulled out our 'roasting bags'—lightweight, foil survival bags—rolled out our sleeping-bag pads, and prepared to spend the night. Our dinner was a granola bar."

At 5 A.M., in a heavy rain, Lynn said, "Let's go." The hunters finally made it to the last stream, where they sat down to pull on waders. "Between the time we arrived at the crossing and the time we were ready to wade into the stream," Mary said, "the water had risen about ten inches. It was too deep and swift to risk a crossing, so we headed downstream to a spot where the river widened out. It would be less dangerous there, or so we hoped.

"The stream was sixty feet wide there and deep, with slippery rocks, but we had to try to ford. We kept our packs buckled tightly because if they shifted, we could be thrown off balance. Contrary to what experts would recommend, Lynn entered the river upstream from me. He was twice my size, so his feet would remain more stable against the rush of the current. To take a step, he used both hands to plunge his walking stick into the streambed, moved one foot, moved the other, then repositioned his walking stick. I held onto Lynn's pack belt while repeating the process with my own walking stick. We crossed very slowly as water filled our waders and rose to our waist. By the time we reached the other side we were so cold that it was a struggle to breathe.

"We thanked the Lord for bringing us this far, then started toward the next ford. As we rounded a corner, we spotted two trucks outfitted with winches. One truck had a four-wheeler in its bed. We had not known anyone else was nearby. Although their trucks were loaded with gear, the owners let us ride in a pickup's bed atop the four-wheeler."

The same three sheep hunters—Mary, Tom, and Lynn—were luckier on another occasion. They were hunting in the Alaska Range when they spotted a herd of Dall rams. After a tricky stalk, all bagged spectacular rams. "My ram was impressive, with 38-inch horns," Mary said. "Tom's, with 41-inch horns, was truly superb, and Lynn's was downright awesome—its horns measured 43 inches."

Mary K. Anderson is no stranger to luck, but you have to ask if it's really luck after all—or the bottom line on life's balance sheet arrived at when a determined, intelligent, and resourceful woman takes a calm, reasoned, and calculated approach to her life and the hunting she enjoys more than anything else.

A POLAR BEAR FOR A PILOT
PAT AULD APPERSON
Polar Bear

Whether she's tracking a giant polar bear on the Arctic ice cap or bagging the elusive western bongo in Africa, Pat Auld Apperson is a portrait of beauty, spunk, and grace. And she's a leader in the modern conservation movement.

Pat was the second woman in the history of the National Rifle Association to serve as a member of its board of directors, a position she held for twenty-five years in the 1960s and '70s. One of her greatest joys was traveling around the United States as an NRA representative, talking to women who were curious but uncertain about hunting and exploring the outdoors. Wherever she went, Pat spoke about the joy of taking a large animal, field-dressing it, and hauling it back to camp. Hunting for a woman was almost unheard of in the 1960s. Women knew little of work outside the home and seldom ventured into male-dominated hunting camps to test their outdoor skills. Time and again, Pat would speak to the wives and girlfriends of the men who loved to hunt, encouraging them to join their men in the field to hunt and enjoy nature.

"I never received a negative reaction," she said. "They were astounded at my accomplishments. Many men were supportive of women who wanted to hunt, and women told me that after my speeches they were encouraged to hunt too."

Pat asked only that her expenses be covered by the club or organization inviting her to speak at a meeting or convention. Her first invitation came from women who were a part of the Gun Owners League of Massachusetts. This was in the early 1960s, and no NRA official had ever spoken to the women of a pro-hunting organization. She was honored and excited to break the ground for women involved in the NRA, an organization she still supports as a benefactor and life member.

She dedicated her NRA efforts to public education and the advancement of women in NRA before the NRA program Women On Target began, and was chairperson of the NRA's Department of Public Relations. She was also co-chairperson and founder of the NRA Women's Policy Committee. She forged new conservation and safety policies for the nationwide organization during her twenty-five years of public service to NRA, the nation's first pro-hunting, pro-Second Amendment group. Additionally, Pat served on the Hunting and Wildlife Conservation Committee and was

Pat Auld Apperson stands beside her Boone and Crockett polar bear in the Buffalo Bill Historical Center in Cody, Wyoming. She took the bear in 1964 while crawling across the Arctic ice cap.

vice-chairperson of the Membership and the Nominating committees. During her service on the NRA board, she was also a member of the Ethics, Urban Affairs, and Audit committees as well as a member of the Task Force Committee of Field Services.

To be selected as one of seventy-five members of the NRA board of directors, a person first needs to be a life member. She asked a minimum of 250 fellow life members to sponsor her and was nominated to the board every two years. This procedure continued for twenty-five years until her retirement from the board in the late 1970s.

Over the years, Pat also organized fashion shows for various groups and took great pleasure in working with women who were new to the sport of hunting. Her dramatic, colorful, flamboyant, and distinctive outfits became her trademarks. While still in high school, Pat became a model for women's boutique shops and department stores. In her early twenties she attended a radio and television school in New York City and continued modeling. She organized a variety of fashion shows for charities near her homes in Texas and Oklahoma, including shows to raise money for a private San Antonio shooting club. She hosted a radio and television talk show in Tulsa, interviewing celebrities and other newsmakers. Her first husband provided radio and TV equipment to local stations, and Pat used her talents as a show host. At one point in the 1960s, she spoke to L. L. Bean representatives about the need to design outdoor clothing for women, a specialty item that did not exist at that time. A company representative attended an NRA national convention in New Orleans at Pat's urging and displayed outdoor wear modeled by a man and a woman.

Pat, one of only a few women who hunted in Africa at the time, hired a tailor in Nairobi, Kenya, to create clothing she designed that fit her perfectly and which she wore on her many safaris to Africa and India. In Hong Kong and Texas, tailors created hunting jackets for her. Whenever Pat organized fashion shows, she modeled her clothing and asked other women to model the clothing with her. She never established her own line of women's hunting clothing, but her friends were directed to her tailors, who created hunting clothes for them.

When not working to raise money for prohunting and wildlife organizations, Pat and her second husband, Dan, drilled for oil along the Gulf Coast. Her father and uncle had been in oil, first with Gulf Oil and then as independent operators. Pat and Dan were also in the oil leasing business in Texas, New Mexico, and Oklahoma and owned a ranch. She was one of the few women in two male-dominated businesses and never looked back. To this day, she negotiates her own land leases and runs her own oil company, having taken it over when Dan passed away in 1980 after twenty-five years of marriage.

In 1999 Pat married Lee Apperson, a rancher who shares her passion for hunting.

At the age of five Pat held a BB gun for the first time. She fished in the Gulf of Mexico and tracked frogs and turtles in the bayous. She thrilled at the sight of quail, turkeys, and doves taking flight and relished her close encounters with white-tailed deer and pronghorns. Hunting was a natural way of life for Pat—it was something that she knew she would always do. And up to this writing, she has enjoyed a minimum of 150 successful hunts throughout North America, Africa, and India.

One of her greatest experiences was taking a giant polar bear in 1964 at Point Hope, Alaska. At the time, her polar bear was the new world record, and today it ranks as the seventieth largest ever taken. Its skull measures $16\frac{13}{16}$ inches long by $10\frac{12}{16}$ inches wide. Its final score remains $27\frac{9}{16}$ B&C points, only two inches smaller than the current world record.

At Point Hope, Pat lived with the Eskimos in their igloos for fifteen days, in temperatures that hovered around 56 below zero. They were snowed in for three days by blizzard conditions, but on the day of the hunt she was flown 150 miles above the Arctic Circle. They landed on the polar ice cap and tracked her bear

Pat with her guides and the water buffalo she took in India.

across the ice and through crevasses until she was within range. At one hundred yards, she fired her .375 Winchester. The 375-grain bullet hit its mark, but the bear dove into the icy waters beside the ice and attempted to escape. With great difficulty, Pat maneuvered for a second shot and finished the job. Her first reaction was, "He's a monster!" The meat was given to the native people, and the skull and cape were saved for a full mount.

The Aulds collected so many wonderful trophies that they opened a wildlife museum in Kerrville, Texas. It has since been closed, but many of her trophies are on public exhibit across the United States. Her grand slam of North American wild sheep is on display at the Cody, Wyoming headquarters of the Foundation for North American Wild Sheep (FNAWS), and her polar bear can be seen at the Boone and Crockett Club exhibit in the Buffalo Bill Historical Center, also in Cody. Two of her trophy bongos are displayed at Watkins Construction Company in Corsicana, Texas. The remaining collection is in private storage.

Pat's involvement with conservation and prohunting organizations reads like a who's-who of the wildlife world. She is one of the founders of Game Conservation International and a member of the American Sector of the International Conservation Committee. She is an active member of the Texas Bighorn Sheep Society and the Sportsmen's Conservationists of Texas, Safari Club International, Dallas Safari Club, National Water Fowl Hunt Club, Ruffed Grouse Society, and the Foundation for North American Wild Sheep, to name only a few. She is also a life member of Shikar-Safari Club International. Pat was the first woman in the Boone and Crockett Club when she joined as a regular member in 1992. She serves on various B&C committees and attends quarterly meetings around the country.

Throughout her adult life, Pat has participated in a variety of shooting competitions. She organized many Tiro El Pigeon shoots and was graded for her shooting expertise. She was a member of the ladies' Grand National Quail team and the ladies' team of the National Waterfowl Association. She was named as the 2002 Texas Shoot Out honorary chairperson for the 4-H shooting programs and continues her involvement with the Texas Women's Shooting Sports organization, which encourages women to enjoy the outdoors and shooting sports. A favorite of Pat's is a shooting group called the Divas, comprised of dear friends who get together for celebrity shoots.

Pat was the first woman to take a trophy bongo, in 1972. Her bongo hunt remains one of her favorites. "The word Africa rolls like magic off the tongue," said Pat, "and conjures visions of high adventure as no other place can." Her hunt began with a sore throat and flu in Marseilles, France. After a three-day recovery in her hotel, she flew to Bangui, capital city of the Central African Republic, and then by bush plane to Bangassou, surviving mechanical malfunctions and repairs of their plane.

"We met the porters, who had one horse," Pat said. "I insisted that Dan ride, but he refused, so up I mounted, and what a relief!" They meandered through the jungle in single file, arriving in camp at 10:30 P.M. Pat fondly remembers the gracious and friendly natives who brought pineapples, fresh Nile River perch and catfish, bananas, chickens, ears of fresh corn, and mountains of avocados. After twenty-nine days on safari, Dan came home with a bull bongo with horns measuring 31⅛ SCI points and Pat with a 27⅛-point SCI bull. Pat's guide suggested that it helped if a bongo hunter was a little bit crazy. After enduring swift-running rivers, torrential rains, armies of tsetse flies, mosquitoes, and marching ants, Pat wasn't sure if insanity was absolutely necessary, "But now I know it helps."

The same drive that put her in the NRA boardroom also put her with the 4-H Club Shooting Education Project, which involved the organization of state shooting safety programs at the national level. Education is the key to hunting and shooting safety, and Pat Auld Apperson was a national leader in organizing the 4-H efforts to ensure that safety and firearms are inseparable.

When still in her early twenties, early in the history of aviation, Pat joined the Civil Air Patrol (CAP). She worked for a law firm at the time and met a man who was organizing training classes for new pilots. To join the class of twenty young men, Pat needed $200, so she borrowed the money from a bank. She was the only woman in the training class. A radio operator was needed to help pilots patrol the Gulf Coast during World War II, so Pat volunteered, receiving the secret codes each day for the pilots. She was given top-secret clearance for the job. With the money she and the twenty male pilots raised, their local CAP unit purchased two small airplanes that were used to patrol the coastline in case enemy airplanes dared to approach American shores. She often flew as a navigator on missions along the Gulf Coast.

Shortly after completing her pilot's training, Pat met her first husband, Ronnie Durham, and they started a sales office for Cessna airplanes at the Corpus Christi airport. Ronnie and Pat later divorced, and Pat married Dan Auld in 1965, but her involvement with flying continued and her memories of those adventures remain special for her today.

Pat continued to fly for business and volunteer activities until the 1970s, including stints with the Women's National Aeronautics Association and the Amelia Earhart Ninety-Nines. This latter group of women pilots flew to small towns to help local business leaders select

A royal permit was required for this rogue rhino, one of many prize animals that mark Pat Auld Apperson's hunting career.

a tall building atop which the name of the town could be painted to help pilots keep track of their flight patterns (this was long before the days of satellites and the electronic equipment pilots have today). Town names painted atop buildings also provided a safety net for private and commercial pilots who needed to know how far they were from airports in case of mechanical failure.

Pat Auld Apperson is the embodiment of human spirit and spunk. From her early days as a fashion model to her adventures as a female aviator to today's hunter, wildlife conservationist, and philanthropist, she has left a permanent mark that few men or women will ever duplicate.

SHOOTING STAR
CONI BROOKS
American Bison, Pronghorn

Zimbabwe, March 2000: The petite and attractive American hunter was hot on the trail of a big bull elephant. As the air temperature soared somewhere between 100 and 105 degrees F, the threat of rain kept the relative humidity hovering around 100 percent. Utah's Coni Brooks and her professional hunter (PH) slipped quietly through the bush on the broad track of a solitary bull elephant. When the pair finally spotted it, Coni decided this was not the animal she'd been dreaming of and lowered her .500 Nitro Express double rifle.

The elephant must have sensed danger lurking nearby. "He's getting a little cheeky," whispered the PH. Coni's husband, Randy, was following close behind, armed with only a video camera to shoot footage of this up-close encounter with the largest of Africa's legendary Big Five of dangerous game that also includes the rhino, lion, leopard, and Cape buffalo.

"I had dropped my guard," Connie admitted. "We were standing there quietly just twenty yards away when the elephant suddenly whirled and charged!"

As massive as elephants are, never be fooled into thinking that they are slow. An enraged bull can thunder toward a source of aggravation with the speed and power of a bullet train, and at twenty yards you have almost no reaction time. The PH shouldered his rifle and fired in an instant, dropping the bull just nine yards from where the pair was standing. The elephant was still crumpling to the earth as Randy Brooks rushed up, screaming to his wife, "Why didn't you shoot?"

"I didn't want him," Coni Brooks replied, as calmly as if she were attending an afternoon tea.

From that day forward her family has seen Coni in a different light. They may razz her about "rather dying than shooting an animal she doesn't want," but Coni's grace and cool under pressure were remarkable to behold.

This anecdote perfectly illustrates what Coni Brooks is made of. She's feisty, fearless, and eager for any adventure imaginable. In other words, she's a pistol, to use an apt shooting metaphor.

Coni is living proof that good things come in small packages. Weighing in at 110 pounds, she has charged into situations so dangerous they would terrify most male hunters. Her exploits bespeak the resolve and tenacity that have made her one of the continent's most respected hunters, male or female.

Coni once endured a wilting seven-hour stalk on a 115-degree day, pulling up short some sixty yards from a herd of Cape buffalo. The buff were lazing about in the stifling heat, bunched up tightly. Coni waited for the animals to shift slightly to allow her a clear shot at the huge bull she was after. Finally, hot, tired, and increasingly exasperated, she suggested, "Let's rush them and see what happens."

Let's repeat that now: This tiny grandmother of six wants to rush a herd of Cape buffalo, among the meanest critters on God's green earth?

"Can you believe that?" Randy Brooks later asked a reporter. "Coni's tougher than a lot of men I've hunted with."

Cooler heads ultimately prevailed. Later that same trip, the firepower of Coni's .500 Nitro Express and its 570-grain X-Bullet brought down a huge buffalo bull with one well-aimed shoulder shot from sixty yards. "In that heat I was damned miserable, but extremely relieved, too," Coni said. "The bull was magnificent, with a 15-inch boss and a 39½-inch tip-to-tip spread."

On that same Zimbabwean hunt, Coni connected with a bull elephant, also with the .500 Nitro Express double rifle, a gun with such formidable recoil that not many men will line up to shoot it. (Accurate Reloading's Web site lists the .500 Nitro's recoil at 78.3 foot-pounds and its recoil factor as 1605.2, which lumps it in the "very painful" class.)

"You might think that a big, slow elephant would be easy to hunt, but that trip was an eye-opener," Coni said. "They can weave in and out of the brush in the blink of an eye, and can blend into the foliage and terrain as completely as any other wild animal. And they're dangerous. Their only enemy is man. If they scent a human and feel threatened, things can quickly deteriorate."

How did someone this small become such a hunting terror?

"Even as a kid I was always by my father's side when he went hunting and fishing," Coni said. "I was his only child, and I think he enjoyed having me around. I know I loved being with him. We were then and still are best buds."

Father and daughter walked the fields and timber for pheasants and deer. Each summer they'd visit the family's cabin, where they would arise early each morning to fish for trout in a nearby lake. "Daddy always seemed to make sure that I'd catch more than he would," Coni recalled.

She briefly retreated from the outdoors during high school, when she joined the cheerleading squad, but "I never lost my passion for hunting."

At seventeen, Coni met Randy Brooks. "We'd go deer hunting with his family, and attend the horse races together," Coni said. "Randy's grandfather owned race horses. Racing them all over the West was one of his passions."

The couple married when Coni was not yet twenty and Randy was a day shy of his twenty-first birthday. "We were poor, so we'd go out west of town to hunt rabbits and deer and pheasants," she said.

Randy's uncle owned a dairy farm near Grand Junction, Colorado, that became the couple's next destination. "Randy helped out with farm chores, but he also began loading custom ammunition for some local people. A gunsmith suggested that we check out this company, Colorado Custom Bullets, that was for sale. We didn't pay much attention at the time, but we didn't forget what he'd said, either."

Randy next worked as a saddlemaker in New Mexico. Coni, however, was unhappy. She felt they had strayed too far from their

Coni's Utah pronghorn, taken with a .338 muzzleloader and a 160-grain Barnes X-Bullet, would qualify for the Longhunter record book.

families. The couple decided to return to Utah, but not before learning more about Colorado Custom Bullets on their way back. "The company, formerly known as Barnes Bullets, was run by two men from a basement," Coni recalled. "After a two-week crash course in bulletmaking, Randy and I arrived in Utah with everything we needed to produce bullets in our own tiny basement." The Brookses eventually moved their business to a larger facility they built behind their home.

One day Fred Barnes, the founder and inventor of Barnes Bullets, dropped by the operation. "He told us he thought it would be a good business move for us to revert to the name Barnes Bullets, since it had been so well-respected," Coni said. "Mr. Barnes sold us the name for $1, and he also stayed to help make bullets. His expertise and knowledge were welcome. We learned a lot from him."

Connie has spent her entire career at Barnes Bullets as the company grew from a mom-and-pop operation into one of the country's top bulletmakers. "I've held every job there—I ran presses, packaged bullets, shipped orders, worked as the accountant, as the bookkeeper, in order entry, in sales and marketing, and anywhere else to keep the business up and running. Fortunately, other employees now handle those jobs."

From the beginning, Coni and Randy understood that their personal hunting experiences could be used for researching and developing new and improved bullet designs. "A customer from Alaska called one day," Coni said, "and suggested I come there to bear hunt. I thought bear hunting would be too dangerous, too difficult, and not much fun. Randy had made an Alaskan bear hunt, and what he'd gone through to get a scruffy old bear was not at all appealing."

The next time the customer called, he told Coni that a bear guide of his acquaintance had just had a last-minute cancellation and was looking for a hunter. "That was on a Thursday," Coni said. "The guide wanted his hunter in Alaska by the following Tuesday. I hung up and said, 'I don't know if I should go.' 'Tell him yes!' Randy said."

Coni remained uncertain about traveling that far without her husband to hunt bears with a stranger. "I asked my sister-in-law to go with me," she said. "Elane had never hunted a day in her life, but she agreed to go along. She didn't have a clue about what she was getting into, and I didn't dare tell her what to expect.

"We backpacked for ten days, then floated down a river in a raft to reach our hunting spots. The weather was cold and miserable. When the hunt ended, neither of us had shot a bear. The guide felt terrible about it and offered to let us both return the next fall. The hunt had been long, hard, and miserable, but we said yes. That next fall, both Elane and I shot grizzly bears."

Coni knew her rigorous hunting trips would benefit Barnes Bullets just as much as Randy's hunts did. She also discovered while hunting grizzlies that she enjoyed challenging herself. "From then on I was totally hooked on hunting," she said.

Since 1982, when she bagged her first grizzly, Coni has hunted all over North America. Her North American trophies include cougar, bighorn sheep, mule deer, black-tailed deer, pronghorn, bison, whitetail, elk, and brown bear. She has taken superb African trophies, too, including an immense leopard that impressed even her PH.

"I went on most of those trips without Randy," Coni said. "When you own and operate a business as a team, it's difficult to get away at the same time."

Coni's animals include a huge Boone and Crockett bison she killed on Utah's once-in-a-lifetime Henry Mountain tag. She used her favorite gun, a custom 6¼-pound .338 that Randy made for her, to take the bison, which scored an awesome 123⁴/₈ Boone and Crockett points. The bullet that felled the giant was a 225-grain Barnes X-Bullet (the X-Bullet concept was pioneered by Randy Brooks). Coni also used her custom .338 to take an elk that scored 345 Boone and Crockett points, and downed a fine Utah pronghorn with a .338 muzzleloader and a 160-grain X-Bullet. The pronghorn, if entered, would rank high in the Longhunter record-book listings.

Coni and Randy have taught both of their daughters to hunt and fish. "Jessica, who works at Barnes, has hunted much of North America," Coni said. "I can't think of anyone who knows more about firearms and shooting than she. Chandra, our youngest daughter, has also hunted. She and I once went on an Alaskan caribou hunt. Last Christmas we gave her a 12-gauge Browning Citori for shooting trap, a sport in which she excels."

Coni's grandkids will soon be joining grandmother in the field. Her oldest grandson already has gone on a Texas deer hunt, and both he and the next oldest have hunted prairie dogs and are learning to shoot a bow. The oldest granddaughter is a born angler, while the three other grandkids are "still a bit young. As they get older they'll have every opportunity to enjoy the outdoors," Coni said.

Not only is Coni an enthusiastic wife, family woman, businesswoman, and hunter, she's an effective proponent of wildlife and open spaces. When she was elected president of the Utah Safari Club, she succeeded husband Randy. When the couple joined SCI, the Utah chapter had twenty-five members. Today that same chapter boasts over five hundred members, and its most successful fund-raiser generated $186,000 for wildlife and habitat. "If you're going to hunt, you must do something in return," Coni said.

She belongs to the Rocky Mountain Elk Foundation, the Foundation for North American Wild Sheep, and is a life member of the National Rifle Association. She's a firm believer in the Becoming an Outdoors-Woman program, for which she has taught hunting and shooting classes. Utah's Governor Leavitt appointed Coni Brooks to the state's wildlife board. "Board members formulate the policies and regulations that affect the state's wildlife and aquatic species," said Coni.

Coni pitches in whenever brains or even brawn are needed during moose transplants, black bear studies, and water-guzzler installations in arid locales.

"I also helped promote Utah's Proposition 5, which prevents wildlife laws from being enacted with less than two-thirds of the popular vote," she said. "Now it will be difficult for extremists to muster enough support to interfere with critical wildlife issues."

Animal and environmental extremists are a thorn in Coni's side. "They threaten our very way of life," she said, "not just hunting and fishing but rodeo, boating on lakes, snowmobiling, four-wheeling, horseback riding and packing into the wilderness, logging,

Coni's .500 Nitro Express double rifle downed this formidable Cape buffalo in Zimbabwe.

and even the taking of furbearers and the wearing of fur. It's time people joined forces to prevent these extremist attitudes from altering our lives. Hunters can no longer afford to be complacent. They must take these people seriously."

Strong sentiments from a woman who believes in both animal welfare and environmental action. Coni spends her energy and her money working diligently for wildlife in ways that make a real difference. She also is a leader in grassroots efforts to save wild places from being lost forever.

"Hunter numbers are declining because wildlife habitat is dwindling," she said. "Places where not so long ago I hunted pheasants with my father now are gone forever. Mule deer no longer roam many foothills areas because they are crowded with homes. In cases where wildlife depends heavily on a certain piece of property, it's difficult to prevent the landowner from selling out to developers, especially if doing so will make him wealthy. That is why it's imperative that we encourage more hunters to join conservation groups and become involved with their fund-raisers. That's how these organizations can buy and restore habitat and build fences to keep wildlife from being killed on highways. Thank heavens for hunters. Wildlife would be in serious trouble without them."

A perfect day of hunting for Coni consists simply of "being there—nothing can make a day of hunting less than perfect." She killed the Wyoming bull elk that netted 345 Boone and Crockett points on a bitterly cold day with a howling 45-mph wind. "My camera's mechanical parts had frozen," Coni said. "We had to build a fire to thaw it out so we could take photos."

As for entering her trophies in the record books, Coni said that isn't in the cards, at least for now. "Many of my animals are record-book quality, but I haven't submitted them," she said. "I may someday, but just knowing that they score high enough to make the record book is good enough right now. Each one is special to me. Some of my animals don't qualify for any record book, and yet I'm as happy with them as with those animals that do."

Any opportunity for a shot that doesn't feel right—maybe the distance is too long, the light too poor, or the animal is moving too quickly—will be turned down. "If there's a good chance I might miss or wound an animal, it's not worth the risk," she said. "It might be crazy to refuse a shot at a 175-plus white-tailed buck during the last minutes of daylight, as I once did, but I have too much respect for these animals to do anything else."

Coni Brooks counts her hunt for bighorn sheep among her most memorable. "That hunt was so difficult and challenging," she said. "I suffered through one fiasco after another. It was on this hunt that

Coni Brooks bagged her Boone and Crockett bison bull in Utah's Henry Mountains.

I learned sheep go where God won't. You'll find sheep in the most miserable places, and in the most difficult spots to reach."

After hunting six long days in the snow with British Columbia outfitter Ferlin Koma, they spotted a good ram five miles away on a mountaintop. The woman gamely slogged through drifts to close in on her ram. As she was about to shoot, she lost her footing and dropped her gun. Nonplussed, Coni re-aimed her .338 and fired. Nothing. She bolted in another shell and tried again. The gun again failed to fire. The third cartridge finally ignited, and the sheep dropped. Tests later revealed that the primers Coni had used for reloading were defective. More than half failed to detonate. "When I finally took my bighorn ram, I can honestly say I damn sure deserved it!" Coni said.

Once the initial elation of shooting any big-game animal subsides, Coni reserves a moment for reflection. "I feel a bit sad when I gaze at a beautiful animal that I have just killed," she said. "But even if there were no human hunters at all, wildlife still would suffer, most in far worse ways. Deer are hit by cars, and their habitat is disappearing. Habitat loss affects entire populations of animals.

Utah has a large population of cougars, another factor contributing to the decline of deer herds." Coni is quick to point out that the state does not want to eradicate the big cats, but merely to control their numbers to give mule deer a chance to rebound.

Coni Brooks is one of hunting's preeminent spokeswomen.

She believes that more women must become hunters to ensure hunting's future. She did, and has never regretted her decision. "Men who don't introduce the women in their lives to hunting are missing the boat," she said. "Why not share your fun and your passion for hunting instead of fighting about how long you'll be gone or how much a new rifle will cost? Women I know take hunting very seriously. Guides have remarked that women are excellent hunters because they are not afraid to ask for advice and they pay attention to what they are told.

"If you, as a woman, have ever entertained even the slightest thought about what hunting might be like, give it a try. You'll enjoy it. And the memories will last you a lifetime."

MRS. HUNTING AMERICA
JUDY DADDONA

Mule Deer, World Slam of Longbeards

A fast-food advertisement asks the questions, "Did the hamburger come before the customer? Or the customer before the hamburger?" It is likewise intriguing to wonder why hunting seems to appeal to so many women of achievement, like Pennsylvania's Judy Daddona.

Beauty may sometimes lie in the eyes of the beholder, but in Judy's case she has made the "cut" on more than one occasion. In 1983 Judy was chosen over many other young wives and mothers to be Mrs. Pennsylvania. In that capacity she went on to compete as a finalist in the Mrs. America Pageant in Las Vegas. Judy later commented, "It was a 'crowning' achievement."

"Most people who know me see me as very feminine," Judy said. "Some of these people are shocked that I hunt."

Like so many other women featured in our book, Judy is not just a hunter but also is a vocal advocate for the sport. "I have been able to bring some people who were against hunting to understand my position," she said. "With knowledge comes understanding, and with understanding comes acceptance."

Profound words from a woman who started hunting merely twelve years ago. "My husband, Jack, always shared the hunting season with our two sons, John Jr. and Dino. They would travel to the same camp Jack and his family used during his own youth. There they met Jack's brothers and his brothers' sons. It was a great family tradition. I would never have considered intruding there.

"In 1990, though, once the boys had left for college, Jack needed a new hunting partner. I decided to try it for myself. My first experience was a Texas whitetail hunt in January. I already knew how to shoot, so I felt comfortable with a rifle. Jack and I had such a great time together on that trip that I was instantly hooked. Of course, it helped that I harvested a nine-point buck!"

Judy also has hunted mule deer, pronghorn, and black bear, but her favorite is the wild turkey. "There is nothing like the interaction between a hunter who calls and a turkey," Judy said. "I'm purely entertained trying every call I know to convince a smart old gobbler that I'm a nice, sweet lady hen who would enjoy his company."

Judy Daddona was selected for this book because she has taken not only a few spectacular big-game trophies—her huge ten-point (eastern count) Mexican mule deer buck, for example—but also a Royal Slam of Longbeards (mature gobblers), bagged in only thirty-one days. And to top even that accomplishment, she became the first woman to take a World Slam of Longbeards in a single year.

A Royal Slam of turkeys consists of gobblers of the Osceola, Rio Grande, Merriam's, Gould's, and eastern subspecies. To complete a World Slam, a hunter must kill an ocellated turkey as well. As of March 2001, according to the *Turkey Caller* magazine, only thirty-seven people had recorded World Slams of turkeys. Such an achievement places Judy Daddona in turkey hunting's highest echelons.

Judy attended Lehigh (Pennsylvania) Community College and Temple University, then joined her entrepreneur husband to work on a variety of projects. She now is employed as a consultant and legal liaison for a foreign corporation. Her hobbies include travel, golf, reading, sporting clays, playing the piano, charitable work, and family conservation projects.

Judy and Jack have undertaken a land and stream restoration project designed to benefit both Pennsylvania's elk herd and native brook trout. "We're improving a thousand acres of property that adjoin a three-thousand-acre tract of state game lands," Judy said. "We cleared, raked, and limed almost thirty acres recently, then planted it in clover, trefoil, rye, chufa, and other forages.

"We're also initiating a quality-deer-management program to improve the local herd's age class and structure, especially for bucks."

Judy is a member of so many conservation organizations and gun-rights groups—the NRA, National Wild Turkey Federation, Pennsylvania Longbeards of Lehigh Valley, Quality Deer Management Association, National Sporting Clays Association, Wildlands Conservancy, Safari Club International—that when she adds, "and the U.S. Golf Association," it sounds somewhat out of place.

Judy became a junior Gray Lady with the Red Cross at age thirteen and continued as a volunteer with that agency for twenty-five years. She taught first-grade religion in the evening to Catholic children who attended public schools, and was an active booster of her sons' football teams.

Judy Daddona sees the world as a bud that opens a bit more each day, displaying more beauty or wonderment for anyone who cares to pay attention. "Hunting, for me, encompasses so many things," she said. "It's appreciation, admiration, anticipation, and excitement. It's a total immersion into your environment that begins when you step out into the dark before dawn. It's silence, the slight stirrings of soft breezes, the first light in the sky, the chirping of the birds, the unknown fragrances, and all the different trees and plants growing nearby. It's squirrels scurrying through the trees, and the

Judy Daddona and the mule deer buck she bagged in 2000 in Sonora, Mexico.

peace that comes simply from being in the woods. It's also being able to get very close to the game animals or birds you are pursuing. Hunting provides an opportunity to meet people of different cultures and forge lasting friendships with them. No matter where I may hunt, it seems new every time."

When Judy bagged her Royal Slam of Longbeards over a thirty-one-day period in 2001, she hunted from well before dawn until dusk almost every day. Even when she returned home to spend Easter with her family, she went hunting. Here, in Judy's own words, are her accounts of those days when she bagged her longbeards.

April 7, 2001: After working several Osceola gobblers during a day and a half of hunting, and passing up a gobbler with a five-inch beard, Ken Mayes of DK Flatwoods and I set up at the end of a pasture in a blind made of palmetto branches. Temperatures rose to 90 degrees, so hot it seemed like nothing would be moving. As we left the blind to scout, we spotted a gobbler in an adjacent field. I hurried to a tree line opposite the place where we'd positioned our blind and decoys. After a few calls, three jakes ran toward the decoys, then slowly walked away. Twenty minutes later, I saw a wild hog traveling toward the decoys. The hog was followed by a longbeard, which may have thought he was safe staying behind an animal with such a keen sense of smell. Luckily, we'd set up downwind from where the hog appeared. The hog continued across the field while the gobbler strutted toward the decoys. I made a 58-yard shot with my Benelli Super Black Eagle 12-gauge. My Osceola longbeard weighed 18 pounds, 9 ounces, its beard measured 10⁹⁄₁₆ inches in length, and its spurs were 1¼ inches and 1 inch long.

April 10, 2001: I was hunting Rio Grandes with outfitter Doug Borries at the Flying B Ranch in La Pryor, Texas. The weather was very hot here, too. In late afternoon of the first day, three gobblers came in behind us, gobbling and drumming in response to our calls. As they strutted into view, I shot the largest bird. It weighed 19 pounds, 8 ounces, had a 10⁹⁄₁₆ inch beard, and spurs that measured 1¼ inches and ¾ inch.

April 19, 2001: I was hunting Merriam's gobblers in the Rocky Mountains east of Raton, New Mexico, with Tim Barraclaugh of Kiowa Guide Service. After futilely calling for several hours to a stubborn gobbler that would not come, we tracked a different bird in a loop that took us around the mountain. When we returned to where we'd started from, several gobblers were strutting in front of some hens three hundred yards away. We crawled along a creek-bed, then eased up a hill before taking our positions beneath a pine tree. Several soft purrs from a peg-type box call brought a hen on the run. Two nice gobblers followed closely behind her. I bagged my gobbler at a distance of twenty-five yards with my Beretta AL391 Camo 12-gauge. My license permitted me to take two birds, so I was able to shoot another one later on this trip. Two days after I left, a snowstorm effectively ended New Mexico's turkey hunting for the spring. My Merriam's gobbler weighed 17 pounds, 3 ounces and had a 10-inch beard and ⅝-inch spurs.

April 25, 2001: I flew into Hermosillo, Mexico to hunt out of the El Rodeo Hunting Lodge. The lodge was located high in the Sierra Madre Mountains, a 5½-hour trip in a motor vehicle. The ranch was not huge, but it had never before been hunted for turkeys. After I'd spent much time climbing ridges and glassing for Gould's gobblers, I located eight turkeys on an opposite ridge near some cattle. I climbed up there, set up, and called. I'm not sure whether my calling spooked the cattle, but the cattle in turn scared the turkeys, and they ran in my general direction. As four gobblers raced by at about sixty yards, I called, hoping to stop them, but failed. I remained extremely still, and the largest turkey I've ever seen stepped out from behind a bush to strut ten yards in front of me. My gun was already in position from when those first four had rushed past. I didn't have to move at all to shoot this turkey. That huge gobbler weighed 26 pounds and had a 10¾-inch beard; the spurs were ⅞-inch and ¾-inch long.

May 8, 2001: Now I needed only an eastern gobbler to complete my Royal Slam, but it was proving difficult. The season had already started by the time I arrived home from Mexico. In Pennsylvania hunting is permitted only until noon, and is not allowed on Sundays. I would arise each day at 3:30 A.M. and hunt all morning, but couldn't call a longbeard within range. Not until day thirty-one, and my self-imposed month-long deadline, did I finally get my chance. I'd set up my blind in a hedgerow bordering a field. Dawn arrived silently. I used diaphragm calls and a box call for some time before a faint gobble drifted down from a nearby mountaintop. The tom flew off the mountain and across a road, and I could hear him gobbling from the wooded area behind my blind. When the bird was about sixty yards distant, he looked into the field and spotted my decoys. But he hung up there—wouldn't take another step. I used my purr box ever so softly; the gobbler responded to each call, but moved very cautiously toward the decoys. Each step seemed to make him increasingly uneasy. When he'd closed the distance to forty-five yards, I shot. Mission accomplished! My eastern weighed 19 pounds, 4 ounces, it had a 10½-inch beard, and its spurs measured ¾-inch and ⅞-inch.

To complete her World Slam of turkeys in less than a year, Judy next traveled to the jungles of Mexico's Yucatan Peninsula. "This

Judy Daddona and the Holy Grail of turkey hunters: the ocellated gobbler.

was my most thrilling hunt," she said. "We arrived in Merida on 23 March 2002. Biologist Ramon Juarez met us and escorted us 8½ hours into the jungle. Our camp was pitched thirty miles north of the Guatemalan border.

"Camp was rough," Judy continued. "We raised tent roofs with mosquito-net sides and used tree branches to support them. Tree limbs were tied together to form tables, a wash stand, latrines, clothes lines, and towel racks next to the river where we bathed. We hand-inflated air mattresses, cooked our food over a wood fire, and had only one fueled lantern. That first night in camp, I awoke to the screams of howler monkeys."

The local wildlife species here included jaguars, alligators, and poisonous snakes. "Alligators frequented the river where we bathed," she said. "But luckily, I only encountered two venomous snakes the entire trip."

Each day members of the hunting party followed a guide who used his machete to chop a path through the jungle. Since the ocellated turkey, the bird Judy was after, does not respond to calls, the strategy focused on simply getting within range of the birds. As the hunters slipped through the rain forest behind their guide, they'd stay attuned to the many birds calling in the canopy overhead. "We would also be listening for the ocellated's unusual gobble," Judy said. "It sounds like three or four low drumbeats, followed by first an upward and then a downward trill that resembles notes from a flute. We'd chop and hack our way toward the sound, hoping for a chance to shoot. More likely, we would find a nearby jungle opening or old logging road and return there the next morning to await fly-down and hope an ocellated would venture within range.

"The temperature and humidity were so extreme we could hunt only until 10:30 A.M. We'd go out again at around 3:30 P.M. and hunt until dark. We ate lunch during midafternoon, mostly eggs since too much camp meat might encourage jaguars."

Jungle nights were sultry and stifling. "Our sheets were soaked with perspiration by morning," Judy recalled. "The fourth night, a rainstorm blew into camp. Lightning kept us all trapped in our tents, our beds pushed into the center of the sideless shelter. I slept lying across one end of the bed, my boots still on in case we had to flee. My gear and clothing were stacked on the bed's other end."

Another memorable—and dangerous—moment occurred when the Jeep, loaded with the hunters, started over a log bridge. "One log broke, and the Jeep fell partially through the hole," Judy said. "It took an hour of winching to free it." Had the Jeep fallen completely through the hole, the passengers would have plunged into the river below, with perhaps disastrous results.

Judy and two Merriam's gobblers she shot in New Mexico as part of her World and Royal Slams.

On the third morning, Judy bagged an ocellated gobbler that should tie for seventh place in the Longest Spurs category and tie for second-heaviest ocellated in NWTF's next record book.

"Before I returned home I wanted to take the 'Campeche Triple Crown' of birds. I hunted hard the remainder of the week and succeeded in doing so. The Campeche Triple Crown consists of three jungle birds: the ocellated, which I'd already killed; a crested guan with its dark blue head, red throat, and black headdress plumage; and a great curassow with its bright yellow beak and large black headdress plumage."

Judy Daddona is proud of her hunting accomplishments, but she's even more excited about those of her family. Both sons own their own companies, an achievement in itself. "My son Jack and I have a standing appointment each year on the first day of buck season. Daughter-in-law Kimberlee competed in archery in high school, and now she's gearing up to get back into the sport and plans to start hunting with the rest of us. And I'm looking forward to teaching and hunting with both my daughters-in-law, and my granddaughters and grandsons, too, when they're old enough."

Above all else, Judy is thankful for husband Jack. "He's my husband, lover, and absolute best friend," she said. "He taught me to hunt and golf, encouraged me, promoted me, and shared with me. The greatest part of all my experiences has been sharing them with him. And the best thing about completing my Royal Slam was that he was there with me when I pulled the trigger on that eastern gobbler.

"Hunting is not only good for the environment, it's good for hunters themselves. People who hunt increase their knowledge of, appreciation for, and respect for everything in nature. Best of all, hunting promotes family bonding."

And if anyone should know such things, it would be Judy Daddona, Mrs. Hunting America.

WALKING DOWN THE VALLEY WILD

ANNE S. DODGSON

Roosevelt Elk, Black Bear, Cougar

The title's words, inspired by poet William Blake's introduction to his "Songs of Innocence," could be used to describe the hunting life of Utah's Anne S. Dodgson. Anne, a Renaissance woman if ever there was one, explains the poem's meaning: "Should you enjoy some wonderful experience, don't keep it to yourself. Write it down so you can share the spirit of that experience with those who later read your words." Anne, who has inspired both Newfoundland's Larry Smith and African PH Fred W. Duckworth to share with others their fabulous hunting adventures, follows her own muse by writing poetry about hunting.

That's hardly the type of accomplishment you would associate with a hunter who has been awarded more Safari Club International Diamonds than any other female member for the 202 individual species of big-game animals she has harvested to date. Along the way, Anne became the first woman to garner fifteen SCI Diamond awards, including the Trophy Animals of Africa Slam (for which she harvested ninety-two species—only seventy-six were required), the European Deer Slam, the Trophy Animals of South America Slam, the Red Deer/Wapiti World Slam, the Antlered Game of the World Slam (thirty-six separate species), the Oxen of the World Slam, the Pig and Peccary World Slam, Trophy Animals of Asia Slam, and the Gazelles of the World Slam.

Anne was the first woman recognized by SCI at the Diamond Level for World Hunting Achievement. To receive this honor she needed to enter a minimum of 125 separate big-game species in the organization's various record books. Anne also has taken North American Grand Slams of Caribou, Deer, Elk, and White-Tailed Deer, as well as a Cats of the World Slam.

She is rapidly closing in on the North American Super Slam—the "Twenty-Nine" Slam—for which she needs just six animals, as well as the World Moose Slam (needs one) and the coveted SCI Ring, which will be hers when she takes eight more species, a goal she should reach in 2003. Naturally, Anne Dodgson will be the first woman to sample the rarefied air atop this particular SCI summit.

Anne has spent her hunting life walking down the valley wild—perhaps not "piping," as Blake described it, but enjoying every minute of it nonetheless. On the way she has taken some superb trophy animals, including a black bear that ranks No. 50 in

SCI's 2001 Record Book with a score of 19⅜, a mountain goat ranked No. 45 in the same book (score: 28⅜), a cougar at No. 13 (score: 14¹⁵⁄₁₆), and perhaps her finest North American trophy, a Roosevelt elk that ranked No. 3 when Anne killed it in 1998 but now is No. 8 with a score of 331⅛.

It is that elk to which Anne refers when asked to share one of her favorite hunting experiences: "We'd traveled over an hour from the California coast to Santa Rosa in the Catalina Islands," she said. "The date was 9 September 1998, but the weather was terrible. A strong, gusting wind blew most of the day, magnifying the cold and the dampness until we were truly miserable.

"I was hunting that day with Forest Halford, a biologist with Santa Rosa's Multiple Use Management program, and my husband,

Anne Dodgson and the tremendous 331⅛ SCI Roosevelt elk she killed on Santa Rosa Island in the Catalina Island chain. The bull ranked No. 3 in SCI's record book at the time it was killed, and ranks No. 8 now.

Bill. MUM is a cooperative program designed to provide advice to island ranchers who may be considering the destruction of habitat to feed more livestock. Biologists help landowners manage their property for livestock, wildlife, and a diversity of flora. Fees from hunters allow ranchers to increase revenues with the same numbers of livestock, or perhaps even fewer. That's why we were there. I had paid a large sum of money to hunt elk on such a remote and beautiful island."

Early that morning, Anne, Bill, and the guide had spotted a huge Roosevelt bull elk many miles away. They could tell by the animal's wide-sweeping rack that it was a superb specimen. All day long they had maneuvered through the biting wind and over steep terrain lush with long, slippery grasses to get closer to the bull. In some places they were able to drive island roads to close the distance, but in others it was slip and climb, slide and stumble toward their destination. The trio tried three different approaches. None worked. The wind was simply too unpredictable. As evening approached, the swirling currents at least calmed down a bit, convincing the hunters that another stalk just might work. Anne felt gratified that she had refused to even consider another, easier-to-reach bull elk when things had looked impossible. They set off again.

"We closed the distance to just under a mile," she recalled. "Then we zigzagged the best we could to get closer, following the sounds of the bull's bugling whenever we were unable to see him."

The trio finally slipped up to within a hundred yards of the bull. Anne got into the prone position, but holding her .300 Winchester steady was nigh impossible on the steep, slick slope. "Forest finally wedged his body against mine so I could attempt a shot," Anne said. "But every time I'd prepare to shoot, the bull would turn his head to stare down into the valley, and his antlers would cover his body." As the minutes ticked by, the tension increased. After a half-hour or so, the bull finally turned his attention up the slope and Anne saw her chance. Peering through her Schmidt & Bender scope, she found a point behind the bull's shoulder and squeezed the trigger.

The 180-grain Barnes X-Bullet slammed home, and Anne had one of the largest Roosevelt bulls ever recorded with Safari Club International.

Not bad for a woman whose peripatetic childhood had led her all over the West. Anne was born near San Francisco, moved with her family to Twin Falls, Idaho, then graduated from high school in Logan, Utah. She attended Utah State University, where "I earned a Ph.T.—Put Husband Through." Although the marriage didn't survive, Anne and her first husband were blessed with a daughter, Mary Selina.

Some years later, Anne met and married Bill, her husband of thirty-three years. The couple originally wed beneath a mount of Bill's huge Alaskan moose, an omen of their lives to come. They later married again in a Mormon temple.

Anne not only acquired a husband with her second marriage, she also gained Bill's four children from a previous marriage: Cathy, Cindy, Candy, and William Jr. or "Korki." And later Bill and Anne adopted Holley when the girl was eight years old.

While Anne took care of hearth and home, Bill would often be off somewhere hunting. "Before our marriage I had hunted deer with Bill at Bear Lake in Utah, and later we went after antelope together. I enjoyed hunting, and yet I had difficulty coming to grips with my husband's tremendous fascination with the sport," she said. "I found myself resenting the money he spent collecting dead animals to hang on the wall while I stayed at home taking care of the kids."

Anne felt like this despite having been exposed to shooting by her father when she was a child. "My daddy and a police officer friend of his often took me target shooting," she said. "I loved those trips to the range. The gun-cleaning solution smelled so good, and the way they handled their guns made me believe that firearms must be something special."

Anne's father taught her two major firearms lessons: "Whenever I picked up a gun, I had to remember perfectly every rule that he had taught me, lest I kill myself or a member of my family. The second lesson was learned when, in my eagerness to shoot a rifle for the first time, I did not get into position the way I'd been instructed. I ended up on my bottom in the dirt."

Paternal firearms lessons, early exposure to her father's Idaho deer hunts, and participation in her husband's western jaunts notwithstanding, Anne's marriage had reached a critical juncture. "Bill knew what drove him to hunt, but he couldn't express his feelings about it to me in words that made sense," she continued. "Men like my Bill don't write poetry, unfortunately. But I would notice what he spent on a sheep hunt, then weigh that against the cost of a new sofa and matching chairs or the college tuition needed to complete my degree."

Anne finally decided to travel with Bill on some of his hunts, if only to spend more time with him. This change of attitude took place in 1989, just as Bill set off to take a Mongolian argali.

While the pair was in Mongolia, Anne finally connected the dots concerning Bill, herself, hunting, finances, and what was important in life, although she did experience one last moment of trepidation. "As I watched Bill collect his ram, I was secretly lamenting the money he'd spent to do so. I wanted a swimming pool. Bill later invited me to take a ram, too, since we were already in Mongolia. I said no." Anne's refusal would come back to haunt her.

Almost in spite of herself, Anne Dodgson enjoyed the hunt. "Seeing what Bill in his somewhat clumsy, left-brained way was offering me cured my attachment to material goods," she said. She arrived back home scarcely aware that her secret resentments had healed. Accompanying Bill became the norm, and soon so did bagging big-game animals.

"When I'd first started hunting with Bill so many years before, I think he just wanted to give me something to do so I'd feel useful," Anne said. "I started out shooting camp meat or animals to be used for bait. From there I began taking management bucks and bulls. Over time, they added up. Al Cito, who is with SCI, one day remarked that it was time for his organization to celebrate the hunting women who had helped make SCI a success. When I thumbed back through my journals, I discovered that I had taken fifty-seven big-game animals. Soon I began analyzing where I wanted to hunt, what my next trophy should be, and which guide I

This Toklat grizzly, with its dark legs and lighter-colored body, was taken near Matanuska Glacier in 2002.

wanted to hire—still slightly amazed at how my outlook on hunting had changed."

Anne remains grateful to Bill, who is quite a few years older than she, for many things but perhaps most of all for his unspoken guidance as she followed her hunting heart. "Whenever I'd glance back at him while I was on a stalk, Bill would be smiling," she said.

Bill's love and support enabled Anne to hunt places most women can only dream of. Her first African game was a bull elephant, her second a 48-inch Cape buffalo felled with one shot while she was hunting with Fred W. Duckworth. She bagged her Marco Polo sheep at 650 yards, shooting through a ferocious windstorm.

Some of her adventures are difficult to fathom—like the time she and her guide were nearly killed by a rhino. "I was trying to complete my Big Five," she said. "Bill was videotaping the hunt and somehow found himself quite far behind my PH, Rick Van Zijl, and me. The rhino we'd been stalking suddenly caught Bill's scent and charged. I yelled for Bill to throw the camera away and run. Bill tossed the camera, then raced to a nearby tree, where he froze, not daring to move."

When Anne cried out to Bill, the rhino zeroed in on her position, pivoted to face this new unknown danger, and charged. "He was on us immediately," she said. "When he was ten feet away I looked into his eyes and knew I'd be unable to shoot fast enough to save our lives. Rhinos don't die fast, even when hit by a .458. Had I tried to shoot him at such close range, the sound of the shot combined with the pain would have further infuriated him. We'd have been flattened into mudpies.

"I knew I was going to die," she said. "But instead of fear, I felt love for the rhino, and respect. I remained completely still, as close to a tree as I could get, and hoped my PH would do the same.

"The rhino swept past us with such furious speed that he bowled us over like two pickup sticks. He kept going because he didn't know where we were. The ploy had worked. The wind was with us, and he never got our scent."

While hunting in the Central African Republic, Anne contracted malaria. She lost weight and became incredibly fatigued, but still managed to bag the nine big-game species she was after. She returned home still dreadfully sick. Frightened, Anne visited the hospital, where they told her that malaria was not her problem. Recurring fevers that spiked as high as 104.8 degrees over the next month eventually changed one doctor's mind. "He treated me for malaria," Anne said. "I know he saved my life."

Anne shows no indications of slowing down, despite terming herself a "hothouse type of woman." She maintains good health with a strict regimen of exercise, herbs, and wholesome food. She carries water wherever she goes so she can sip on it at will to prevent dehydration. When she's hunting, Anne shampoos her hair and bathes daily, even if she is allowed just a few cups of water in a basin. She never forgets that she's a woman first and foremost, and takes pains with her appearance even in the field. At the close of each day she records her thoughts in a journal or sometimes composes a new poem. "I feel so close to my Maker at the end of each hunting day that I feel compelled to express myself on paper before going to sleep."

Anne's poetry speaks from the heart of the complexities she has found in life and nature. These two verses from her poem "Learning Leopard Ambience" are a good example of her work:

> Settling down on hollow golden reeds
> since used for a leopard blind
> Lying upon my back—anticipating his attack
> While the African night presses heavy across my face
> Shivering against the cold
> Pulsing stars hang low in unfamiliar space.
>
> Remembering at first sound of the bullet's whack
> Hidden ghostly pachyderms timeworn presiding
> Renounce the bullet's crack through high trumpeting noses
> Warning you don't belong
> Your presence imposes!

Anne Dodgson's interests are eclectic. She loves horses, her teacup poodle, classical music, great literature, the symmetry found in nature, and pondering Einstein's Theory of Relativity. She championed hunters' rights in Australia and completed a course for automobile dealership owners; she gardens, cultivates bonsai, and is one of SCI's Master Measurers.

Anne loves to hunt but hates to kill, although she has made an uneasy peace with the idea that in order to have hunted, one must kill. "The actual hunting is much more important to me than the kill," she explained. "Hunting is so much more than killing. It's the venturing out into places you've never before seen, the dare even to try. It's learning about firearms and how to safely use them. Hunting is the final stalk—the 'Are you really up to this?' question that only you can answer.

"I now understand that it is only the hunter's license that bestows true value on wildlife," she said. "It is a concept that the rest of the world is just beginning to comprehend."

Giving back is important to the Dodgsons, and second nature for Anne. She has fought the good fight for conservation

Anne Dodgson bagged this nice white-tailed buck in Missouri.

issues and hunting rights through SCI and the National Rifle Association. She's organized countless fund-raisers, sat on the SCI's Utah Chapter Board of Directors, helped spearhead the drive to save Angola's giant sable antelope, and fought to preserve the rodeo events that were being protested during Salt Lake City's 2002 Winter Olympics. A life member of SCI, SCI Sables, FNAWS, NRA, Grand Slam Club, and Ovis, she also belongs to the Rocky Mountain Elk Foundation, the Mule Deer Foundation, and Pheasants Forever. During the 1980s the Dodgsons helped plant wild turkeys in Summit County, Utah. Anne underwrote the funds needed to purchase fifty wild Sika deer that were earmarked to be euthanized in Australia. She then paid to have them shipped to and released on free-range habitat. She has underwritten to the tune of $50,000 a course devoted to the principles of the American Constitution because of her great interest in the Second Amendment.

As SCI's Utah Newsletter editor, Anne was a vocal advocate for increasing the state's mule deer populations while managing herds to include more older bucks. Battles with both the Humane Society of the United States and People for the Ethical Treatment of Animals soon followed, but with Anne's help a coalition of Utah sportsmen helped place Utah Proposition No. 5 on the ballot. This proposition, which passed with 68 percent of the vote, mandated the use of scientific wildlife management principles to guide oversight of the state's wildlife, not the emotional pleadings or rantings of anti-use organizations.

Anne's pet issues are related to either conservation principles or the Second Amendment. "Any hunter or firearms owner who does not help raise funds to protect our sport and our rights is not a true and constant advocate," she said. "The most important people in the conservation and Second Amendment rights movements are hunters who may only hunt once a year, sometime target shooters, and people who simply enjoy owning guns. These people vote, they can make things happen, and they should become active in local politics to further our goals."

What about that long-ago wish for a swimming pool? "Oh, I have the pool," Anne admitted. "Now I wish I'd have shot that Mongolian argali instead. I can't believe I turned down the opportunity.

"People are slowly beginning to realize that the human race needs our wild places and wild creatures," Anne said. "Without them, our human minds and souls would be much diminished.

"As long as sport hunting pays a big part of the tab for maintaining wilderness areas and wildlife, and as long as the politically correct among us won't pay their share, I will remain a sport hunter and be proud to call myself by that name."

William Wordsworth aptly summed up the life led by Anne S. Dodgson, poet, Renaissance woman, hunter, and conservationist:

> And so I dare to hope,
> Though changed, no doubt, from what I was when first
> I came among these hills; when like a roe
> I bounded o'er the mountains, by the sides
> Of the deep rivers, and the lonely streams,
> Wherever Nature led. . . .
>
> A lover of the meadows and the woods,
> And mountains; and of all that we behold
> From this green earth; of all the mighty world
> Of eye, and ear—both what they half create,
> And what perceive; well pleased to recognize
> In Nature and the language of the sense,
> The anchor of my purest thoughts. . .

HOMESTEADERS IN MONTANA
PATRICIA M. "PATTY" DREESZEN
Pronghorn, Mountain Caribou

Settlement in the new state of Montana had just begun when Patty Dreeszen's family first set foot on land outside Billings in the Stillwater Valley. Her maternal grandfather, Albert Bennett, was two years old in 1896 when he traveled by prairie schooner with his parents from Edgemont, South Dakota, to the Stillwater Valley. Trout fishing was her grandfather's passion, but hunting was not a major focus in her family's traditions, although her grandfather did hunt to put meat on the table. In the 1930s he was one of the veterans of the famous "Firing Line" at Gardiner, Montana, where he took several elk. Her grandparents left Montana in the 1940s, moving to Oregon.

Patty's paternal grandparents, Caleb and Emma Mills, had also come from South Dakota, migrating into south-central Montana in 1907. They homesteaded near Red Lodge, Montana, where Patty's father was born in 1916. William eventually became a mechanic and, while working in Absarokee, Montana, met and married Ardilla Bennett in 1937. Soon after, they moved to Billings, where William Mills worked for the State Highway Department and then for Montana National Guard, retiring in 1976. Patty's mom spent most of her time as a homemaker, raising Patty and her older brother and sister.

Patty's grandparents were ranchers who hunted some, but she had little exposure to hunting until she met her future husband, Doug. Patty was a secretary for the Billings Police Department when Doug joined the force as a patrolman in June 1969. Several months later, on their first date, Patty knew this was the man she would marry. It happened in May 1970.

Doug wanted to share his love of the outdoors with his new wife. He came from a long line of hunters, beginning in the 1860s when some of his ancestors arrived near Bozeman and eventually migrated to the Billings area. Long before Doug could hunt, he remembers sitting with his chin over the back seat of their car watching the road disappear behind them as his mother drove the family to a favorite hunting spot. Doug always hunted with his dad and waited with high anticipation for the season to begin.

For the first eight years of their marriage, Patty hiked along with Doug, enjoying the companionship, but in 1978 she decided it was time to pick up a rifle and hunt. She began with a Ruger M77 chambered for the .270 Winchester, its stock shortened three inches to better fit her. She later had the rifle fitted with a customized Brown Precision fiberglass stock and topped with a 3–9X Leupold scope. Quality gear for women was hard to find when Patty began hunting, so she used her talents as a seamstress to make down vests, coats, duffel bags, and even a backpack they still use.

"Doug has always been a good mentor and a great influence on me," Patty said. "He has always taken the time to show me how to do it right." The couple has hunted nonstop with each other since 1978. They have no children, but their love of hunting and each other has sustained them through the decades.

Over the years, they have hunted in Montana, Wyoming, Mexico, Canada, and Nevada, but her favorite place is still Montana because of its wide variety of game and outstanding hunting opportunities most of the year. In her home state Patty has taken elk, bears, mountain goat, antelope, deer, and bighorn sheep and has purchased mountain lion tags, although she has yet to fell one. Her favorites are mule deer, antelope, and bighorns. She readily admitted that one of her biggest adrenaline rushes ever came from

Patty Dreeszen with her B&C mountain caribou that scored 416⅞ points, well above the B&C minimum of 390.

discovering she had drawn a bighorn sheep tag. "That's a big deal," she said.

Patty and Doug do all their own research, from working through the complicated process of applying for a variety of special tags and licenses in a variety of states, to scouting the hunt areas. That research time has paid off big in hunt success and is an important part of their total hunting experience. Patty has collected mule and white-tailed deer, mountain goat, elk, black bear, a desert sheep, Dall sheep, bighorn sheep, Coues deer, bison, mountain caribou, and lots of antelope.

Patty's favorite hunt of all time was the 1989 trip on which she took a Wyoming bighorn. Hunting at the 11,000-foot elevation required spending time getting into top physical shape. Doug and Patty saw her sheep with two other rams the day before she took it, but the animals were three miles away and the sun was setting. Early the next morning they dropped down into a basin in the same area and spotted the sheep on the mountain above them. It was difficult to stalk uphill without spooking the rams. Twice Patty backed

Her 1988 pronghorn scored 80⅝, which also made the B&C record book.

An awesome Montana mule deer brings a giant grin from Patty Dreeszen.

off before finally getting into shooting position. Around 5 P.M. she saw the biggest ram stand up, jump off a rocky outcropping, and then return to butt heads with the two others.

Two hours before dark, Patty was able to take three shots that brought down the largest of the rams. Unfortunately, the hunters were miles from their truck and darkness was fast approaching, so Doug and Patty decided to camp at the base of the mountain with the horns, cape, and meat. They skinned the animal for a life-size mount, and the next day Patty packed fifty pounds of ram and Doug packed the remaining ninety-five pounds of meat, horns, and cape back to the truck for the long drive home. Over the years, Doug and Patty have taken thirteen wild sheep between them and have a "Couple Grand Slam."

Another of Patty's best-remembered hunts took place in 1984 and resulted in a mountain caribou that easily made the Boone and Crockett Club book with a final score of 416⅝ points. They were in the Northwest Territories with outfitter Bob Woodward along the South Nahanni River drainage near Little Dal Lake. Patty's caribou was the third largest taken

One of two bighorn sheep Patty has taken over her years of hunting.

during Boone and Crockett's Nineteenth Awards period (1983–1985) and ranks fiftieth in the world, according to the all-time record book, *Records of North American Big Game*, Eleventh Edition. The new world-record mountain caribou scores 452, which illustrates the size of Patty's animal. Her trophy's main beam measures 53⅛ inches long on the right and 52⅛ inches on the left. Its inside spread is 38⅞ inches.

Patty and Doug spotted three bulls on the far side of the lake on the first day of their hunt. She selected the largest of the three bulls and stalked within a hundred yards, crawling over tundra and rolling ground. Doug collected one of the other bulls, also a B&C trophy with a final score of 392⅝. They fired simultaneously to drop their trophies. What a first day.

Two pronghorns Patty has taken over the years also are Boone and Crockett trophies. Her favorite hunting areas are the plains of Montana's Fergus County, where she took her 82⅜ buck in 1986 and an 80⅜ buck in 1988. "I love to hunt antelope—the stalk, the weather, everything about it," Patty said.

On her 1986 hunt, Patty saw a buck below her just after sunup and crawled a ways toward it before firing a single shot to drop the buck in its tracks. She about froze to death until the sun came up, but the animal was worth the suffering.

Patty said she hunts to get out in the outdoors and be with the man she loves. Hunting has brought her face to face with animals that most people see only on the Disney Channel. Photographs are an easy way to preserve her memories, and she uses them to encourage other women to hunt. She has been an inspiration to others who were reluctant to try. In the '90s Patty was a hunter-safety instructor near her home and an instructor for a Becoming an Outdoors-Woman workshop. She is eager to share her love of hunting and hopes that her photographs and stories of success will motivate more women to go afield. Patty and her husband strive to take good-quality kill-scene photographs. And her advice is to take plenty of photos—use at least a roll on a harvested big-game animal. There will always be one or two shots that will stand out. She reminds people that poor, distasteful photos can turn nonhunters into antihunters.

Patty and Doug are active in the Montana Chapter of the Foundation for North American Wild Sheep, attending meetings, participating in auctions, and working on conservation projects. Doug was a founding member and past president of the chapter and a contributor to the 1999 book, *Putting Sheep on the Mountain*, which traces the history of FNAWS from its beginnings in 1974 through its first twenty-five years.

These days, Doug and Patty have returned to their ranching roots, owning and operating a small farm and raising registered black Angus cattle. Doug retired as a captain from the Billings Police Department in 1993, and Patty retired as the administrative aide to the chief in 1995. In 1997 she began a new career as a loan assistant for a bank.

They both enjoy gardening, but theirs is no ordinary garden. The quarter-acre plot produces so many acorn squash, corn, beans, cucumbers, beets, tomatoes, pumpkins, carrots, and beets that Patty spends much of the fall canning and pickling the fruits of their labors. One of the Dreeszens' giant pumpkins grew to one hundred sixty pounds and three feet tall.

Life on the plains of eastern Montana is good for Doug and Patty. They savor their times together in the field and look forward to spring in their garden. The cattle graze on grass, and the Dreeszens plan future hunts.

TWO MUSKOXEN FOR THE BOOKS
CAROLYN ELLEDGE
Muskox

Few hunters ever see a muskox, let alone hunt one, but Carolyn Elledge collected two bulls for the Boone and Crockett Club record book. Her 109⅛-point bull remains the largest muskox ever taken by a woman and ranks ninety-seventh largest in the world.

With her hunting abilities well established with her interviewer, Carolyn quickly turns the conversation to her love of husband George and their sons, Jay, Austin, and Hunter, and daughter Samantha. Jay died in a tragic automobile accident in 1987 when he was only seventeen, but his influence remains strong in the minds of Carolyn and George, who hunted many times with Jay before his death. Today, the hunting enthusiasm of Samantha (born in 1967), Austin (1989), and Hunter (1986) propels them into the field with their parents to enjoy each hunting season.

"If the boys and I can dream it up, Carolyn is game," George said. "We've gone deep-sea fishing—and landed a 150-pound marlin—had three Kodiak bear hunts; Dall sheep hunts; bighorn hunts; deer, turkey, blackbuck antelope, caribou, and goat hunts; horseback riding in Africa; scuba diving, glacier trekking, river rafting, glider flying, backpacking, you name it. She is one tough little gal."

This 5-foot, 2-inch mother of four, George's wife since 1966, earned a degree in music performance from the University of Alaska with a specialty in flute, but has focused her musical talent on religious services at their churches. Carolyn shared her musical talents at the Worldwide Church of God in Anchorage from the moment they moved back to Alaska in 1968, and then at the First Presbyterian Church of Houston when she and George returned to Texas in 1992.

Carolyn's life began in then-rural Calallen, Texas, which is now within the city limits of Corpus Christi. Her father and mother owned a sixty-acre farm filled with chickens, pigs, red Angus beef cattle, and five beloved milk cows. Carolyn's daddy, Walter, was a full-time lineman for Southwestern Bell Telephone while her mother, Mamie, took care of the farm with the help of Carolyn and her older sister, Barbara. Seven days a week, Carolyn and Barbara rose at sunup to milk the cows and tend the chickens before they trudged off to school. Every afternoon after school, the girls had more chores to do. When Carolyn first started milking the cows at the age of six or seven, she was afraid of the big animals until her older sister showed her the proper techniques. Today Barbara remains Carolyn's mentor and best friend.

Carolyn grew up around guns but never hunted until she met her future husband. She was an outdoorswoman from an early age, though, and found hours of entertainment climbing the scrubby mesquite and other trees indigenous to south Texas. No rabbits or squirrels were available to hunt. Only the occasional rattlesnake crossed her path. The family shotgun was always nearby, propped against the refrigerator as a defense against predators that tried to make off with the family's prized chickens. Carolyn never learned to fire the shotgun and her sister was the one to use a .22, so it was up to George to teach Carolyn the ways of guns.

The two met in a cow pen when she was sixteen and he was a swashbuckling eighteen-year-old college freshman home for the summer to help his father. George's father, J. W., was a small-town entrepreneur who always dreamed of new ways to make money. One of his schemes was to turn a piece of his property, located next to Carolyn's farm, into a feedlot for cattle, so naturally he recruited

Carolyn Elledge kneels beside her second muskox bull.

his son to help. George fed their cattle a unique combination of hay, cottonseed meal, and blackstrap molasses—a sticky mess. Carolyn's dad had the clever idea of dipping the hay into the molasses and then into the cottonseed meal. The two men went into partnership, and their teenage son and daughter became the "feeders."

The flies and sticky feedlot food were tough enough on the two teenagers, but the constant rain and high humidity that summer only added to the muck and mess. Of course, George drove a sexy white Impala convertible with red interior. How could a young woman resist? George was a city kid who enjoyed working as a cowboy. He loved horses but wasn't particularly smitten with cows. On their first date, a few weeks after beginning the feedlot business, George showed up in a brand-new Oldsmobile 98, an "old-person car," not the white Impala. He wanted to impress her with a fancy car, but her heart was set on the Impala. But after spending hours with George in a cow pen, sticking to everything she touched, Carolyn figured their relationship could only get better on that first date.

Two months after George and Carolyn met, he left for the University of Texas and she returned to high school. During the next four years, George finished a degree in finance and Carolyn started a music degree, first at Del Mar College and later at the University of Texas. Romance blossomed, but George discovered Alaska while on a sheep hunt in the fall of 1964. He finished his degree at Texas and left immediately after graduation to work for Beneficial Finance in Anchorage. When George asked her to marry him in 1965, Carolyn couldn't imagine living in Alaska, but she eventually joined him after they were married in May 1966.

Carolyn was homesick in Anchorage—Alaska was so different from south Texas. Anchorage was a dirty little frontier town with few paved streets and little sunshine. It took two weeks for a telephone to be installed. For a few days electricity came from an extension cord connected to her next-door neighbor's house. She was a long way from Mama and didn't know a soul. She secured a secretarial job at a small engineering firm shortly after arriving but soon started feeling sick to her stomach. Although the pair had not planned to start a family for five years, Samantha was born one year and two weeks after they were married, and thus ended Carolyn's career with the engineering firm.

Two weeks after arriving in Alaska, the couple began their hunting activities by going on a walk-in Rocky Mountain goat hunt up a 9,000-foot mountain. The hunt was so arduous that Carolyn laughingly claims she got pregnant to avoid mountain hunting ever again—at least until the children were older. She didn't hunt regularly until 1979, when her two oldest children could come along.

Carolyn with her one and only Alaska brown bear. 1982.

George's dream of becoming a pilot finally began to come true when he got a slot in pilot training, and in December 1966 they headed for Del Rio, Texas. Pilot school went well until it was determined that George's eyesight was no longer twenty/twenty. He was offered a slot in navigator school, where he could wear glasses, and left for Sacramento a few days after Samantha was born. Carolyn stayed with George's parents until George was settled in and she felt more like traveling. After George became a navigator and was hired by Amoco, a major oil explorer in Alaska, the couple continued their life there.

During one of her early hunts, Carolyn realized that she loved the peace and quiet hunting gave her. Lying in a tent or looking at the stars, Carolyn collected her thoughts and came to see that in hunting camp, unlike housework, her work was finished for the day when darkness fell. "I just like being out there," she says. "I've always gone with my husband, and I like shooting and putting my skills to the test." Her children have come along on most of her hunts and become skilled hunters themselves, a fact she points to with pride. When their family grew to include two sons, the Elledge family added to the permits collected and the meat enjoyed.

Carolyn's first Boone and Crockett muskox was taken on Nunivak Island off the west coast of mainland Alaska. She and George flew by Twin Otter to Bethel, Alaska, and then to Mekoryuk on the day a Russian missile shot down a Korean airliner in September 1983. This was Carolyn's first hunt with native Alaskans and her first view of muskoxen. Permits were offered in the fall and spring, and her

Carolyn with her New Mexico pronghorn in 2001.

permit was for the fall. Fall hunters are transported by open boat from Mekoryuk, on the north end of Nunivak, to protected coves up to sixty miles away on the south end.

Hunting for muskox in the fall is tricky business. When the ocean waves build, there are few places to safely beach a boat, and the services of a local transporter who knows where to find protection are mandatory. Crashing waves and frigid water are the order of the hunting day. A boating accident in these conditions can be fatal. George served as Carolyn's guide, and the couple hired a native, Henry Jack, to transport them to the best hunting locations on the island. The weather was so foul in Mekoryuk that they had to wait several days for the winds to die down before boarding the rickety boat for the trip to their hunting site. Traveling in an open, wooden, sixteen-foot boat in the Bering Sea is quite an adventure. At the landing site, Henry had to wait for the wind to die down before they could safely beach. Travel time from Mekoryuk to the hunt area was around four hours on rough seas with swells exceeding ten feet. Winds toward the end of the trip were estimated at over fifty mph. The deteriorating conditions forced the group to pull into a protective cove short of their planned destination. Carolyn wondered out loud, "With two babies at home, is this really smart?"

Carolyn always had faith in George, so she toughed it out and helped make camp in the cove around 6 P.M. This was a self-guided hunt, the hunter providing all camp gear and food. Henry and George set out to scout the area for muskox bulls, returning a few hours later to say they had spotted a small herd of cows and calves. Carolyn and George decided to take advantage of the improving weather and conduct a stalk to see if bulls were hanging out nearby. As Carolyn prepared to sneak up on the hairy beasts, she discovered that the terrain is devoid of trees or brush; high grass provided the only cover for a stalk. (Earlier in the day they had met a native woman at a fish camp who had never seen a tree.) The hunting party came up from the narrow beach and climbed a near-vertical cliff covered in grasses. As they crept closer to the small herd, Henry excitedly pointed out a massive bull grazing in the grass. Carolyn couldn't see the bull even though she was less than a hundred yards from it. Roly-poly sand dunes were everywhere, hiding the fuzzy herd from sight. Carolyn moved in extremely close to the muskox and fired her .30-06 with a 180-grain bullet.

Nothing happened—the tough old bull didn't even buckle. But finally it dropped after several shots by Carolyn. George knew immediately that Carolyn had taken a really big head, but he didn't know how big until his tape measure confirmed that its green measurements would make it the largest muskox ever taken on the island. The next day Henry helped Carolyn and George prepare the meat and cape for the trip back to Mekoryuk. Unlike most wild game, muskox meat is marbled; that of old bulls is quite chewy but has a pleasant herb flavor.

Two years later, in 1985, Carolyn again drew a muskox permit. Once again George was her hunting guide, but this time they hired Sam Weston as her transporter. She returned to the same general area, and again the weather delayed her hunt. They remained in Mekoryuk until sea conditions improved and allowed them to reach the narrow beach with steep cliffs heading upward to tall grass. They spotted two bulls on a peninsula that jutted into the Bering Sea, and began a stalk. Focused intently on the two bulls, they failed to notice that their boat had not been tied properly and was drifting out to sea! A fisherman in a boat near the beach saw the dilemma and brought their boat back to them with all the camping equipment still safely packed in the hull. A near disaster diverted, Carolyn turned her attention to the larger bull feeding in the tall grass. She was able to crawl to a good position and downed the massive bull with two quick shots from her .30-06.

George and their son Jay finally drew muskox permits for the spring of 1987 (spring up there means minus 40-degree temperatures). Both George's and Jay's muskoxen made the Boone and Crockett Club's Tenth edition of *Records of North American Big Game*, with final scores of 103⅜ and 104⅝ points, respectively. Both trophies are on permanent display at the Fort Richardson Wildlife Museum in Anchorage, Alaska, in the exhibit titled "America's Arctic Warriors."

Carolyn continues to build hunting memories as she and George enjoy the bounty of Texas, where they have lived since 1992. George attained the rank of Colonel while flying C-130s as a navigator for the Alaska Air National Guard and retired after twenty-eight years of flying all over the world. A few years later he retired from Amoco after a thirty-year career in Alaska and Texas with numerous assignments in Russia.

For Carolyn, the best part of hunting has always been her family. Boxes and boxes of photographs coupled with approximately one hundred mounted trophies permanently preserve those adventures and provide hours of satisfaction as they reminisce about their life together. Over the years, Carolyn has taken a caribou, a brown bear, numerous whitetails, a bull elk, Rio Grande turkey, blackbuck antelope, and a pronghorn. She has drawn permits for Dall sheep but has never taken one, but she points with pride to her children, Jay and Samantha, who filled their Dall tags with her at their side. Samantha, Hunter, and Austin still accompany their parents into the field.

"I love to hunt because I love to be outdoors," Carolyn said. "I've always had my personal guide, George, and have never had to hunt alone. I know our family has profited immensely from the time we have spent hunting together in the remote reaches of our beautiful country." The Elledge family bonds with the joy of hunting.

HOW'D YOU GET THIS WAY?
GLORIA ERICKSON

Polar Bear

The hunting that day had been incredibly tough. The hunter and her guide had labored up jagged mountains, then leaped, clambered, and slid down the other side. The hunter, who was scouring this northern British Columbia hellhole for Canada moose and mountain goat, already had tumbled down one rugged hill, but recovered nicely by scrambling to her feet, still smiling. Her feet were so sore they seemed to scream for relief. The shintangle— low-lying vines that snagged the pair's feet—was everywhere, and merely remaining upright was a constant struggle. The day had been long, arduous, and frustrating, but stopping to rest now was unthinkable. "We knew we weren't anywhere near the trail," Gloria Erickson said. "Had it gotten dark while we were still stumbling down that mountain, we would have been in one heck of a fix."

Gloria's guide kept glancing anxiously back at her. He finally blurted out the question he'd been longing to ask all day, "How'd you get this way?"

"What?" Gloria looked at him, somewhat confused.

"How did you get this way?" The guide chose his words carefully as he considered the God-awful terrain the woman had negotiated that day. "If a guy had been with me today, he would have either refused to go any farther or wanted to kill me. You? You just keep on going."

Energizer Bunny comparisons notwithstanding, Gloria replied, "Well, I might not be so mellow if I didn't know these hardships were temporary and that I'd be going home soon. If I had to live like this every day of the year, well, I don't think I'd be so congenial."

That latter statement is debatable, particularly if you know anything at all about Gloria Erickson. For starters, Gloria is intelligent, articulate, and motivated to do more than simply observe from the sidelines. In fact, this woman has more irons in the fire than a Ted Turner cowboy on branding day. Gloria is acquainted with every mover and shaker in the nation's major conservation, environmental, and hunting organizations. She knows more folks than any sane person ought to know, yet remains intimately involved with all the humdrum details that must be attended to before ideas can be transformed into accomplishments. And yet Gloria somehow still finds the time to share a joke, spout off with an obscure but spot-on quote, or let you in on some of the homespun philosophy that forms the basis of all that she stands for.

Likening Gloria to either dervish or dustdevil would be easy, except that both spin wildly out of control and that is hardly an apt description of the pert Nebraskan. This dynamo of the modern conservation movement moves, one could say, faster than a speeding bullet. She is arguably more powerful than any other American woman on today's conservation scene. And during the past three decades she has overcome formidable obstacles to attain the myriad goals she has set for herself and for the organizations she has endowed with her blood, sweat, tears, money, and time.

And she's not finished yet. Gloria Erickson, 1999 Budweiser Outdoorsman of the Year, doesn't seem to know the meaning of the phrases "slow down," "rest on your laurels," or "call it a day." Thank you very much, she might say when so advised, but not when there's still work to be done to preserve or restore wildlife habitat or otherwise aid the wild creatures of the air, earth, or water.

Biology and education major, science teacher, farm wife, farmer (a good farm wife must also be a farmer), conservationist, angler,

Gloria isn't just interested in hunting—"I'm passionate about it," she said. She's shown here with a plains mule deer.

gardener, photographer, and hunter are just a few of the hats Gloria has donned since striking out from her mother's Nebraska farm over three decades ago.

Gloria's first move as a young woman landed her in south-central Wyoming, where she taught school and learned to hunt. "I never officially hunted when I was younger," she explained. "But I did play cowboys and Indians and pioneers. During those games we'd pretend to put meat on the table, so hunting was never foreign to me.

"When I was eleven my dad died. My mother could have leased our land to a neighbor, but she decided instead to farm it. We kids knew from that point on that we'd all have to take an active role in running the farm."

One of Gloria's earliest hunting memories was driving the family's old car down field edges while her brothers hunted pheasants. Harvested birds would be tossed inside to lighten the boys' load. "An unwritten farm rule stated that when a youngster's feet could reach the pedals, she was old enough to drive," she said. "So I started driving when I was eleven."

Wyoming life agreed with Gloria, who still calls the Equality State her adopted home. "I used to hunt on Elk Mountain between Rawlins and Saratoga," she said. "I learned a lot of lessons there. The first was that if you look at an animal long enough, your eyes will see whatever you want them to see. I discovered that if I stared at a bedded bunch of cow elk for a long time, I might have sworn one of them had sprouted spike antlers. Of course it hadn't," she said, still grateful that she wasn't convinced enough to pull the trigger.

Another lesson, learned atop the most formidable peak in the Medicine Bow range, was that if you have the right deer license, the season's open, and you spot a big buck—shoot! "My friends warned me that morning not to shoot any deer on top of the mountain," Gloria said. "Any one of them would have shot the monster muley I later sneaked up on, and done so without a thought about how to get it out of there. But I was new to hunting and I didn't want to anger my friends, so I passed on a buck so huge its antlers resembled an elk's. The buck didn't know I was there for several minutes. When he finally realized it, he vanished almost immediately."

Wyoming can take much of the credit for making Gloria the woman she is today. She can describe the precise moment in which she felt herself transformed. "I was twenty-four years old," she said. "I'd gone mule deer hunting with my friends. Our group had separated, but we'd made plans to meet later back at the truck. I started off by myself and was soon trekking up a steep ridge. As

I trudged along, I looked down and saw this nice buck at the bottom of a ravine. He had no idea any human was in the area.

"I became so excited with buck fever that I started to shake," Gloria continued. "My brain had gone to mush. I now had to go through my checklist of must-do details so I could get this deer."

The buck was lying straight downhill at approximately two hundred yards. "I'd been taught to take a leaning rest," Gloria said. "But the sagebrush was so high I couldn't see the deer from a supported position. I eased over to a different spot where I could see over the sage and sat down. When I rested my .243 on my knee, the view through the scope was bouncing everywhere. I forced myself to be calm and then shot."

The deer raced away like a creature possessed. "A classic heart shot," said Gloria, "but I didn't know that at the time. All I could think was, *Oh, no, I missed him!*

"I climbed down, thinking *Please be dead, please be dead.* And when I reached him he was stone-cold dead. I yelled for the others, but no one came. I would have to field-dress the buck myself.

"That was a watershed day in my life. I realized then that I really can do anything, and what's more, I can do it by myself. I will never forget that feeling. I found the buck, shot the buck, tracked the buck, and then dressed him out. The amount of confidence an experience like that provides can carry you through the rest of your life."

Gloria minces no words when she speaks about the activity so near to her heart. "I'm not just interested in hunting," she said. "I'm passionate about it. Participating in the natural world the way a hunter does is good for the soul. It's good for your spiritual life, and it's good for your physical life. Hunting is one of the most important aspects of my existence.

"I've always wondered why feminists don't embrace women as hunters. But then I realized that feminists are more interested in having the government act as a safety net to catch them if they fail. What, I ask, is more crucial to becoming an independent woman than actually being able to feed yourself and your family without relying on someone else or a government agency to do it for you?"

Gloria met Lloyd, her husband of the past twenty-eight years, at a high-school football game. He was impressed to discover that this attractive teacher hunted, and even more impressed a couple of weeks later when she cut up his deer. "Man, I'm not letting this woman get away," Lloyd told anyone who would listen.

"Yeah," said Gloria, "but it was the last deer I ever cut up for him."

The two were soulmates, each being both farmer and hunter. An ideal match most of the time, they spiced up their lives with the occasional squabble between two strong-willed individuals. Lloyd and Gloria still realize what a treasure they have in each other. "He likes me at home fixing him hot meals at the end of the day," Gloria said. "I do that, of course, when I'm home, which isn't all that often." Gloria got more than a husband when she married Lloyd. She also became the proud stepmother of his son, Chris, ten at the time, who has since grown up, received a degree in agriculture, and is helping run the family farm. Chris's wife and son, Caden, age two, now live in the Ericksons' family home place, while Gloria and Lloyd live in town.

Gloria is president of Nebraska's Council of Sportsmen's Clubs, served as the Nebraska Game and Parks Commission Chairman, and is involved in foundation work for Nebraska's All-Bird Alliance, a coalition formed to enhance and restore habitat for grouse, pheasants, quail, and songbirds. She is on the Rainwater Basin Joint Venture's management board. She also was president of Safari Club International's Nebraska chapter as well as an SCI regional vice-president, and was a National Rifle Association committee member

Gloria's Canada moose was taken during a hellacious hunt through some of the roughest terrain in British Columbia.

and is a life member. She belongs to almost every conservation organization with a charter, and has devoted much of her recent free time attempting to hammer out solutions for the chronic wasting disease (CWD) now threatening the wild deer herds of many states.

"I always say that if I take on a job it must meet three criteria: It can't pay anything, it must take up a lot of time, and although it need not be controversial when I agree to do it, it absolutely must become controversial," she said, only half-joking.

Indeed, the finger-pointing and hard feelings resulting from the discovery of CWD in Nebraska's wild deer population continue to be a source of consternation for this champion of conservation, especially since most indicators seem to point at game-farm animals as likely agents of infection. "The state holds wildlife in trust for the people," she said. "How can anyone be upset at efforts to protect that wildlife?"

Gloria Erickson takes her responsibilities seriously, yet she's always ready, willing, and able to have a good time, especially at the many conventions and symposiums to which she and Lloyd travel. "I buy a lot of raffle tickets," she said. One can only imagine what "a lot" means, considering the prizes she's won. They include her favorite gun, a .338 she won at a Foundation for North American Wild Sheep convention; a wild-bison hunt on Idaho's Shoshone-Bannock Indian Reservation; and many spectacular Safari Club International hunting adventures, including an all-expenses-paid safari for Africa's Big Five dangerous game animals, a Grand Slam of sheep, and a North American Bear Slam.

Husband and wife have enjoyed many great hunts together. One of Gloria's favorites was when both Lloyd and she bagged big bull bison on the Idaho reservation. Before Gloria won the bear slam, though, they both realized that she would probably have to hunt many of the bears without him. "Lloyd suffers from asthma," she said. "The doctor told him he couldn't go on the polar bear hunt. Being so far out on the ice with only a dogsled for transportation was simply too risky." Since Lloyd had already killed both an Alaskan brown bear and a grizzly, he decided not to go along on those hunts either.

When she traveled to Yakutat, Alaska, to hunt with Ken Fanning for her glacier bear, a rare color phase of the black bear, she did so with one of her female friends. As the hunt neared its conclusion, one of the elusive trophies was spotted on the other side of a lake. After a hasty conference, the two women decided to stay a few days longer so Gloria could try to get this bear. Ken had to radio out to inform the waiting husbands. "I've rescheduled hunters before," he told the women, "but I've never had to cancel appointments with hair stylists and manicurists." Despite the extension, Gloria never did take a glacier bear.

On another occasion, Gloria was waiting to board a plane in a British Columbia airport. As she sat there, rifle case at her side, a soft-spoken man and his wife approached. "Excuse me," he said. "What instrument do you play?"

"A .338," she said, well aware of Canada's restrictive gun laws. Saying "oboe" would have been oh-so-easy and politically correct to boot, but Gloria Erickson never has been one to sugarcoat the truth.

As for her 1997 polar bear hunt, "It was the greatest experience of my life," she said. "I'd talked to a half-dozen men who had gone on similar hunts, and most told me it was the worst experience they'd ever had. One said, 'It's going to be the toughest thing you've ever done. You'll have to be mentally prepared and mentally tough. You'll be cold all the time, you won't see much wildlife, you're away from your own culture, and then things will really get bad. And I hope you like the color white because that's all you're going to see.'

"How wrong he was," Gloria said. "It's not all white but shades of blue and green and gray. Pressure ridges formed by freezing sea water cause the ocean to assume such fantastic shapes, it's like hunting on the moon. It was gorgeous!

Gloria Erickson: tired, happy, and proud of the high-scoring SCI polar bear she took while hunting from a dogsled with the Inuit.

"And the Inuit are such wonderful people. You might think they would be chauvinistic, but that wasn't the case. When I was introduced at a meeting of the village elders, I explained through an interpreter that I wasn't there to prove that a woman could do this or that; I was there to experience how they, the Inuit, have survived for thousands of years, although I would try to do it with a .416 Remington and not a harpoon. They understood, and I think they liked hearing it. They are just like us. They enjoy being with people who have a genuine interest in them and what they do."

Gloria endured two days in an Arctic whiteout. On the sixth day of her hunt, she told her guide that she only wanted a big male bear. "I didn't want to kill a female, no matter what," she said. "We were riding along on the dogsled and suddenly cut this bear track. I knew when I saw it that it had been made by a big bear."

Gloria's Inuit guide urged the sled dogs along the fresh tracks. Several hours later, the guide and his hunter spotted the big bear on top of a pressure ridge. The guide released two of his dogs. They ran up and began worrying the large carnivore. Gloria and the Inuit meanwhile took the dogsled to the far side of the pressure ridge. When she was finally in shooting position, less than thirty yards from the huge white bear, she tried to find a rest while her guide leaped up and down on the ice, shouting, "Shoot him, shoot him!"

"I shot once, and the bear disappeared," Gloria recalled. "When we climbed over the pressure ridge, it lay dead on the other side." Gloria's big bear, which ranks very high in SCI's record book, missed qualifying for the Boone and Crockett book by a single point.

What did she tell the hunter who had said polar bear hunting would be the worst experience of her life? "I asked, 'Have you ever done Christmas? Talk about tough! The cooking, the cards, the shopping, the decorating, the baking, the wrapping. Everything on your two shoulders. Compared to Christmas, polar bear hunting was a walk in the park'. '

Gloria Erickson is a special woman, and has so many fabulous hunting tales to share that she said she may someday write her own book. Her outlook on life is so positive and she expresses her feelings about hunting so well that it would surely be a bestseller. Anecdotes that everyone can relate to provide a glimpse into the workings of this independent spirit's mind.

"One afternoon not too long ago," she said, "a woman friend and I went duck hunting. It was a cold, blustery day, but we had good shooting. As we prepared to leave, I noticed our decoys had blown out farther into the lake. I had to fetch them, but as I waded out farther and farther in my hipboots, the water got deeper. Just as I was about to grab the first decoy, my foot slid in that lake-bottom gumbo and I fell. Water filled my boots and one arm was soaked clear up to my shoulder. I stumbled back to shore, frigid to the bone, and said, 'It's just a damned good thing this was my idea or somebody's butt would be in a grinder right now.'

"It's easy to blame someone else for our problems if we think we're not in charge," she explained. "But if it's our own decision—if we're in charge—we'll just smile and move ahead."

A LEAGUE OF HER OWN
KATE FIDUCCIA
Quebec-Labrador Caribou

Cornell University was probably the farthest thing from Kate Fiduccia's mind when she spotted the blackish blur moving through the patch of golden alders. Kate carried not only her rifle but also Utah's once-in-a-lifetime moose tag. The blur, she knew, was a bull moose. What she had to do now was make the most of this opportunity.

Thousands of miles from Ithaca, New York, home of Cornell, Kate's alma mater, far from the New York home she shared with husband Peter and son Cody, and far from her Manhattan job as an editor with ABC News, Kate made her decision. She hustled down the steep slope, keenly aware that she must move fast if she was to ambush the bull. A rutting bull moose's long-legged stride, Kate knew, could easily carry the animal well away from the place where she'd last spotted it. Like so much else in her life, the bull had appeared rather unexpectedly. Through the years, however, Kate has come to realize how important it is to remain open to unanticipated possibilities that may suddenly present themselves. That is how, on this brisk October 7, she found herself in Utah hunting moose on her birthday. That birthday turned out to be one of Kate's most gratifying.

"I'd always been an outdoorsperson," Kate said. "I enjoyed canoeing, skiing, fishing, and camping. Quite frankly, I hadn't thought much about hunting. When I met Peter in 1979, my feelings toward hunting could best be described as neutral." When she met Peter, she was seventeen and had just graduated from high school. She had applied for a job as the front-desk clerk for a motel, managed by Peter Fiduccia.

"We hit it off right away and began to talk about many different things, including hunting," Kate said. "I found the way Peter explained hunting to me made it very interesting. The idea of hunting sounded rather intriguing, and I wanted to try it for myself. The next year, when I was eighteen, I went hunting for the first time."

She enjoyed her first taste of hunting, but believed she owed it to herself to pursue the educational goals she'd established. A few years later she graduated with honors from Cornell's Hotel School with a degree in business and hotel management. Kate then spent two years as manager of protocol and restaurant administration for the Morgan Guaranty Trust Company in New York City.

Peter and Kate married in 1986. During their courtship Kate continued to absorb as much as possible about both hunting and fishing. She soon discovered she had a natural affinity for both sports. During their early days together the couple pursued white-tailed deer and wild turkeys in rural areas of New York state. Peter so thoroughly enjoyed hunting and fishing, and had such a great desire to communicate his love for and knowledge of the outdoors, that he began to toy with the idea of creating his own TV show that would revolve around his many adventures afield. Peter soon was hosting one of the first TV shows dedicated to hunting and fishing, which he called *Woods 'N Water*. Soon after the show's inception, Kate joined its staff. Her organizational, creative, and writing talents were an ideal fit for television. A short time later, in recognition of her contributions, she was promoted to the show's executive producer. A mere six months later, Kate had attained equal billing with Peter as the series' co-host. Her outdoor exploits were featured prominently each week. Showcasing a beautiful young woman like Kate resonated with both male and female viewers. "Our audience often writes that 'the entire family watches your show'," Kate said. That was the type of audience response the Fiduccias were seeking.

The more Kate hunted, the more she began to feel that she had been born to be a hunter. "I enjoy hunting because it's a challenge," she explained. "When I head out into the backcountry, I enjoy challenging the terrain as well as being challenged by it. To be a good hunter means learning everything possible about your chosen quarry. Hunting's survival aspect is appealing, too. I sometimes imagine what I'd have to do if an emergency arose. Building a strategy to counter a game animal's senses is another fascinating element of the sport, as is preparing and cooking the wild game that I take." With Kate's extensive background in hotel management, a field in which gourmet cooking and aesthetic presentation of food are both highly prized, it's no wonder she gravitated toward instilling a proper appreciation of wild game's benefits and preparation in hunters and their families.

Kate left Cornell's Ivy League atmosphere behind to head up a league of her own where she reigns as one of the nation's most respected wild-game chefs. Her star is still rising in a firmament filled with cookbooks published, it sometimes seems, by every writer with access to a word processor.

After the phenomenal success of his *Woods 'N Water* TV series, Peter Fiduccia next decided to establish the Outdoor Edge Book Club. Each month club members have a chance to buy a particular outdoor title focusing on a different aspect of hunting, fishing, or general outdoor experience. Kate contributed a chapter on wild-game cooking to Peter's 1994 book, *Whitetail Strategies*. This chapter received such an enthusiastic response from readers that the Fiduccias were inspired to include a wild-game cooking segment on their TV show. Called "Going Wild in Kate's Kitchen," it was filmed in the co-hosts' own rural New York kitchen. Viewers let the Fiduccias know how much they appreciated this new and personal addition to *Woods 'N Water*. "Some viewers even wrote in to tell us that 'Going Wild in Kate's Kitchen' had changed a family member's entire perception of hunting, and even persuaded a wife, daughter, or son to try hunting themselves."

These rave reviews inspired Kate to write her own cookbook, *Cooking Wild in Kate's Kitchen*. It became one of the bestselling game cookbooks ever, and encouraged Kate to write another, *Cooking Wild in Kate's Camp*.

Kate's ventures into venison cuisine have paid off handsomely. Peter's book-club membership eagerly awaits Kate's next volume of game-preparation tips, venison recipes, and details such as favorite accompaniments for each entrée. Her recipes display

Kate Fiduccia's magnificent Quebec-Labrador bull missed qualifying for Boone and Crockett by a mere five points.

tremendous creativity and are well suited to a variety of palates. Baked ziti with venison shares the stage with the Greek-influenced venison moussaka and interesting-sounding recipes such as sweet moose loin roast. Kate's comments and reminiscences about the origins of her recipes, the color photos of her finished creations, and scores of memorable scenes from hunting camps and hunting trips make this cookbook truly special. The introduction to Kate's Venison Tamale Pie provides a good example of her personal touch:

> Here's a dish that takes a little bit of extra time because of the cornmeal crust. But it's well worth the effort! It was during a whitetail hunting trip to south Texas that I first tasted true tamales. We were hunting at the Lazy Fork Ranch and the cook prepared many dishes native to her Mexican homeland. Although I wasn't able to get the exact recipe from her, this one comes close—and I haven't had any complaints on the receiving end when I serve it!

"Venison is one of the healthiest meats available today," Kate said. "A four-ounce piece of venison contains only 3.6 grams of fat; moreover, it has not been injected with preservatives. Deer are not fed hormones or antibiotics, either, so I feel perfectly safe eating and serving venison to my family and friends."

One could say that Kate's skill with venison was preordained. She is directly descended from the Beekmans, a family of early Dutch settlers who helped found New York City. In those days people relied a great deal on venison. Perhaps a flair for the preparation of this oft-maligned meat was encoded in Kate's genes.

Kate Fiduccia compiled quotes to be used in *The Quotable Wine Lover*, a featured selection of the Paperback Book of the Month Club. She also has contributed articles and recipes to magazines such as *Outdoor Life* and *Deer and Deer Hunting*. She long ago joined the Outdoor Writers Association of America (OWAA), where she is recognized as an expert on TV, videography, photography, and writing.

A person who hunts and is proud of it is rarely asked to be a guest on network TV. Kate's contract job as a news editor for ABC News, though, has provided her with access to news glitterati like Brian Williams of MSNBC and the staff of the *CBS Evening News*. She has been a guest on both programs, and has been in the spotlight as a hunter of note in feature articles printed by *The New York Times* and *Newsday*. To paraphrase a well-known adage, one TV appearance is worth a thousand words, especially for an audience comprised largely of nonhunters that is exposed to a young female hunter who has accomplished so much and hails from their own state. Such exposure and influence by hunters are increasingly rare. The rural population is decreasing as more people flock to megalopolises, while the precious habitat that supports wildlife—and would allow more people a chance to experience hunting—continues to disappear at an alarming rate.

Five years ago at this writing, birthday girl Kate Fiduccia hustled down to the bottom of that slope, where she wasted no time in locating fresh tracks made by the bull moose she'd spotted from the mountaintop. Those tracks led her to a wallow, and from there the bull's fresh trail was clearly visible. 'I caught up with him as he was traveling along a grassy edge and through some scattered snow," Kate said. "I set up, made my shot, and bagged my first Shiras moose. I was so excited! Only two nonresidents each season are allowed to draw Utah moose tags. Once you draw a tag, you can never apply for another."

Her thrilling experiences with moose keep this species at the very top of Kate's to-hunt list. "Calling and rattling for moose is my favorite thing to do," she said. "I can hunt whitetails almost anywhere, even close to home. But there's just something about the way a big bull moose responds to calls and antler thrashing that really appeals to me. Before shooting my Utah bull, I had an encounter I'll never forget. I'd been slamming my moose antlers together and then thrashing them

Kate, Cody, and Peter Fiduccia pose with Peter's Quebec-Labrador caribou.

into the brush when a big bull just charged right in. He was really fired up. A cameraman was filming the action for our TV show, but this time his camera was out of position and he was unable to get any of the excitement on film before the bull spotted us and ran away. I can't adequately explain what a thrill it was to have that big bull race in to me like that."

Kate's favorite gun is the Thompson Center Encore, a single-shot rifle in .30-06 caliber. She also bowhunts, often with both Peter and Cody. "I shoot a Golden Eagle Spitfire compound set for 55 pounds of pull with 80-percent letoff," she said.

Kate also makes the most of opportunities that arise in her somewhat rarefied New York social circles. "Most New Yorkers are slow to connect a woman with hunting," she said. "When they discover that I'm a hunter, they seem genuinely surprised."

Although she approaches each conversation with high hopes of bringing that person to a better understanding of hunters and hunting, Kate is pragmatic about her chances of doing so. "It depends upon the person I'm speaking with," she said. "Some people don't want to know anything about hunting, and don't want to know why I hunt. These people are unlikely to change their attitudes, no matter what I say. In such a situation I prefer to say nothing. Everyone is entitled to his or her own opinions."

Give Kate an opening, though, and she'll rush on through. "I believe it's better to educate than agitate," she said. "If people seem open to what I have to say, it seems fairly easy to influence them in a positive way by explaining why I or other people hunt.

"A few years ago a journalist from *Newsday* signed up to attend one of my Becoming an Outdoors-Woman courses," Kate said. "She made it clear that she was neither pro- nor antihunting, but simply was interested in learning about it. I really believe that the way I taught the course, emphasizing why and how I hunted and making the presentation fun and enjoyable for participants, worked wonders on any attitudes she may have been harboring. This journalist later wrote an article for the paper based upon her BOW experiences. The spin she put on hunting was extremely positive. That made me feel very good."

Kate doesn't revert to the usual justifications for hunting. "I explain that some women work out at the gym and others play volleyball. I hunt. Hunting is my sport. Of course, there also is the wonderful camaraderie you find when you're outdoors with your family and friends. And there's also the great meat I can prepare, serve, and eat. But the main reason I enjoy hunting is because it really is my sport."

Kate's favorite place is an out-of-the-way spot in the woods near her New York home. "I've seen so many animals there—

Kate's Texas whitetail made everybody happy.

deer, black bears, coyotes, bobcats, foxes, turkeys. Being there gives me a sense of peace. It's beautiful, and it brings back so many great memories."

On a hunting trip to Whale River, Quebec, Kate bagged her most spectacular trophy to date: a Quebec-Labrador caribou. This great bull narrowly missed qualifying for Boone and Crockett's all-time record book with a net score of 370 points.

Kate and Peter have raised their son, Cody, to have a thorough appreciation of the many different facets of the outdoor experience. "Cody started fishing when he was three," Kate said. "He was nine when he shot his first deer, a Sika doe. He's twelve now and has added two white-tailed bucks." Not in New York, Kate was quick to point out. The minimum legal age for hunting there is fourteen.

Kate and Peter try to plan hunting trips with their son in mind. "This season we'll travel to Saskatchewan for elk," she said. "We also have arranged to hunt whitetails at the end of October on Quebec's Anticosti Island. I really believe Cody benefits from these trips. Anticosti, of course, is full of beautiful woodlands and plenty of game to spot, but the island also is loaded with fossils. We'll search for fossils together."

Kate's Utah moose remains her most thrilling hunting memory. Close behind, though, is the Texas whitetail that barged in when she was least expecting it. "The buck's rack was huge, ten or twelve points, and colored an unusual dark chocolate brown. I could have shot, but again my cameraman wasn't ready, and the deer vanished.

"I didn't mind," Kate said. "Through the years, I've discovered that the animals that linger longest in my mind are always the ones that got away."

WILD BLOOD
ERNA FILLATRE
Rocky Mountain Elk

The inside of the duck blind was cold and dark. A man and his small daughter huddled within, content to be able to share the predawn stillness. The man produced a Thermos of hot tea. Steam curled above the tea as the man poured two cups and handed one to his child. A sweet fragrance filled the blind as the young girl blew upon her tea to cool it. She glanced outside, trying to impress upon her memory everything about the moment: the pale seam along the eastern horizon, the wind gusts rattling the bent and twisted cornstalks, and the way her father bent his neck to search the lightening sky.

The seam had fractured now, and an opalescent glow was flooding the charcoal sky. A cloud of ducks rose, tiny specks above a distant tree line, but the flock turned and melted away into a grove of tamaracks. Somewhere in the distance, other ducks were crying faintly.

Years later, Erna Fillatre would recall that duck-blind morning as one of life's defining moments. "I remember when the ducks finally flew in," she said. "The tea tasting so good. My father shooting, and how I loved to eat the ducks he brought home. That wonderful morning grew in my mind and my soul until it formed the lifelong basis for my fascination with nature, the outdoors, and the hunt."

Erna, who grew up in British Columbia, would have to store up enough memories of her parents to last her entire life. They died within two years of each other when Erna was a teenager. Before her beloved father passed away, he gave her some advice: "Always be independent. Never rely on anyone else to do things for you." When he died, Erna remembered his words and decided to use them as the template for her life.

Erna graduated from school in Calgary, Alberta, then returned to British Columbia, where she worked for twenty-five years at her own painting and interior decorating business. During this period she met and married a hunter. In her late thirties, she went along as a spectator on a mule deer hunt organized by her husband and one of his friends. "They each got a buck right away," Erna said. "Witnessing the kill was exciting, but I wasn't sure I would be able to pull the trigger myself."

Erna gave the carcasses a wide berth before curiosity about field-dressing the animals finally got the best of her. She eventually took photographs of the field-dressed animals, then helped load them into a pickup truck. Enjoying the venison from her husband's buck during the coming year helped convince Erna. "I knew I wanted to become a hunter," she said. "And I wanted to hunt on my own."

A wealth of information exists for any would-be hunter, if you know where to look. Since Erna was married to a hunter, she already had access to hunting magazines and books. Her favorite "teachers" have been Jim Zumbo and Dwight Schuh, and she eagerly scoured their articles searching for any "magic bullets" that would help her become a better hunter.

In 1984 she took a giant step forward when she enrolled in a British Columbia hunter-training course. The instructor was proficient in the areas of high-powered rifles, benchrest shooting, and the handloading of ammunition. Erna decided to learn how to handload, too. Handloading requires incredible attention to detail and the willingness to put in long hours for a reward that other people might not understand. The handloader must select the right bullet and powder to use in her cartridges. She must experiment with various powder loadings to get the desired ballistics. That suited Erna Fillatre to a T. "I wanted to learn everything, from loading my own cartridges to butchering the animals I shot," she said. She did her homework and purchased a .270 Husqvarna bolt-action rifle from an old friend.

"I made a vow that I would kill an animal as humanely as possible," Erna said. "I would get as close as I could before shooting, and wait for the proper moment so that I might kill with one shot." One-shot kills require a lot of rifle-range practice. "My shoulder was many times bruised and sore after I'd shot sixty or more rounds in a single session," she said. Once Erna gained accuracy from the bench, she started shooting offhand from various positions at balloons positioned on boards. "The stance I liked best, and the one that felt the most natural, was one I could quickly assume: I would drop down and sit on my right leg while resting my gun across my left knee. When I wasn't at the range, I'd practice with a pellet rifle, shooting flies off the shed door." When Erna became proficient at both killing flies and breaking balloons, she knew she was ready for the real thing.

Year one came and went. Erna didn't see a legal animal. "Thank goodness," she said, reflectively. "I would get myself into such gnarly places that if I had shot an elk, I don't know what I would have done."

Her second season afield resulted in Erna's first big-game animal: a deer. "That's when I discovered how much work is involved in getting a deer out. Before taking a shot, I began considering how far I'd have to pack the animal out. This is important if you hunt alone." Getting game out can be a problem even for a man, and it can be a major problem for a petite woman like Erna.

Although her first big game was a deer, the game animal that truly made her pulse race was the bull elk. While elk hunting late one afternoon, she thought it might be a good time to practice bugling. "My first bugle was one of those little brass coils," she said. "My only instructions came from books and audiotapes. I blew the bugle every ten or fifteen minutes on my way off the mountain. I didn't think I sounded much like an elk, but as I neared my truck I heard a bloodcurdling squeal. I spun around, and the trees behind me were swaying violently. I was so scared, I just sat down and froze. After many minutes, I finally was able to make a feeble little squeal with the coil. The bull screamed back instantly—

Erna mainly taught herself to hunt elk, with spectacular results.

he couldn't have been more than thirty yards away! The two of us exchanged threats and insults until it was too dark to shoot." Erna never did see that bull.

Erna took one of her first bulls after inadvertently slipping right into the middle of a herd. "The wind was in my favor," she explained. "They were feeding, so I just remained quiet until the herd passed me. Once they'd all gone, I followed them up the next ridge. I saw a light-colored bull feeding as he climbed, so I sat down and rested my .270 upon my knee." Erna aimed carefully and squeezed the trigger. The raghorn bull ran downhill just a few yards and then toppled over in a clump of trees. Elk are tough, but Erna had killed this one as planned, with a single, well-placed shot. Her hours of practice on the rifle range had paid off.

"I enjoy hunting so much," Erna said. "The natural world is so amazing, and hunting puts me there. I try to think like the animal I'm after, and this gets me totally focused on the moment.

"I see and experience so many incredible things," she continued. "Once, a squirrel ran along a log and then right up my

Erna bagged this raghorn after it stepped out to rake a sapling with its antlers.

leg. We stared at each other, but I finally broke out laughing. That squirrel left in a hurry. A nonhunter would rarely, if ever, experience such things."

Erna enjoys hunting for other reasons, too. "Hunting hones necessary skills, like stalking," she said. "You begin to think like few modern people do anymore. My mind calms down, and all is right with my world. The rigorous exercise helps get me in great shape, and when I harvest an animal with one shot, I feel a tremendous sense of accomplishment."

Erna, who was a director of the Lake Windermere Rod and Gun Club in British Columbia, endured the curious looks and cautious statements of male club members when she first aspired to hunting. "It wasn't only that I am a female, but I don't fit the typical hunter image since I am slim and small-framed," she explained. "Their attitudes changed, though, after I started killing bull elk season after season and began winning the largest-elk trophy at the annual big-game banquets."

Erna is so much more than simply an excellent hunter with trophy animals to her credit. She is also an accomplished fly fisher and sculptor, and enjoys hiking, horseback riding, meditating, and tinkering with things that are broken. Her byline has appeared in various places, including *Bugle*, the Rocky Mountain Elk Foundation's magazine. She has volunteered to help biologists trap and radio-collar elk for research projects.

Erna has learned a lot through the years about bugling simply by doing it. "I'd gotten up late one morning," she said, recalling one learning experience. "The weather was awful: windy, cold, and drizzly. I debated whether to go back to bed or go out and get cold. I finally drove to a friend's place in good country full of small ridges and draws where elk like to congregate, particularly during breeding season. I hiked up a ridge and bugled. The wind swallowed my call—I could barely hear it amid the sound of the trees swaying in the gusts.

"I crossed another, more heavily timbered ridge, and blew on a second type of bugle I'd packed that day. When I'd heard no reply after fifteen minutes, I returned to the first ridge. Now it was pouring and I was cold and soaked, but I tried the third and last bugle I'd brought along, a cow call. I noticed movement through a fringe of poplars along a game trail and blew into it softly, and suddenly a four-point bull came out directly below me to rake a sapling with his antlers. I killed him where he stood, less than forty yards away."

Using similar tactics, many of which she devised herself, has during her fifteen years of hunting allowed Erna to take numerous mule and white-tailed deer as well as many branch-antlered bull elk, including several four-points and five-points, three small six-points, and two trophy-class bulls—one a royal six-point and the other a spectacular imperial seven-point. Although Erna has entered neither trophy into the record books, both are large enough to attain a high SCI ranking. Erna has gained a reputation as perhaps the most accomplished and best-known female elk hunter on the continent. And she does it all on her own!

"Every animal I harvest is a trophy," Erna explained. "Taking that seven-point was nice, but I honestly didn't set out to do so."

Erna's story about that monster bull is both exciting and spiritual. She wrote it for *Bugle*, which titled it "The Hardest, Easiest Hunt." Here is the gist of that story:

During a scouting foray in late August, she found fresh elk sign in a grove of poplars in one of her favorite spots. The rubs were still sticky with sap, and bits of bull hair adhered to the violated tree trunks.

On opening morning Erna was nearby, listening and waiting. But it was a dry hole. "After nine more days of hard hunting, I still hadn't connected," she said. "I'd been close, but something always seemed to go wrong."

That evening, Erna stopped to ask a local rancher if he would let her hunt on his property. The place contained many lush hayfields, one of them bordered by a brushy creek that butted up against a dark forested area.

"The rancher told me they hadn't allowed hunting there for about seventeen years," Erna said. "But he knew my reputation for hunting alone and taking only one clean shot, so he granted me permission."

The next day, Erna was back at the ranch by 4:30 P.M. A spate of hot weather had made conditions extremely noisy, so she decided to take a stand rather than tramp about in the dry timber. "I positioned myself on a slight rise above a hayfield," she said. "I moved three or four times to get into just the right spot."

Erna, thinking like an elk, believed the animals would approach the hayfield from the creek, jump the fence, and enter the field about 150 yards upwind from where she was waiting. At 7 P.M., that's exactly what happened. One elk followed another until ten cows and calves were bucking, mewing, and feeding in the hayfield right in front of her.

With the wind still in her favor, Erna had no fears about the animals scenting her. She was watching them when she heard a thud behind her and smelled the strong, musky odor of elk. With no time to put on her facemask, Erna covered her features with a gloved hand. No sooner had she done so than the cows and calves started moving downhill to her right and as close to her as sixteen yards. The jig was almost up when a calf crossed the fence behind

Articles by Jim Zumbo and Dwight Schuh taught Erna much of what she needed to get started in elk hunting.

Erna and walked right in front of her. "I could see droplets of moisture roll from its nose and land on the ground," Erna said.

"I lowered my eyes until I was staring at the space between the calf's head and feet. I thought it would never move, but I finally heard the twang of barbed wire below me, signaling that the calf had jumped into the hayfield."

For some reason, women hunters seem to be extremely in sync with game animals. More than one woman has expressed the notion that human "brain waves" seem to be detectable on some level by game animals. Erna believes game animals possess an uncanny ability to discern danger by zeroing in on a hunter's thoughts. "One reason I hunt alone is that I have no distractions," she said. "I can remain 100 percent focused on what I am doing; my senses are a lot keener when I am by myself. I often allow my intuition to take over, and that has worked to my advantage on many occasions. I try to empty my mind of predator-like thoughts, because my state of mind seems to directly affect my success. When I behave like a spectator or just another creature in the woods, I find that I can approach much closer to game."

Erna was in full instinctual mode when the calf passed so near she could have reached out and touched it. With her arm and hand cramping from being held so long over her face, she had just started to shift into a more comfortable position when she heard a guttural grunt behind her.

"I continued to look straight ahead, despite an overwhelming urge to turn and see what had made this noise," she said. "My peripheral vision caught a huge set of antlers, then a large, light-colored body. I moved my head slightly and was able to count seven points. Behind this bull stood a six-point, a five-point, and then a spike. My heart was pumping like a frightened bird's. I breathed in deeply to calm down."

Within minutes, these elk joined the others less than fifty yards from where Erna waited. Rather than shooting immediately, the woman simply enjoyed the animals' antics for more than half an hour. "I actually had to pull myself back into the hunter frame of mind. I put my .270 up to my cheek and aimed at the seven-pointer standing broadside in the field."

Something—who knows what—prevented Erna from squeezing off a shot, despite numerous attempts to do so. She changed her mind and decided to harvest the smaller six-point bull. As she put her cross hairs on the animal, he began weaving in and out of the cows, making it a risky shot. When he finally stopped, a cow stepped between the bull and Erna.

Dark shadows were spreading over the scene, and Erna knew she had no time to waste when a sudden alarm "bark" sounded behind her. Something had scented her! The field emptied of elk, except for the big bull, which trotted from the middle of the field but stopped at the fence. Erna made her decision and fired. The bull humped, took three or four steps, and collapsed.

"The cows were looking at him from across the fence," she recalled. "I felt incredibly sad."

Erna collected herself, then walked down to the magnificent bull. "I thanked him for his life," she said. "Then awe turned to excitement."

At first, Erna Fillatre had been unable to take the life of such a beautiful and spectacular animal. "In the end, though, he gave it to me," she said. "This had been the hardest, easiest elk hunt I've experienced.

"Taking an animal's life is an act of great significance," she said. "Although I have 'made it right with myself' as another predator on this earth, I realize I owe it to the animal to give it as quick and painless a death as possible.'

Erna is no longer married, but she has found a new hunting partner in her significant other, Lyle Dorey of the Rocky Mountain Elk Foundation. Together they have shared many adventures, including an attempt to establish a helicopter medevac service in Honduras. Today the pair resides in Alberta, where Erna continues to hunt on her own and philosophize about her involvement in a sport that can at times seem paradoxical to even the most conscientious hunters.

"Once the season opens, I eat, sleep, and breathe hunting. Camo clothing is my only wardrobe, and I love it. It's difficult to return to wearing street clothes again, or to go from elk urine back to perfume. When elk season ends, I go through withdrawal.

"But, oh, how my life begins again in earnest during the last weeks of August," she said in conclusion. "Preparing for the hunt is almost as much fun as being in the woods once the season begins. I truthfully can say that as I breathe in the late-summer smells and watch those first leaves turn to gold, the anticipation of each coming fall and each pending season sets the wild blood flowing through my veins. As long as my legs still carry me out into the bush, I will be a hunter."

ROCKY MOUNTAIN HIGH
JANET GEORGE
Mule Deer, Rocky Mountain Bighorn, Whitetail, Pronghorn

When two avid bow hunters, one female, the other male, meet by chance while on their own individual treks after bighorn sheep, the karma involved must be acknowledged. First, hunting bighorns is never a cakewalk. Second, only the most self-assured hunters would ever make plans to hunt bighorns, the ghosts of the scree, with a bow. Yet that's exactly what each of these people, independent of the other, had decided to do.

What are the chances they would meet in the quaint little town of Georgetown, Colorado?

Three years later, in 1988, Janet and Scott George accepted another challenge when they made their vows as husband and wife. In Scott, Janet had found someone who enjoyed hunting and wildlife as much as she did. Scott knew there weren't many women anywhere like Janet. The next ten years passed in a blur. Janet, a biologist for Colorado's Division of Wildlife, and Scott, a general contractor, spent their spare time applying for licenses, planning and making bowhunts, and reminiscing about hunts completed. Their lives became a whirlwind of shared adventures, more exciting than either could have imagined on that fateful day years before in Georgetown. Janet's life as a hunter, however, had begun even earlier than that.

"When I was a kid, shooting BB guns and bows fascinated me," Janet said. "My dad was a pheasant hunter, and my family has supported my interests all the way."

At the age of nineteen, Janet enrolled at Colorado State University in Fort Collins. She was married to her first husband at the time, but he didn't seem nearly as interested in hunting as Janet was. She yearned for a real honest-to-goodness Rocky Mountain high-country elk camp.

"I was in school, but my schedule allowed me to hunt some mornings, evenings, and weekends," Janet said. "I had several close calls with elk that first year, and a few of those were pretty exciting. But I didn't need excitement to know that this was what I really loved to do. I'd always enjoyed shooting a bow, and I liked the incredible challenge of sneaking up close to animals. Bowhunting for elk was everything I thought it would be. Though I didn't get anything that first year, I couldn't wait for the next season to begin."

The following year, Janet's husband got his own bow. When elk season arrived, she, he, and one of his friends pitched camp in an area they previously had scouted out. Early one morning, Janet arose well before first light so she could use the darkness to slip close to where she suspected the elk might be. She had discussed her plan with the two others, but they chose to remain in camp. It's a good thing she didn't allow herself to be tempted by the prospect of a lazy morning in camp. About an hour after sunrise, the young woman shot a five-point bull elk she'd bugled with an arrow at twenty yards.

"It was the first big-game animal either my husband or I had ever taken," Janet said. "Once the bull was down, the situation became rather humorous, as well as exciting, since neither of us knew exactly what to do next."

Janet felt conflicted about the act of killing. "It had taken me a long time to actually kill a sparrow with my gun, and when I did, I felt terrible seeing it lying there. Even now I feel bad after I shoot something, but I realize that dropping a game animal with either a bullet or an arrow is probably the most humane death we can give it."

Wildlife determined her education as well as her avocation. In college Janet was torn between a career with animals and

"I've taken several Pope and Young white-tailed bucks, but I don't think any of them meant more to me than my first white-tailed doe," said Janet George.

becoming an electrical engineer. Wildlife won out, and at Colorado State she majored in zoology and went on to earn a master's in wildlife biology.

The five-point bull elk marked Janet's "coming out" as a bow hunter. She took another five-point elk and a mule deer doe, then became intrigued with whitetails when she learned that they can be so much warier than either mule deer or elk.

"I'd been reading about hunting from stands," Janet said, "and decided I wanted to take my first whitetail from one. I found a good spot along the South Platte River, set up my tree stand, and shot a white-tailed doe from it. I can't begin to describe what an accomplishment that felt like. Since then I've taken several Pope and Young white-tailed bucks, but I don't think any of them has meant more to me than that doe."

Doing it all herself, as when she shot this wonderful bighorn ram with an arrow, gives Janet George an incredible feeling of accomplishment.

Janet enjoys the thrill of the chase, whether she is packing a bow, rifle, or shotgun. "I use the rifle when my goal is to bring home meat," she explained. "I don't think anything is healthier than lean wild game."

Janet so far has taken eight Pope and Young animals: a caribou, a mule deer, three whitetails, a Rocky Mountain bighorn, and two pronghorns. She killed another caribou that would have made the book, but its antlers were in velvet. At the time, Pope and Young was not accepting entries of caribou in velvet.

Janet George is so enamored of wild sheep that she uses a variation of the bighorn's Latin name, *Ovis canadensis canadensis*, as an e-mail address. She has applied for Colorado archery bighorn licenses every year she's been eligible, and so far has drawn three tags. Her craving to use a bow and arrow to shoot a Rocky Mountain bighorn in the Colorado high country was satisfied in 1989. That moment ranks among her most exciting bowhunts.

The date was 4 September. Before the sun's rays had gained enough altitude to penetrate the canyons in Deadman's Gulch, Janet was already looking for her ram. The evening before, she had watched a lone ram with almost a full curl feeding near a talus slope. It had seemed nervous, often pausing to look in all directions.

Now Janet glassed the cliffs where she'd seen the ram the night before. Sure enough, she spotted the loner and continued to keep him in her sights until the animal bedded down at about 9:30 A.M. That's when the real work began. Janet had to mark in her mind's eye the exact spot where the ram had bedded, then calculate the best way to traverse the cliffs and boulder fields so that she would come out on a ledge directly above the resting animal. As soon as she felt confident of her route and landmarks, she crossed the small creek rushing through the valley below and began her climb. It was 9:40.

"I climbed until 11:30," Janet said. "When I reached the target ledge, I eased out on it, but the ram was nowhere in sight. I decided to wait until noon to see if he would appear. I thought perhaps he had moved into the shade of a tree or an overhanging rock. I didn't want to move too much for fear the ram might spot me.

"Noon arrived, and still no ram. I moved slowly east, and then realized that I had come out too high up on the ledge. When I looked farther down the slope, the ram was bedded 150 feet below me.

"Very carefully I edged down the slope and moved out onto the ledge directly above the bighorn. When I peeked over the rim, he was just forty feet below me, bedded about ten yards out from the base of the cliff. A Douglas-fir limb blocked any shot at the ram's chest. As I eased out onto a narrow pinnacle to get a clear shot, the ram turned his head. I froze."

In mountain landscapes you often hear brittle sounds like rock hitting rock or tree limbs scraping against each other, but Janet thought the slight sound of dry lichen being crushed beneath her boot heel had perhaps alerted the bedded bighorn. After what seemed an eternity, the ram's head nodded and returned to its napping position. "By wedging my boots in cracks, I crept farther out on the pinnacle. When I was just a foot from the end, the fir bough still screened too much of the ram's chest to risk a shot." Willing herself not to look downward at anything but the ram, Janet took one minuscule step after another until finally she was poised on the pinnacle's far right corner. Forty feet of air separated the broadhead from the ram.

"I concentrated on a spot behind the ram's withers and an inch to the left of his spine. Then I drew and aimed instinctively, and shot."

The ram bolted from his bed, charged forty yards along a sheep trail, then turned and lurched down into a boulder field before coming to rest on a huge boulder.

"Taking a bighorn ram had been one of my dreams since reading Jack O'Connor's sheep-hunting stories during my

Janet George has become perhaps the most successful high-country female bow hunter on the continent.

childhood," Janet said. Her ram green-scored 1704/s under the Pope and Young system.

When Janet and Scott George's son Owen was born four years ago, his parents were elated, even though a child would definitely cramp their style for a while. "I think he's going to be a hunter," Janet confided. "He enjoys looking for animals with us, and thinks shooting his little bow at our Styrofoam dinosaur target is just the coolest thing in the world. Whenever I take him hiking, though, I outfit him in orange because he can disappear so quickly, and he knows how to blow the safety whistle he carries everywhere."

After Janet gave birth to Owen, she decided to see if she'd lost her edge. "I hadn't gone on a backpack hunt for some time," she said. "When I finally drew my long-awaited goat tag, I wondered if I would still be up to the rigors of a solo backcountry bowhunt.

"Goats live in extreme country, but they're usually stalkable," Janet said. She backpacked into her area, set up camp, spotted a good billy, and had the animal down and tagged before her friend, Nance Howard, had hiked in as planned to meet Janet at her campsite. "Nance had agreed to come in to help out with the packing chores in case I was successful," Janet said.

Her job as a biologist keeps Janet close to nature and wildlife every day of the year. But the days she lives for and longs for are those when she can become one with the wildlife, the wind, and the weather during yet another unforgettable wilderness adventure.

THE FAMILY EXPERIENCE
LESA HALL
Pronghorn, Black Bear

"I am who I am today because of my dad and my husband," said Lesa Hall, owner of and graphic designer for *Trophy Hunter* magazine. Hunting together has always been a large part of the close feeling she has for her family.

Her father, Kent Roberts, took her into the field starting at the age of nine. At the time, she was her dad's "son" because her sister Dana never went hunting and other siblings Jena, Tara, and Brad came much later. Years later, Lesa and her father and brother hunted regularly, and those adventures continue today, with the added company of her husband, oldest daughter, and son.

Lesa's father, who started fishing commercially in 1966, the year she was born, worked in Alaska each summer. But in 1978 he built a summer cabin so his family could be closer to him while he worked. Starting at age twelve, Lesa worked each summer in a fish cannery with her sister. By the age of sixteen, she was working eighteen hours each day and making good money. She earned a reputation as the fastest fish gutter at the cannery and was always the one to get the job done. "I've smelled rotten salmon, so antelope and bear are nothing," she said.

Rusty Hall came into Lesa's life on 1 December 1983. While sitting on her boyfriend's lap at a party, Lesa couldn't take her eyes off the handsome young man playing poker nearby. Rusty Hall stood out because he wasn't drinking, swearing, or chewing tobacco. And "He had a wrestler's body," added Lesa. She and her best friend made a $5 bet on whether she could get a date with Rusty within one week, which she did. At the time, Lesa was a senior in high school and Rusty attended Snow College, majoring in engineering after serving a Church of Jesus Christ of the Latter-Day Saints mission in South Dakota.

Exactly seven days after the party, Lesa and Rusty went on their first date, and in December Rusty proposed. They were married on 1 June 1984, in the Provo, Utah, Temple, just one day after Lesa's graduation from high school. Even her father knew their marriage was destined to happen and thought her relationship with Rusty provided a healthy example of love to her siblings. Rusty joined Lesa's father in Alaska on the fishing boat in 1984 while she continued to work in the cannery to earn money for Rusty to finish college. The newlyweds set up house near Snow College, and Lesa delivered the first of four children on 1 April 1985. Three years later, Rusty graduated from Utah State University with a degree in industrial technology and began a professional career as an engineer with Thiokol. Their life only got better as they added three more children to their family: Kade in 1988, Jenika in 1991, and Kylah in 1992.

Just as Rusty's professional career was taking off, he dreamed of founding a hunting magazine dedicated to great stories and photographs of big game across North America. His and Lesa's passion for hunting prompted him to begin the magazine *Trophy Hunter* in the fall of 1993. Rusty's salary at Thiokol supported the growing young family, so the duties of magazine management fell in the lap of Lesa, who balanced running a company and raising four children for five years. In 1997 Rusty finally made the break from his secure job to manage the magazine full-time. Lesa taught herself to design the magazine, thus saving charges from independent designers. The successful magazine is a great credit to the Halls.

After marrying Rusty, Lesa took a break from hunting to concentrate on raising their children. In 1990 she began hunting again. Lesa has killed four barren-ground caribou, one antelope, three black bears, one white-tailed buck, one Alaska-Yukon moose, one Coues deer, a cow elk, nine turkeys, and a muley buck. Her pronghorn and

Lesa Hall with her outstanding caribou taken in 1997.

Coues deer rank in Boone and Crockett, while one of her bears ranks second among muzzleloader kills in the state of Utah. Lesa drew hunting permits right after the delivery of two of her children. She actually hunted for Utah mule deer one month after delivering Kylah in November '92 and filled her mule deer tag in '91 when Jenika was six months old. She would nurse, go hunting, nurse, and go hunting throughout the season. Now her two oldest children, daughter Tana and son Kade, join her on many hunts.

Lesa loves a challenge, so beginning in 1997, she added to her schedule the duties of graphic-design director for *Race Review* magazine and regularly designs brochures and other publications for a variety of clients.

All the while, Lesa was suffering from severe headaches that tormented her daily for nine years, twenty-four hours a day. A few weeks after a major surgery, believe it or not, Lesa went on a turkey hunt. "I'm crazy like that," she said, shrugging.

Lesa continued to hunt despite her medical setbacks. Rusty paid for a variety of dream hunts in 2001 since her headaches were

Lesa Hall, left, and her daughter, Tana, celebrate a successful hunt.

continuing at an alarming rate and they didn't know what the future might hold. There was a turkey hunt in Nevada and Wyoming, and a caribou hunt with their children in Alaska. Lesa wanted her children to experience what she loves to do so much and the bond that she had with her father. Lesa also went moose hunting in the Northwest Territories, black bear hunting in Utah, and Coues deer hunting in Mexico. She especially enjoyed the bear hunt, which daughter Tana dubbed "Mother's Day Bear" and described in a story for Lesa's magazine.

That hunt began with Lesa being drawn for a coveted black bear tag. The first weekend of the hunt, Lesa, Brad, and Tana met up with their guide, Wade Lemon, and assistants Ed and Dan Hickman. They chased a bear for twelve hours up and over many canyons but never caught up with it. The next weekend, Lesa and Brad went to the hunting area without Tana. Saturday afternoon, Lesa called to ask Tana to come and help locate a decent bear, so Tana, having had her license for only two weeks, hopped into her car and made it to the site a few hours later. They split up to cover more country the next morning. Wade, Kaylah, Brad, Lesa, and Tana went up one canyon while Dan and Ed went up another. On top of a ridge, Tana joked that it was Mother's Day and Wade had better hurry and find a black bear for Lesa or she would beat him with a stick. Farther up that ridge, the dogs struck the scent of what turned out to be a giant bear, which took the hunters down into a deep hole. The going was tough, but they finally reached the bear. Lesa let fly a round from her muzzleloader, but it took two additional shots to down the boar for good. Its skull measures $19^{13}/_{16}$ inches and will rank approximately twenty-fifth in the world when listed in the next edition of the *Longhunter Muzzleloading Big-Game Record Book.*

Lesa's New Mexico pronghorn hunt in 1997 resulted in the ninety-second largest buck ever taken, according to the 1999 edition of the Boone and Crockett Club book *Records of North American Big Game.* Tony Grimmett and Paul Stewart were her guides in Socorro County. At first light they spotted a huge buck. He ran with another buck and a doe. During a four-hour stalk, Lesa twice missed the big one, and wondered if she'd have another chance to redeem herself.

Tony, Lesa, and Rusty returned to the same spot the next morning. As Tony glassed left and Rusty right, Lesa looked straight ahead and whispered, "Please tell me that's him!"

Sure enough, the buck had returned to his home territory. Twenty minutes later, Lesa fired once, using her lightweight .30-378 made by Mountain Rifles Inc., and the buck dropped. Lesa's buck is noteworthy for its mass. The right horn measures $16^{1}/_{8}$ inches long and the left measures $15^{7}/_{8}$. The circumference at the base of

Logan, Lesa, and Rusty with her Alaska-Yukon moose from the Northwest Territories.

both horns is 6⅝ inches. Only six other women have taken pronghorn bucks that score higher than Lesa's.

Lesa also fondly recalls the Alaska-Yukon moose hunt she and Rusty made in 2001 with Nahanni Butte Outfitters in Northwest Territories. Glassing from a high vantage point in the middle of a valley, they spotted a Dall ram and several bull moose, including the one eventually taken by Lesa. It was bedded in pines on the far side of the valley. They stalked across the valley and into willows below the bull's location. Guide Clay Lancaster blew on a cow call, and a series of low grunts came in reply. A tree shook violently, and the bull increased its grunting as it moved to their left. They circled that way and set up again. Antlers flashed above the brush, and Clay told Lesa to get ready. As the bull stepped through a small clearing, Lesa fired a single shot from her .30-378 and the bull dropped. The rack has an outside spread of 61 inches.

The entire family got into the act when Lesa, Rusty, Tana, Kade, Grandpa Roberts, and Uncles Woody and Brad traveled to the Bear Trail Lodge in King Salmon, Alaska in 2001 to hunt caribou. This was the first time Lesa's children had hunted with the men who had inspired her hunting career. As outfitter Mike McCrary flew them to the hunting area, they saw bears, thousands of caribou, and a few moose. As Tana described it in *Trophy Hunter*, "There were caribou everywhere. I couldn't believe it. There had to be literally thousands all around us. But they were far from camp. I don't think I have ever been as excited to get out and hike my butt off before." Within a few days, each hunter had a respectable caribou. Their spare time was spent fishing the Naknek River. "Uncle Woody caught about 80 percent of the fish. He was lucky," Tana quipped. She considered herself one of the luckiest sixteen-year-olds in the world for the opportunity to travel to Alaska with her parents and family. She especially loved hunting with her grandfather as Lesa had done for so many years.

Lesa and Tana have favorite moments from that memorable hunt. Lesa's father shot a caribou with his bow, and Brad came running back to camp to get Tana to help pack the caribou out. Tana had been sleeping in the tent and came out in nothing but her red longjohns and hiking boots. She threw on a backpack, grabbed one more for the meat, and said, "Let's go!" Lesa said, "I will never forget Tana running across the tundra in nothing but her red longjohns."

Lesa also recalls moments involving son Kade, especially the look on his face when he harvested his first big-game animal—the biggest caribou of the trip.

There's a lot more to Lesa than hunting and magazine design. She enjoys antique cars, family outings, fishing, and spending time with her mother and sisters. And she readily admits that she loves her chickens. "Calamity's Hen House," so named by Lesa and her four children, is artistically painted to resemble the cabin featured in the old Doris Day movie *Calamity Jane*. For the past two years Lesa has cared for forty-four chickens, and just recently received two hundred more, filling Calamity's Hen House.

Lesa hopes to continue hunting for as long as her health allows. She doesn't know what the future holds, but if her will to get better is as strong as her will to hunt, she will do just fine.

FIRST-TIME HUNTER WITH
A FIRST-PLACE BULL MOOSE
MARY A. ISBELL
Shiras Moose

A new hunter seldom sees, let alone collects, a Boone and Crockett anything, but first-time hunter Mary Isbell, twelve years old at the time, did just that on 30 August 2000.

"Most of us only dream of taking such a fine trophy," said the late C. Randall Byers, chair of the Boone and Crockett Club's Records of North American Big-Game Committee. "There are younger hunters with trophies in the record book, but none with such an impressive Wyoming moose. Hats off to Mary's dad and other parents who introduce their children to shooting and hunting at such a young age."

"Mary's bull scores 185⅝ points," said Jack Reneau, director of big-game records at the Boone and Crockett Club, "and ranks in the top fifteen Wyoming moose ever recorded. It received the first-place award during the 24th Awards Program banquet at Bass Pro Shops, Springfield, Missouri, in June 2001." Reneau added that close to one hundred Wyoming or Shiras moose were accepted by the B&C records program from 1998 to 2000, and Mary's moose ranked No. 1 among those. When the eleventh edition of the Boone and Crockett Club's all-time record book is published in 2005, her moose will rank approximately twelfth largest in the world.

Mary comes from a long family tradition of hunting, starting with her Grandpa Isbell, who taught Mary's father, Doug, the ways of the woods. This hunting tradition has passed to Mary (born in 1987) and her three older sisters, Ashley (born in 1979), Becky (1981), and Ivy (1984). The girls all started with .22s at the age of five and progressed to other rifles. By the time Mary and her sisters were ten years old, Mary said they were working with .243s. Soon they progressed to .270s and .30-06 rifles.

"It was just so neat to go out together," Mary said. Her ancestors traveled by Conestoga wagon in the mid-1800s to Utah, where they settled and raised their family. Hunting was how they fed everyone. When Doug graduated from medical school at the University of Utah, he and Heather relocated to Idaho Falls, Idaho, where he set up his practice.

Mary enjoys school, especially the electives like cooking, sewing, and plastics, where "you can make things with your hands." She thinks about a career in medicine like her father, who is an obstetrician and gynecologist, or as a teacher like her mother. Fifth grade would be her choice of grade level. Becoming a nurse practitioner attracts Mary to the medical field.

She has an assortment of pets, including two potbellied pigs, dozens of multicolored rabbits, five horses, and a tabby cat named Peeper. Mary quickly admits that her favorite part of growing up is doing "stuff with my family." Her mother, Heather, a former schoolteacher, cares for the brood and encourages her daughters to enjoy all aspects of the outdoors, although she has not hunted.

Mary also is an accomplished horsewoman. She and the two family horses, Tiggy and Missy, compete in American Quarter Horse Association- and 4-H-sponsored riding and horse events. All four of the daughters and Heather are accomplished horsewomen who have won numerous awards, ribbons, and trophies for their skills. They compete in Wyoming, Idaho, and Utah.

Music, piano in particular, also holds a special place in Mary's heart. She gives concerts at school and entertains friends and family with nimble-fingered renditions of classics and popular music. Her

Mary Isbell (left) and Ivy Isbell with the Canadian black bear Mary shot in June 2002.

parents report that she is an honor student entering high school, where she looks forward to joining the debate team, on which older sister Ashley competed and was twice a state champion.

The Isbell family fate must be to draw moose tags. In the same year that Mary drew her tag, sister Becky also received one and collected a nice bull that weighed approximately nine hundred pounds. Ashley drew a moose tag in 2001. The family traveled to Texas that year, and Mary collected a respectable white-tailed buck with sixteen scorable points and a gross Boone and Crockett score of 169⅜. In June 2002, the girls and their father traveled to Canada for a long-anticipated black bear hunt on Queen Charlotte Island. All four of the girls have hunted with their dad for as long as they can remember.

"I've hiked with them over some of the most difficult country you could imagine in southeastern Idaho," Mary said. "My dad loves the steepest, roughest, and rockiest mountains he can find." The daughters have given some of their most arduous challenges

Mary (right) with some of her friends and family who shared in her joy when she downed this massive moose on 30 August 2000. From left: Bob Hudman, Craig Heiner, and Doug Isbell.

nicknames like "death mountain," "heart-attack hill," and "heatstroke mountain." The Isbell family travels to such places, though, because that is where trophy animals live. Since Ivy is closest in age to Mary, the two girls have often hunted together, but in October 2002, it was Becky and Mary who hunted pronghorns together in western New Mexico.

In Idaho, where Mary lives, a hunter must decide which special permit to apply for—a moose, sheep, or Rocky Mountain goat permit or the deer, antelope, or elk permit. Each year as application deadlines near, the Isbell family finds itself in deep debate about which permits they want.

Mary's success in 2000 actually began in the summer of 1999, when her father and a few of her older sisters hiked in an area of Bonneville County and he spotted a breathtaking bull moose near a cabin where the family had gone to camp. Dad returned to the cabin breathless and described this amazing animal. He led Mary and the others back to the location, and together they viewed the moose through binoculars. From that moment forward, they all decided to apply for moose tags in 2000.

"As I listened to the excitement in their voices, I could tell this one must be very special," Mary said. "Dad is very objective and knowledgeable about evaluating trophy game and doesn't usually get as excited as he was this time." Her father's Boone and Crockett trophies include a 407⅜-point barren-ground caribou at Wolf Lake, Alaska in 1993 and a 394⅜-point barren-ground caribou near Mulchatna River, Alaska in 1988. He also took an outstanding pronghorn in 1998 in New Mexico that scores 84⅜ points.

When Mary and Becky learned they had drawn moose tags for that fall, they couldn't believe their good fortune. Family friend Craig Heiner also drew, so the entire family and friends started planning the hunts. Tradition dictated that Mary carry her grandfather's .30-06, so she practiced shooting it all summer with Becky, who also planned to use the rifle, a Model 70 Winchester bought in 1945. Doug had modified the stock in 1982 and developed some handloads with 165-grain Nosler Partition bullets. The older sisters had used it to take some nice animals, including trophy moose.

Throughout the summer, the girls practiced their shooting, hiked, rode horseback, and searched in the woods where the giant moose had been sighted the year before. Two weeks before the start of the season, family friend Bob Hudman called to say he'd seen a bull moose that took his breath away. As he described the location, the Isbells recognized the area and vowed they would keep track of the moose until the season opened. But the bull simply vanished days

Mary Isbell and a fine Texas whitetail.

before the opening. Nonetheless, they resolved to be in the area early on opening day. Heather and Doug made arrangements for Mary to miss school that day. Craig Heiner offered to join the hunt without a rifle even though he, too, had a moose tag.

Everyone met at the Hudmans' cabin near the Tex Creek Wildlife Management Area on opening morning. The party included Mary, Heather, and Doug Isbell; Bob, Sandy, and Charity Hudman; and Craig and Debbie Heiner.

"We traveled by ATVs to a place where we could glass. It wasn't thirty minutes before the monster was spotted," Mary explained. She tried to sneak in front of it but couldn't get a clear shot. They watched it through their binoculars as it walked into a stand of aspen in the next canyon. As Mary prepared herself for a shot, the wind howled and light rain sprinkled them. The moose didn't have a clue it was being "surrounded" as Doug guided Mary to a rock she could use as a rifle rest. He told her to wait until the wind died down. The moose was 250 yards away. Mary's heart pounded. Bob and Craig stood ready with their video cameras. After what seemed an eternity, Mary decided the time had come and fired. The single shot hit its mark and the bull collapsed—but jumped up again. Simultaneously, Doug and Bob yelled for Mary to shoot again. A second well-placed shot did the job.

"The next few minutes were pure chaos," Mary said. "My dad, Bob, Craig, and Sandy were all acting crazy with the excitement of this great animal." Bob, Craig, and Sandy hiked to the moose while Doug and Mary stood watch in case it jumped up again. When all finally was quiet, Doug and Mary made their way to the kill site. Mary, who stands 5 feet, 4 inches, reached the mountain of a moose and marveled at its size. Craig kept screaming that it was a monster. Bob and Sandy returned to the cabin to alert the rest of the group. Many rolls of film were used as every moment of the hunt was recorded. Then the task of field-dressing the 1,200-pound animal began, and later the eight humans packed out the meat, cape, and antlers. At the check station, officials and other hunters gathered for a closer look. Standing beside the moose was our 115-pound heroine. The moose remains one of the largest animals in the Isbell family collection.

Mary's moose has a spread of 48 5/8 inches, with thirteen normal points on the right antler and fourteen on the left. The width of the right palm measures 13 6/8 inches and the left palm measures 14 7/8 inches. The moose will remain one of the hunting highlights in Mary's life, but her experiences have only just begun.

The impressive collection of mounted big game on display in the Isbell family's Idaho home includes a massive bull elk in the 380-point range, six trophy mule deer bucks, a life-size mount of Doug's desert sheep, shoulder mounts of two Dall sheep, one Stone sheep, a bighorn, six white-tailed bucks, an Alaska-Yukon moose, numerous pronghorns, Doug's B&C caribou, and life-size mounts of a Kodiak brown bear and two black bears. Mary's Shiras moose has a place of honor in the trophy room. A separate building connected to their house includes dozens of additional North American trophies taken by Doug and his four daughters. Utah taxidermist Jay Ogden of Richfield created most of the mounts, including Mary's moose, but Atcheson's Taxidermy of Butte, Montana, mounted some.

Mary hunts because she loves the adventurous experiences with her family and friends. As she matures, she appreciates the closeness she feels with the creatures she comes face to face with in their natural habitats. Stalking close to wildlife, in many cases, is for her more enjoyable than filling a tag. Mary Isbell and other youngsters like her are the future of hunting in America.

BEAUTY AND THE BEASTS
MADLEINE KAY

Coues Deer

"For who could ever learn to love a beast?"
—*Beauty and the Beast*

Madleine Kay's hands were so swollen that she was afraid she'd be unable to shoot her custom-made handgun with any degree of accuracy. Her hand trouble had started the preceding day. After she and boyfriend-guide Mike Fejes had been dropped off in a remote Alaskan riverbed deep in the Chugach Mountains, they had started up the slope. Their goal was the magnificent glaciers that clung to the high mountain cirques ringing the area's steep-sided valleys. Such wild and desolate country is favored by the elusive mountain goat, an animal Madleine had decided to hunt.

That uphill climb was Madleine's first experience with the native plant known to Alaskans as devil's club. The plant lives up to its name. Its thistles penetrate exposed skin, causing wounds that can fester badly. Unaware of the plant's devilish effects, Madleine was less careful than she should have been. By the time the pain and suffering set in, it was too late. The damage to her hands and fingers had been done.

After spending the night in a spike-camp tent pitched precariously on a mountainside, Madleine and Mike made it to the ridgeline the following morning. "The glaciers were breathtaking," she said. "But we didn't see any goats."

Trouble followed trouble when later that day an early season snowstorm blew into the Chugach range. "Mike had been an Alaska guide for years," Madleine said. "As soon as it started snowing, he pitched our two-person tent." To reduce the weight of their packs, the couple hadn't taken much food along during the arduous climb. Now they were doomed to spend thirty-six hours in a tiny tent. The time was passed sleeping, talking, and using a knife to pick the remnant devil's club out of Madleine's fingers and hands.

"The next morning the sun came out," Madleine said. "We started out and soon cut the tracks of what appeared to be a good goat. We began tracking him and some time later spotted him up ahead on the ice of a glacier. I got into the prone position, found a rest for my .270 JDJ (a Contender built by well-known gunsmith J. D. Jones) with its Leupold 4X scope, and prepared to shoot. The distance was about two hundred yards. I squeezed off a shot, and down the goat went.

"I was so happy," she said. "As Michael and I were discussing the best way to reach the goat and pack it out, something strange happened. The goat's carcass, which had been lying motionless on the glacier's ice, began to move." Sliding slowly at first, then faster, the carcass gained momentum as Madleine and Mike watched in horror. Apparently the animal's body heat had melted the glacier's surface just enough to turn it into a waterslide. "My goat disappeared as if he were on a ride at Disney's Magic Mountain," Madleine said. "Four hundred feet later, he disappeared completely. I was in shock. My goat was gone."

The goat had plummeted down a chute and into a subterranean ice cave, where any recovery would be not only doubtful but also fraught with danger. "We returned to our tent to try to work out some kind of plan," Madleine recalled. "Making it worse was the fact that we'd brought no equipment along to attempt such a feat."

As if on command, the drone of a small plane suddenly could be heard. It was Mike's buddy, Sam Fees. "He must have spotted us standing there," Madleine said. "He was supposed to check up on us and drop some food if we hadn't checked back with him in a

Madleine Kay poses with the trophy Alaskan moose she killed with her .454 Casull.

certain amount of time. Sam circled back around, and then we spotted a box falling from the plane. We retrieved it and found inside two roast-beef sandwiches, two Cokes, and a two-way radio. Even today I can honestly say that was the best roast-beef sandwich I have ever tasted."

Mike radioed Sam and asked him to return with ropes and picks for the goat-retrieval operation. Sam went Mike one better. He offered to drop off a packer at the mountain's base to bring in the necessary equipment and help out during the retrieval.

The packer arrived early the next morning, and he and Mike started toward the glacier. "I waited alone in camp, wondering if I would ever see my goat again," Madleine said. "I even worried that a bear might already have found the carcass and carried it off."

Later that afternoon, the men returned victorious. "I wouldn't have done this for anyone but you," Mike said. He meant it, too. (Some years after this event, he and Madleine were married.) Mike explained how he'd salvaged Madleine's goat. He'd first had to venture inside an ice cave where the carcass had become solidly frozen to the ice. The animal's skull had broken and one horn was missing. Ever resourceful, Mike worked by the light of his flashlight to cape out the animal's head and shoulders, a nerve-wracking job under ideal circumstances and mind-numbing in the icy, dangerously unstable cell in which he found himself confined. After this portion of the animal had been carried from the cave, Mike crawled back inside and slid around on his belly until he finally located the animal's missing horn.

Madleine Kay has spent her life in pursuit of beauty in one form or another. Even her Alaskan mountain goat was part of this quest.

Madleine's parents met and married in Istanbul, where her mother's Armenian ancestors had made their home for more than three hundred years. Her father, a member of the U.S. Office of Strategic Services (OSS), brought his young bride home to St. Louis, Missouri, where Madleine was born. When the youngster was four years old, she already was displaying a budding talent for art. She drew pictures of animals and pored over other artists' renditions of beasts both wild and tame. "I could already tell when something was wrong with their artworks," Madleine said. "If a beak didn't seem exactly right for an eagle, or if a wolf looked more like a coyote, I knew it. Even at such a young age I remember how much I enjoyed observing animals and studying their anatomical features and the way they moved."

When Madleine was eight her parents relocated to California, but the girl did not abandon her art or her fascination with wildlife. "Once I'd graduated, I got a job as a technical illustrator," she said. "One day a jeweler friend of mine was looking at my work and mentioned that I had an extremely good eye for detail. The next thing I knew, he introduced me to another jeweler who was skilled as a carver and a gemologist."

Madleine became this jeweler's apprentice. "I started out altering existing pieces. I learned about waxes and gem-setting, and I slowly began to understand." She watched and she learned and applied what she was seeing to her own art. Her ability to capture the essence of the wildlife that laid siege to her imagination is perhaps unparalleled in the world today. Her time-consuming technique is basically self-taught. When she began creating her own line of jewelry, which she called Zoo Babies, Madleine's initial clientele were the zoos and parks where people could view the real-life animal babies that her painstakingly crafted pendants and charms depicted.

The inspiration behind the creation of fine jewelry doesn't arrive in one fell swoop. It's a process that begins when the seed of an idea sprouts in the artist's imagination and she begins mulling over the best way to bring it to fruition. She must determine the precise manner in which she will carve the wax, cast the gold, cut the mold, and what accent gems or materials should be used to best enhance it all. Working with dental tools and inlay waxes, Madleine has perfected her methodology through thirty years of trial and error. Although she once sculpted bronzes, a number of

This central barren-ground caribou was one of her first kills.

which were commissioned by corporations and wildlife associations, she found the work too time-consuming. Some of Madleine's work has been selected by Knott's Berry Farm and Universal Studios to be reproduced as charms for their gift shops. Awards given out by Safari Club International and Disney Studios are based upon Madleine's models. Another outlet for her creativity is gorgeous, privately commissioned custom jewelry. She makes to order many spectacular one-of-a-kind items that sometimes are based upon her clients' visions and sometimes include the claws, teeth, bones, and other parts taken from their animal trophies. Madleine prefers to create her art in fourteen-karat gold, although she will work in eighteen-karat gold if the customer requests it.

A portion of the copy in a brochure Madleine uses for advertising purposes reads: "The detail of my pieces is what makes them unique. I have always enjoyed the outdoors and take pride in being an active sportswoman. People who appreciate wildlife can see this . . . in every item."

Detail. The same motivation that churned within her as a small child still drives Madleine Kay today. If it isn't perfect, the artist isn't satisfied. The quest for artistic perfection is what inspired Madleine to book her first African photographic safari more than twenty years ago. She was able to capture on film animals in their natural settings so that her sculptures and molds would be even more lifelike and accurate. She particularly admired African plains game for the many different configurations their exquisite, spiraling horns assumed, and for their intricate markings so unlike those of most North American wildlife.

During that safari, Madleine realized that there was another way she could improve her anatomical knowledge of her wildlife subjects—how an animal's neck actually emerges from its shoulders, the curve of a leg, or the subtle variations in the ways animals turn their heads. Extreme close-up shots of the sort that only a hunter could stage while shooting an animal would help at least as much as photos of animals in their native habitats. Since the photo safari was being held in Namibia, in a camp run by a professional hunter, Madleine approached him about possibly shooting a gemsbok or oryx. She borrowed a .300-caliber rifle, which she set about mastering. When she felt confident in her abilities, she bagged a lovely gemsbok with its gaudy coloration and razor-sharp ebony horns.

"I shot my gemsbok in 1983," she said. "I returned to Africa in 1985 to take my first leopard, and also that year I shot my first North American animal, a central barren-ground caribou.

"I don't have to hunt or kill every species of animal, but some animals I am fascinated with," Madleine continued. "I enjoy looking at the trophies I have taken, not only for reference purposes but because they are so beautiful."

Madleine became a hunter well before she'd ever met Michael, the man with whom she now shares her life. They met while she was attempting to further her knowledge of wildlife anatomy from the inside out by learning taxidermy from one of Michael's friends. Globetrotting after big game is a passion the couple shares, and she remains an enthusiastic hunter today.

Madleine's idea of a perfect day of hunting would be to see a spectacular trophy in some remote setting, stalk close enough for a shot, and then put the animal down with a single bullet. "Hunting is knowing that you can get as tired and as dirty as you must. You don't have to hunt every day to survive. Hunting for me is embodied in the thrill of the chase."

Madleine is well known for her skill with high-powered handguns. Two favorites are the scoped .270 JDJ and a .454 Casull. Accuracy matters a great deal to her—details, remember?—and so she practices for months prior to a hunt. "Shooting my gun hundreds of times both offhand and from the prone position is something I feel I must do to be a good and ethical hunter," she said.

Madleine hunts not only for the thrill of the chase but also to see animals in their natural elements. "An artist must do more than simply observe animals in a zoo," she explained. "She must understand every aspect of their existence, how they have survived in a particular climate, even how they have evolved over time. An artist intensely involved with her subjects will also be extremely concerned about whether they and their habitats will exist in the future."

Madleine uses not only the flesh but also the capes, horns, and antlers of the animals she kills. Once an animal is down, she makes a voluminous film record of it and all of its visible parts, even to the point of arranging them in various positions so that if necessary she will be able later to create lifelike renderings for her art. Madleine Kay calls her creations "dimensional" art, and indeed they are. Details lost in ordinary two-plane representations literally leap out at you from her three-dimensional renditions. She has mastered better than any of her contemporaries the techniques required to make gold castings that display miniature versions of animals with antlers and spiraling horns that truly resemble the real, breathing McCoy. This is no small feat. And the problems that can arise when removing the piece intact from its mold are formidable.

Madleine has taken many trophy-caliber animals. If there were a separate record book for handgun-taken animals, hers would rank well up in the standings in many different categories. The only animal she feels sure would make the B&C book is a Coues deer, of which she has only poor photos. "We were hunting in Sonora, Mexico, one day," Madleine said, "driving around in an old Toyota truck. I couldn't open the door, so I decided to climb out the window. When I did so, my tennis shoe caught on the frame where the window should have been but wasn't, and I fell to the ground, landing hard on my back and barely missing a big barrel cactus. When I laughed in relief, I felt some pain."

The pain worsened as the hunt wore on. "One day I was riding horseback with my guide," Madleine continued. "The country was mountainous and very brushy. We suddenly spotted a good buck on the next mountain. It was so brushy that I don't think the buck was too worried about us." Madleine climbed down and finally had an opportunity for a clear shot. Using her custom rifle, a .257 Weatherby action fitted by Rifles, Inc. to a fiberglass stock, she placed two bullets into the buck's chest. "He dropped immediately. My adrenaline already was flowing, partly because of all the pain I was in, and now we had to cross the valley and try to find the animal on a brush-covered slope."

Madleine Kay with the horns from her "ice goat."

Madleine explained that Coues deer are well-adapted to this country and their coats blend into the terrain. When the guide and his hunter approached the general kill area, they came up empty-handed. Much of Sonora is an arid, brutal land. The two settled down to wait, hoping the dead buck would attract some of the country's ravenous vultures. "That is the only way we were able to locate my Coues deer," Madleine said. When the hunter finally walked up on the buck, she knew he was special because the antlers looked so massive on the diminutive body (the Coues is considerably smaller than a standard whitetail). Though the buck carried a very large rack for a Coues deer, she explained that hunting for a score is meaningless to her. "I hunt because I enjoy it and because it enables me to become better acquainted with each of these animals."

When Madleine returned home and the pain still had not ceased, she visited a doctor and learned she had broken the large rib that curves directly beneath her shoulder bone. No wonder breathing had been such agony!

Madleine has hunted the world over. In China she took a Tibetan gazelle now ranked in the world's top ten, and would have scored on a blue sheep were it not for a communication problem with her native guide. Other credits include a Stone sheep, a Dall sheep, a moose, a polar bear, two caribou, and many other species. "My most difficult challenge was hunting at seventeen thousand feet in China," she said.

"For who could ever learn to love a beast?" Madleine Kay, for one. She has loved them her entire life and on many different levels. It is this love that has made Madleine Kay a great hunter, an informed conservationist, and one of today's premier wildlife artists.

MS. SURE SHOT
SUE KING
Axis Deer (Texas)

Yes, it's Ms., not Miss or Little Miss, both of which were used on occasion by Chief Sitting Bull, Sioux Indian chief and Custer nemesis, to describe Annie Oakley, nineteenth-century sharpshooter. If you talk to Sue King, be sure to use Ms., or there'll be hell to pay later.

Similarities abound between Annie and Sue:

Annie Oakley would secretly follow her brother when the boy went squirrel hunting well over a century ago. When discovered, Annie would plead to stay.

Annie shot a rifle for the first time when she was just eight years old. Her aim was so true, the bullet cut the throat of the squirrel that had been romping along the family's rail fence.

Annie went on to achieve national and world acclaim as a member of Buffalo Bill's Wild West troupe. She outshot everyone on a regular basis and became a media darling. Years after her death, Annie Oakley's star gained added brilliance when Richard Rodgers and Oscar Hammerstein wrote the musical *Annie, Get Your Gun.*

Perhaps no one is writing a Sue King musical, but someone should consider penning a biography about Ms. Sure Shot, a woman who has helped throw into reverse many popularly held but wrong-headed attitudes about women, guns, and hunting. Sue's proactive approaches to these topics have inspired many in the media to reevaluate the significance of each in our country's culture.

Sue has been successful because she rarely backs down. She may not always win, but if she doesn't at first, it's likely she eventually will. Sue truly believes, to paraphrase the motto of the old Texas Rangers, that "No one in the wrong can stand up to someone in the right who just keeps on a-comin'." And she knows she's in the right.

Oh, yes—has it been mentioned that Sue King is a Texan?

Like so many other Texans, Sue enjoys guns. She likes to look at them, touch them, buy them, shoot them, and hunt with them, and has ever since she was a tyke—and no mention of Freud would be very much appreciated by this wife and mother of two. Her interest in guns and hunting comes naturally to someone born in and raised by a family of hunters, men and women alike. When Sue was three she went on her first hunt. While her father was serving overseas during World War II, her mother was inspired to take a series of photos of a young and pretty Sue marching and saluting as she held her own small gun smartly and safely, the way she'd been instructed to handle it. Small wonder the photos were an immediate hit with Sue's father.

"I get more pleasure out of hunting now than I did as a child," Sue said. "I am suited for it. There is so much to enjoy—the solitude, the hours spent observing animals going about their lives and not knowing a human is near, the feeling that you've become a natural part of the earth's cycle and are not merely an observer, the challenge of doing it right, the surge of adrenaline at the moment I commit to the shot, and the feeling of accomplishment when a hunt is completed well and honorably. People tend to enjoy what they do best, and I'm a good hunter."

Sue has been married for many years, more support for her belief that if something is worth doing at all, it's worth doing well. Highly intelligent, well-organized, dedicated to increasing public awareness of Second Amendment pro-gun issues and women's involvement in firearms-related activities, yet never one for self-recognition or self-aggrandizement, Sue must have been a

Sue King's Texas free-ranging axis deer is one for the books.

formidable romantic challenge for fellow Texan Robert J. King—Jerry, the man who eventually won her heart. In Sue Jerry found a woman who was a deadeye with pistols, rifles, and shotguns, a lover and companion who had hunted since the age of three, and one so intellectually curious that as a Lamar University undergrad she studied forensic speaking and political science, then later delved into the nuts and bolts of advanced classical rhetoric while enrolled in a University of Wisconsin master's program.

What was the key to her heart? "One of my criteria for dating a boy was, Can he outshoot me?" she said. Jerry made the cut.

Sue King, like Annie Oakley, is equally at home pointing a shotgun, peering through a scope mounted on her favorite long-distance rifle, or brandishing one of the pistols with which she can shoot the whiskers off a flea. She has won numerous shooting awards, including High Handgun at the 1995 National Shooting Sports competition, and was rated top gun in the .410 preliminaries as well as High Overall Average Female for all four gauges at the Grant Ilseng Open. While competing at ESPN's combined Sporting Clays and golf tournament, Sue won High Individual Overall Lady, and her ladies' team twice has taken home first-place trophies. Sue has twice captained the Browning Ladies Sporting Clays Team at the National Sporting Clay competitions to second-place finishes.

"I've won lots of stuff, but that only means I was lucky on that particular day," she said.

Sue's hunting tastes are universal. "Whatever I'm hunting at the moment is my favorite game animal," she said. "Each species presents its own unique challenges, and is best hunted with a particular firearm. I find prairie dogs as much fun as whitetails, whitetails as much fun as feral pigs, and right on down to varmints, pheasants, quail, or doves."

Sue has pigeonholed many wonderful memories during a lifetime of hunting. "One January I was hunting the *brasada*, the brush country, along the Rio Grande in south Texas. It's a harsh country but full of history. It's also home to big-antlered whitetails. I'd come to this particular place searching for the buck that belonged to the huge tracks I'd found the day before. I was waiting beside a tank—that's Texan for pond—under a sky so blindingly blue it hurt the eyes to stare at it, and near an oak motte vibrating with brilliant red cardinals and Mexican green parrots. The buck I'd been looking for appeared. It wasn't his size alone that awed me so. It was his kingly bearing, the way he so clearly expressed his dominance in the deliberate way he moved. I pulled myself together and made a slam-dunk shot. That evening we celebrated around the campfire by enjoying a few outright lies well told and an appropriate amount of kitchen whiskey."

Sue King's SCI-class whitetail scores 151 B&C points and was taken in South Texas.

Sue said she relives the taking of this fine buck, her largest whitetail to date, every time she glances above her kitchen fireplace to the place of honor where its head now hangs. The buck scored over 150 Boone and Crockett points and qualifies for SCI's record book.

Also in Texas, Sue has taken both an axis deer and a Corsican ram large enough to be listed in the *Exotic Big Game Record Book.* Through the years, a variety of exotic wildlife species native to other lands has been transplanted in Texas and other southwestern states—usually after native populations of these animals or their foreign habitats fell on hard times. Animals like nilgai, oryx, axis deer, mouflon, and aoudad now range freely in many Texas locales. You are as likely to find them on unfenced or traditionally fenced properties, as Sue did, as you are on high-fenced operations.

Examine the rack on Sue's big axis deer, and there can be no doubt that it places well up in the record book. When asked about its actual score, Sue said, "Oh, hell! My axis and my Corsican ram are both listed in the exotics record book, but I'm no longer sure of either score. And who knows where the paperwork is anyway?

"I don't fit the definition of a trophy hunter anyway," she continued. "I'm not even sure I want to be classified that way. I don't hunt to take trophies. I hunt for other reasons."

Women, it seems, hunt for reasons intensely personal to them, or motives that are difficult to communicate to others. Most women are not driven to bag the biggest or the best, although some admit feeling a profound sense of accomplishment when they "make the book."

Sue King objected strongly at first to being included in any book with the word "trophy" in its title. She consented only after being reassured that the book would be much more than just a celebration of trophies and trophy hunters. The subtitle word "trophy" was chosen to appeal to the continent's diehard hunters; one requirement for inclusion was that each featured hunter had to have taken at least one trophy-class North American game animal. That stipulation provided a way of separating dedicated female hunters from those who are not.

Some of Sue's hunting exploits could have landed her in the hospital, or worse. During an NRA women's feral pig hunt in Pierce, Texas, she had started the day by telling the other participants, "Ladies, these animals can be dangerous. Feral pigs are unpredictable, extremely aggressive when mad or wounded, and entirely capable of hunting *you!*"

Like Miss Cleo gazing into her crystal ball, Sue had accurately foreseen her own next day afield. One second Sue and Brian Watkins, a freelance cameraman assigned to go with her, were stalking through the brush; the very next moment they were being charged at close quarters by a grumpy 250-pound boar. The animal hadn't been previously wounded; it was merely annoyed at their approach. Thanks to many years of experience in expecting the unexpected, Sue reacted first and thought about it later. The boar was nearly on top of the pair when Sue aimed her Marlin .44 Remington Magnum from the hip and dumped the animal almost in Brian's lap with her first and only shot. "It was like shooting Low House 8 from the hip," Sue remarked once the hubbub had died down. Brian had kept his video camera trained on the action, so Sue can relive this hair-raising episode whenever she starts taking either good health or life for granted.

Sue is an NRA Benefactor, and a life member of the Texas State Rifle Association (TSRA), the U.S. Sporting Clays Association, and the National Sporting Clays Association. She is a director of the NRA, the TSRA, the Greater Texas Sportsman's Coalition, and the Women's Sportfishing Foundation, as well as being a member of the Houston Safari Club. She is certified as an NRA Training Counselor in shotgun, personal protection, and handgun. As the retired executive director of the Women's Shooting Sports Foundation (WSSF), she is primarily responsible for the great gains made by that organization. While Sue was on board with the WSSF, the Ladies Charity Classics and Couples Charity Classics shooting events raised hundreds of thousands of dollars for local charities while also ensuring that local press provided plenty of positive media coverage for the shooting sports. For these and her many other achievements, Sue was given the NRA's prestigious Sybil Ludington Freedom Award for 1999.

The list of her accomplishments is much less interesting than Sue's many interactions with nature. Take the evening an owl decided to roost on top of her head, or the scare provided by a cougar that skulked close behind the woman as she walked back to camp at dark after hunting the Sabine River bottoms. "Being followed by that panther was the most frightening experience I can recall," she said.

The mother of twin sons, Charles and Lee, has never gone out of her way to avoid danger, or the irritation of pesky reporters who resort to ambushing firearms-rights advocates when they least expect it to extract hasty sound-bite comments. Reporters love sound bites and will go to great lengths to set someone up to respond without thinking to a series of previously composed, rapid-fire questions about shooting, hunting, or the Second Amendment. Sue doesn't get mad; she gets even. This resourceful woman conceived of and developed a diabolical program for dealing with "ambush reporters" as part of her mentoring duties for enrollees in the Texas State Rifle Association's Media Training Seminar.

After one particularly grueling interview, one trainee remarked, "It's hard to be a soldier in the pro-gun cause."

"Then stop being a soldier and start being a general," Sue replied. "Find your particular passion, and then lead the charge."

Sue is a dedicated angler and loves to read. Among her hobbies are counting alligators and creating large piles of wood shavings during frenzied bouts of sculpting.

A question about her favorite hunting spot produced a record-class quantity of hemming and hawing. "My God," she said. "There are simply too many great places. If I had to choose one, though, it would be the Texas brush country along the Rio Grande. I love it because there is so much wildlife of all kinds, including birds and varmints. I always see something new there."

You might expect that Sue would find it difficult to list fewer than a half-dozen of her favorite guns. "Let's see," she began. "I like my Remington 7mm-08 for deer, my SuperLight Belgian

Who wouldn't be pleased with these two bucks, both taken by Sue.

Browning Superposed 12-gauge for pheasants, my Winchester 28-gauge Quail Special for quail and doves, the Remington 1100 12-gauge for ducks and geese, a Remington .22-250 for prairie dogs, the .425 Browning presented to me at a recent Shooting, Hunting, and Outdoor Trade (SHOT) Show, the single-shot .22 that was my first real gun, the .454 Casull for hunting hogs, the .44 Remington Magnum carbine I used to hip-shoot that silly pig. . . .

"If you'd like the rest of the list, just say the word."

A new phase of Sue King's life began with her recent involvement with the Katy Prairie Conservancy. This organization, founded in response to inchoate plans to convert Texas's unique Katy Prairie wetland area into an airport, is a coalition of unlikely allies. There's the Sierra Club, a group believed by many hunters to be the refuge of extremists and tree huggers. And there are representatives of both the Houston Chapter of SCI and the NRA. Representing the NRA? None other than Sue King.

Did she take flak for aligning herself with the "enemy?" "Oh, yes," she said. "But the exchange of ideas is the best prophylactic against ignorance and stupidity that I know of." Sue is hoping that by working with the group's leaders, its members will become aware that hunters do indeed put their money where their mouths are—in this case, to fund the preservation of a valuable resting stop on one of the country's major goose and duck flyways.

Sue's personal contribution to the Katy Prairie Conservancy was to earmark for its use the entire 1998 proceeds of WSSF's largest and richest women's clay shoot.

"Sue King is a strong woman," said Marge Hanselman, the Sierra Club's conservation chair in Houston. "She is also one of the most avid conservationists I know. We stick to issues on which we can agree, and work together to preserve wildlife habitat."

As the founder and former leader of the Women's Shooting Sports Foundation, now realigned with the National Shooting Sports Foundation, Sue continues to beat the drum to get other females involved. "Hunting is the perfect sport for women. Neither the gun nor the game animal gives a hoot about gender. Women can hunt as well as or even better than men. That's a fact."

She doesn't waste any sleep over those who don't understand hunting. "Sure, I've run across folks who don't understand why I hunt. That's OK, because I can't for the life of me understand why they don't understand. As for the antihunting crowd, I've converted about as many of them as I've turned pigs into lollipops."

Sue King keeps her fingers firmly fixed on America's hunting and shooting pulse. One problem looming on the horizon—one she fears might sway the nonhunting public toward the antihunting point of view—is the sale of living, large-racked wildlife on high-fenced game farms in Texas and elsewhere. She believes the practice has helped taint trophy hunting: "On some Texas operations, if a deer grows a rack in the two-hundred-point Boone and Crockett class, he'll be sold for a large sum of cash to some so-called 'hunter.' If ranchers discover a two-year-old buck with a better-than-average rack, the *vaqueros* will be ordered to babysit the animal so that no harm befalls him until his antlers grow large enough to attract a big payday. Once a 'hunter' with enough money to buy the buck is located, ranch personnel will do everything but pull the trigger for him, and they might even do that. This isn't a real hunt. It's a kill. Any animal taken like this isn't earned—it's just another high-priced status symbol."

Sue King has never shied away from tough issues—one reason the respect she is given is so heartfelt. Like Annie Oakley before her, Sue King is a straight shooter. And her aim has always been true.

LUCKY LADY
KANDI KISKY
White-tailed Deer

"Some guys have all the luck!" begins an old Rod Stewart song. Well, Rod, ladies can be lucky, too, and the luckiest one I know is Iowa's Kandi Kisky. Kandi started hunting eleven years ago, and since then she has created much of her own luck by working diligently to become one of the best female deer hunters on the continent.

Kandi's husband, Don, introduced her to hunting when the two still were dating. Ask Kandi today about her most memorable hunting moment, and she says, "That's easy—the morning I was six months pregnant and crawling after a gobbler.' Son Kaleb was born a few months thereafter.

Don and Kandi met and married while they still lived in Missouri. They longed for greener pastures, though, and looked to Missouri's northern neighbor, Iowa, as an ideal place to move to. Once you get to know these two, the reasons they give for making this transition are understandable. They wanted a less-populated locale, especially one with fewer hunters. They also hoped to find a place with either good numbers of trophy white-tailed bucks or the potential to produce them. If the deer population already had a good buck-to-doe ratio, so much the better. Sparsely populated Iowa, known for its huge whitetails and family farms, filled the bill nicely.

The Kiskys moved and soon either owned outright or managed a total of 3,200 fertile Iowa acres. Each year they planted the tillable portions of their land in soybeans or corn. Soybeans provide the protein boost whitetails need to grow large antlers, and waste corn can supplement the diets of winter-stressed whitetails to help them survive. Access to so much phenomenal whitetail habitat stirred the glowing embers of the family's interest in quality deer management. That interest eventually flared up into a second profession when Don began videotaping not only the tremendous whitetails and plentiful wild turkeys found on the family's farm but also his and Kandi's hunts so they could relive the excitement after the season had closed. Kandi, too, learned to operate the camera, and the desire to share their adventures with others seemed like a natural progression. Kisky Video Productions was thus born.

Kandi and Don didn't really need to implement a detailed blueprint for growing bucks on their land. The rich, loamy soil, high-protein crops, scant hunting pressure, and scattered cover were all the animals needed to thrive. The Kiskys believe in maintaining the

Kandi used her muzzleloader to kill this nice buck with a gross score of 141.

excellent buck-to-doe ratio and age-class structure already present. To that end they make certain that each season they harvest not only bucks but also the required number of does. By following accepted wildlife management principles, Kandi inhabits a whitetail paradise that will probably remain so for many years into the future. She knows how lucky she is to be able to hunt such dream country for big bucks.

A year in the life of Kandi Kisky begins in early January after the last day of Iowa's whitetail season. She and Don barely have time to catch up on sleep lost during the various deer seasons before they begin traveling to the many hunting and archery shows held each late winter. While working these shows, the two talk business, entertain clients, and market their video products. They return home just in time to prepare for spring planting—repairing machinery, ordering and storing seed and fertilizer, and all the other details of a farmer's busy existence. Planting season can be frenzied, yet all family members take time off to turkey hunt, which regenerates them. Don and Kandi also spend time videotaping friends who visit their farm to enjoy the soft spring days, the lengthening daylight, and most of all the hunt. The year's activities climax at harvest time when the crops are gathered and sold. Soon afterward, the Kiskys will be hard at work preparing for the whitetail archery, shotgun, and muzzleloader seasons. They have hosted hunts for some well-known folks, including the late racing legend Dale Earnhardt, Realtree's Bill Jordan, and M.A.D. Calls' Mark Drury.

During the past eleven seasons, this young woman has harvested some truly spectacular bucks with both muzzleloader and bow. She has used her .50-caliber muzzleloader to kill whitetails with racks grossing 175⅝, 167, and 150 Boone and Crockett points, and two other bucks whose racks each score right at 140. Every one of Kandi's black-powder bucks has sported a rack large enough to qualify for listing in the Longhunters record book of black-powder trophies. Kandi's largest buck to date will almost certainly qualify for Boone and Crockett listing. But Kandi isn't worried about that. The buck is a tremendous trophy, no matter its score, and just seeing the mounted rack is more than reward enough.

The bucks Kandi has killed with a bow have so far included one whose rack gross-scored 150 and another that grossed 140 Pope and Young points. Both bucks qualify for entry into Pope and Young's record book should Kandi ever decide to register them.

Kandi Kisky, proud hunter, and her 140-class muzzleloader whitetail.

Kandi follows simple tenets that any new hunter can easily adapt to her own routine. She attributes most of her success to remaining well aware of all the subtle details that could foul up a hunt. She watches the wind at all times and keeps her clothes free of human odor by washing them thoroughly in a good scent-free detergent. "I spray down with anti-odor products, too," she said. "When clothing is clean and scent-free, I keep it that way by storing it in sealed plastic bags. Don and I wear knee-high rubber boots to eliminate any scent trail we might otherwise leave behind as we walk to and from our tree stands. If a big buck smells even a hint of human scent, it will turn around and leave. This next season we plan to use Scent-Lok odor-adsorbent clothing—we've heard so many good things about it."

Kandi's choice in muzzleloaders is a Knight .50-caliber Disc Rifle outfitted with a Redfield Lo-Pro 3–9X scope. She shoots sabot slugs. Her archery gear includes a Hoyt Intensity compound bow with the draw weight set at 48 pounds. With a draw length of just 24⅝ inches, Kandi may be small, but her Graphite Pro 35/55 arrows tipped with 85-grain, three-blade Thunderheads fly straight and true.

Early in 2002, Kandi experienced hunting's ultimate rush when she scored on that nine-point 175⅝ behemoth whitetail mentioned previously. She plans to have this beautiful buck scored for both the Boone and Crockett and Buckmasters record book.

The story of that memorable hunt is worth telling. The date was 6 January 2002. Kandi and Don had been driving around that evening, searching for a place that might give them a better than average chance to score on a buster whitetail. Don stopped the truck at the base of a hill so that it would be hidden. The two got out and slowly climbed to the top of that hill to see if any deer were feeding in the large corn-stubble field just beyond. Daylight was waning rapidly by the time they topped the hill's crest, but they could see deer everywhere. Near that field would be an ideal place to set up when they would be able to return.

Two days later, on 8 January, they were back. After checking the wind and finding it ideal, Don and Kandi made a beeline to a line of trees, where they quickly and quietly positioned two tree stands close to each other so Don could video Kandi's evening hunt. The temperature was around 70 degrees, hardly optimum deer-hunting weather and highly unusual for the upper Midwest during January. "Hunting food sources usually works best when it's bitter cold," Kandi explained. "But we had to hunt whatever the weather conditions because deer season would be ending in just two days."

Not until whitetails started pouring into the field from every direction did the Kiskys gain confidence in their decision. They hadn't been waiting long when Kandi saw a huge buck exiting the timber to her left. It ambled over to a smaller one and stopped.

"Take him," Don said. Kandi placed her muzzleloader on a rest, then braced herself for the shot's recoil. "But I couldn't shoot, I was in such a state," she said. "On the video you can hear how loud my heart was pounding. I was so excited, but I somehow managed to calm myself down enough to shoot." Blue smoke exploded from the muzzle of her gun, and startled whitetails fled in every direction.

At the shot, the buck had been standing about 130 yards from her tree stand. The yardage wasn't worrisome, thanks to the Knight Disc Rifle, noted for its long-range capabilities. But dusk was turning into darkness, and the couple knew time was not theirs to waste. They climbed down from their tree stands, switched on their flashlights, and began searching for blood, hair, deep tracks, or any other clue that would reveal a good, solid hit. The search was over almost before it began. The tremendous buck lay not forty yards from where it had been standing when Kandi shot. They were familiar with this animal, having kept track of and even filming it through the years as it had grown into the magnificent creature now lying at their feet. Not many years had passed since the day Kandi had dubbed the animal "The Big Seven," but now the monstrous rack sported nine long points and was as thick as a man's forearm.

The Kiskys live and breathe big whitetails. They are as careful with their crops of deer and turkeys as they are with their corn and milo, perhaps more so. "We manage this land to produce the finest deer it can grow," Kandi said. "We try not to harvest any buck until it is at least five years old."

Kandi's life is a whirlwind of activity. She helps out with the farming, takes care of their neat, country-themed home, and is also a wildlife cinematographer and producer for their company, Kisky Productions. In her spare time she dabbles in Web site design and outdoor writing. She also belongs to the Parent-Teacher Organization at her son's school, helps out with Little League and Bible school, and is a teacher's aide for Kaleb's grade-school class. Hobbies include collecting Longaberger baskets and Boyd dolls.

The Kisky family's hunting circle enlarged as soon as young Kaleb was old enough to toddle around with them during shed-hunting excursions. The boy takes great pleasure in pulling out the various sheds he's found, and will tell you the story of each one in great detail. Kaleb has already bagged his first wild turkey, during a hunt with his parents in spring 2002.

Shed hunting is important to the family, both as quality time together and as a way to scout out and identify the various bucks living on their land. "We've found up to a hundred shed antlers in a single year," Kandi said. "By watching our bucks when their antlers are in

The culmination of Kandi Kisky's hunting career to date came the instant she fired at this magnificent B&C-class whitetail.

velvet and then when they have hardened, and later finding identifiable sheds in a particular spot, we get a good idea of where each buck likes to hang out, where his core area is. By saving shed antlers, many of which we can match into pairs, we record many of our bucks' antler cycles. Learning how deer grow their antlers from one year to the next, and seeing how antlers vary in size and configuration, is just so much fun for all of us."

Kandi says there is no real secret to shed hunting. "Most of our antlers have been found in the transition or edge zones where a field meets the timber. Concentrate on the area that extends ten yards into the field and ten yards into the timber.

"While you're looking for sheds, you'll see old rubs and scrapes you might not have known existed. And you can bet the bucks will be back there when autumn comes again."

Kandi has become an impassioned advocate of hunting, particularly for women. "Some of my friends don't understand why I hunt," she said. "I explain that taking deer each year is good for the herd, and that on every trip afield I learn more about nature and wildlife. Learning about those things helps you gain respect for them. Hunting also allows me to spend quality time with my husband."

Kandi is concerned about the changes taking place as North Americans lose their connection to the earth. "Reading about nature in books or watching it on TV isn't enough," she insists. "Most people have no idea how wildlife lives or dies. Most children never have the chance to try hunting for themselves, either because their parents don't hunt or because they live with grandparents who may be too old or single mothers who don't know where to start. Not enough of today's hunters take the time to introduce a child to hunting, so we slowly are losing one of our oldest traditions."

Kandi's solution would be to pass laws or amend regulations to allow children younger than eleven to go hunting accompanied by mother, father, or legal guardian. "Once kids reach eleven, so many other interests are competing for their attention it's difficult to get them excited about hunting. We must reach them before they're eleven."

Lucky lady? In many ways, yes. But like so many of the fortunate in our midst, Kandi Kisky realizes that luck will carry you only so far before skill becomes a necessity. This is a lady who is both lucky *and* skillful. And she has the trophy bucks to prove it!

RAINBOW LACES AND TELEVISION
CHASE MARTIN
Central Barren-Ground Caribou

"Thank God I'm a country girl," goes the song, and Chase Martin is just that.

Born in 1980, Chase was introduced to hunting and fishing a few years after learning to walk, thanks in large part to her father, Jerry Martin. Jerry hosts the popular half-hour weekly show *Bass Pro Shops Outdoor World* on Outdoor World Television and periodically invites Chase and her brother, Flint, born in 1976, to join him on the show to highlight outings they have shared. Her TV appearances, which include some of her favorite hunts, are a culmination of experiences she began sharing with Jerry as a kindergartner.

"I was probably five or six when I started squirrel hunting with my dad," Chase explained. She wasn't old enough to carry a gun but quickly found her way around the woods. She learned what sounds to recognize and how to walk quietly on the forest floor. She was too small to carry the equipment, but she knew she liked being in the outdoors.

"I love the outdoors so much that I wanted to pass on our family's traditions," Jerry explained. He never pressured Chase into hunting or fishing but made sure he exposed her to everything he loved to do. She took to fishing and hunting like a retriever to water. His son, Flint, tends to enjoy the outdoors by himself, so Chase has become Jerry's true hunting buddy. Jerry and his wife, Jill, named their daughter Chase Myriah in honor of their Indian heritage (his wife is Blackfoot and Cherokee, and he is part Cherokee) and a favorite song from the movie *Paint Your Wagon* entitled, "They Call the Wind Mariah."

"I really believe women can enjoy the outdoors as much as men," said Jerry, "but they may look at things a little differently than men do. I've learned a lot from Chase because she observes things differently from me. She has opened my eyes." The key to getting more girls into the woods and into hunting, he added, is to get the mothers out there. Some of his fondest memories and greatest joys in life have been when he was hunting with Chase. "Chase is so special because *she* loves the outdoors," he said. He also admits that the media often portray women hunters differently from men, but this attitude is "coming around." Advertisers and sponsors know that the majority of hunters are men, so more men are portrayed in magazines, books, and TV shows. But he sees that changing as more girls and women venture out into nature.

The first thing Jerry taught Chase was to stop moving in the woods when he stopped, so they sound more like an animal moving than a couple of humans crashing through the woods. Her challenge was to avoid making a racket by stepping on sticks, dry leaves, etc. She learned to communicate in a low tone or by hand signals—a hard lesson for a young girl, but she persevered. She passed her hunter-safety course at age nine or ten, and two months after her eleventh birthday, she killed her first white-tailed buck— a nice eight-point—on her Grandpaw Martin's farm in Thayer, Missouri. She used a .223 Ruger rifle with a synthetic stock to lighten the carrying load.

At age eleven, Chase Martin, right, and her father, Jerry, drag her first buck out of the woods.

Over the years, Chase has hunted white-tailed bucks, does, squirrels, and rabbits in her home state of Missouri and once in south Texas. She has caught a ton of fish and been on a few turkey hunts, but has yet to take one. "They're pretty tricky," she says, laughing. "They can sense you and know exactly where you are."

Hunting with a daughter is rare, even in families that hunt. When Chase tells her friends and acquaintances that she hunts with her dad, they can't believe it, or if they do believe, they're taken aback. A lot of the women she knows are antihunting and assume that a hunter is not a pet lover, an impression with which Chase strongly disagrees. She worked for a pet store and quickly discovered that the women workers were extreme antihunters. They pictured every deer they saw as a beautiful Bambi, but failed to understand that deer are not beautiful when they are starving to death because the population is overcrowded. "Bambi definitely put a damper on deer hunters, especially female deer hunters," Chase said.

Until the age of ten, Chase and her family lived in Springfield, Missouri, but then moved out into the country. Chase liked school— everything except math—but her regular routine always revolved around being outside. She feels more relaxed in the woods where she can be alone with her thoughts.

White-tailed deer remain her favorite quarry, but the hunt on which she took her record-book central-Canada barren-ground caribou will be etched in her mind forever, as it will for Jerry.

Jerry and Chase flew from Missouri to Winnipeg, Manitoba, and then switched to a "puddle jumper" that landed nine times before they got to where they were going. The final leg found the father-daughter duo in a Twin Otter bound for Courage Lake, a premiere location for trophy caribou. Chase's sixteenth birthday, 9 September 1996, occurred during this special hunt, which promised to generate a lifetime of memories.

They were guided by Ken Gangler of Beverly Hills, Florida, who had made arrangements to hunt on Indian property that had not been hunted by whites for years. It was cold when they first arrived late in the afternoon, but not as cold as it would become. In snow and sleet and a light wind, they set out to scout around and get the feel of the land. Right off the bat, Chase spotted a monstrous bull across the inlet of the lake, so they crossed the lake in a Zodiac boat. As Chase stalked toward it, she fell into the inlet up to her neck—and the windchill factor was about 40 degrees below zero.

"It was cold, so cold, but I saved my gun," Chase laughed. She held her rifle, a .50-caliber Knight Wolverine muzzleloader,

Sweet sixteen and conqueror of a record-book caribou bull.

above her head as she sank into the ice and muck. Somehow she pulled herself together to fire one round using a bullet she had handloaded, but she shook so badly that she missed. All six layers of her clothes were soaked, her teeth were chattering, and her hands froze to the rifle barrel as she hunched over in the Zodiac boat for the breezy trip back to camp. All she could imagine was a warm blanket and dry clothes. In camp, Jerry had to help Chase remove her boots and open the tent flaps so she could collapse into the comfort of a space heater and sleeping bag. She peeled off layer upon drenched layer, stripping to the skin and crawling into dry longjohns. She made a makeshift clothesline to hang up her clothing to dry for the next day's hunt.

All the while, Jerry was chuckling. "He thought it was pretty funny," she said.

Chase says she was so cold she technically did not warm up until she returned to Missouri. The next morning, her clothes were only semi-dry and her boots were still wet, so she switched to four layers of dry clothing and black low-top sneakers with rainbow shoelaces.

As Chase thought about what she would say to her dad, who was drinking coffee at the mess tent, about the fact she had no boots for the day's hunt, some hunters shouted that caribou were behind the camp. A herd of about fifty cows, calves, and bulls wandered by. Chase hurriedly threw on her coat and grabbed her gun, and she and her guide, Chester, ran a little way behind the camp to spot them. She immediately saw a massive bull, very white, that was bigger than the one she'd seen across the inlet the day before. It was walking with a smaller bull. Chester and Chase came up around and flanked them to get a broadside shot. The bull was about 110 yards away. To get into shooting position, she hunkered down and walked around a line of squatty tundra trees into a small clearing. Chase realized that in the rush of getting out, she'd forgotten the shooting stick she used to steady her rifle, so Chester sat and volunteered his knee as a rest.

"Go for the one in the white cape," Chester said as Chase prepared to fire. She told herself to settle down, flicked off the safety, took a deep breath, rechecked her sights, and gently squeezed the trigger. The bull had been grazing the whole time and was taking a step forward when the bullet hit its mark. It ran only about five yards and dropped.

"He never even knew we were there—didn't have a clue," Chase said.

Chester then played a dirty trick on this country girl. He told her to poke the caribou with the gun barrel to make sure it was dead. What he did not tell Chase was that caribou swell up immediately after death Chase knew the animal was dead, but the dutiful hunter poked it with the gun, and instantly moss blew out of its nose and mouth. Chase jumped back, and Chester broke out howling. He was still chuckling when the rest of the hunters walked up to them.

Chase was told not to field-dress the caribou because they swell up so quickly their abdominal cavity will pop. She skinned out the cape and quartered the carcass, removing the backstraps and loins. The remaining meat was given to the tribe whose land they were hunting. Tradition dictated that the first caribou killed was dinner that night, so the entire camp dined on tenderloin. From start to finish, Chase and Chester had traveled about a mile from and back to camp.

Chase was the first in camp to fill her caribou tag. The bull scored almost 30 inches above the minimum for entrance into the Boone and Crockett Club and nearly 100 inches above the minimum for entrance into the *Longhunter Muzzleloading Record*

Flint, seventeen, and Chase, thirteen, on the 1993 hunt on which she collected the "mud buck."

Book. With a final score of 374⅝ points, Chase's central-Canada barren-ground caribou would rank in the Longhunter book as the third or fourth largest in the world and approximately eighty-second in the world if entered in the Boone and Crockett Club. The greatest spread between the main beams of the 12x12 bull's antlers is 32 inches, and both main beams measure more than 48 inches in length. Quite a gift on Chase's sixteenth birthday.

What advice does she have about motivating women to hunt?

"There is a stereotype about women in the field, and I was hoping our society would be past it by now, but it is not." She knows she was lucky to have supportive family and friends, especially her dad. Chase wants to see more articles featuring women in hunting magazines and books. More families, especially men, need to take their children hunting, including their daughters. Depicting women hunters in the field can inspire and encourage other women to do just as well as the men, Chase thinks. She vows to take her children hunting, but quickly added that she won't force them if they don't want to do it. She will accept their decision, but she will teach them to respect hunting and to appreciate its value as a wildlife management tool. As an example of her dedication to motivating other women to hunt, Chase donated her magnificent bull to the Bass Pro Shops Outdoor World store in Springfield, Missouri, where it is on permanent display.

Chase knows no other woman her age who hunts. She has only male hunting companions, who themselves have wives and girlfriends who will have nothing to do with hunting. She has always hung out with the guys.

"Surprise, surprise," she said with a chuckle.

Her father, though, knew firsthand that a daughter was as good as a son in the field, and their family's positive experiences are passed on to his television audience. He periodically features Chase on the show; a recent segment showed her discussing the need to harvest does in areas overpopulated with deer.

Chase says she has never felt discrimination in the field, but has sensed that some men were slightly uncomfortable with a woman in camp. She also notes that few hunters invite her to go out with them, though she would love to be asked. Maybe, she thinks, men are not sure whether women can take care of themselves and may require special treatment or instruction.

"Frankly, these feelings are understandable, seeing as how so few women hunt," Chase said.

Her future? Chase plans to attend Drury College in Springfield, Missouri, with a possible career as a nurse or something involving animals. Health care was a big part of her life in 2001 and 2002, when she spent time with her grandparents as her

One of Chase Martin's first fishing trips at age five or six with brother Flint and father Jerry. Flint is napping behind Chase.

grandfather's health failed, and later cared for her mother when Jill was seriously burned Demand for nurses is great, and Chase hopes to secure a full scholarship for her studies.

Jerry Martin's job demands much travel, so her time with him in the field is sometimes the only time they have together for weeks on end, especially now that she is a young adult.

One of her best memories is of a deer-hunting trip with her dad when she was thirteen. The sun was setting as they trudged through deep mud to reach what Chase dubbed a "Dad and me" stand, which means a platform where Jerry sat behind Chase and she leaned back on his knees. Soon they saw just the antlers of the biggest buck Chase had ever seen in her life as it ghosted through the woods below her stand. Though she couldn't see the body of the buck, she developed a major case of buck fever. Her dad grabbed the gun to keep Chase from shaking so badly and possibly dropping it. The buck wandered down the hill, and Chase's heart sank, thinking she would never see it again. But a short time later—almost at the end of legal shooting time—the buck walked back uphill toward them. Chase caught her breath. Jerry urged her to settle down, and she fired once, using her lucky gun, the .223 Ruger. The buck dropped about a hundred yards from them.

It was a major chore to lug this two-hundred-pound field-dressed buck from the woods as darkness fell, even with the help of a three-wheeler that had brought them to the tree stand. With the buck in the back rack and two human riders, the weight seriously unbalanced the vehicle, so Chase rode on the handlebars. "Of course, we got stuck in the mud," Chase said with a laugh. Jerry got off to push the rig out of the mud and soon wore a ton of mud as the wheels splattered muck all over him. "We got to laughing so hard that it took us an extra half-hour to settle down. Three times the deer fell off the back and we had to get off and hoist it up again." Naturally, they got stuck in the mud each time. To this day, Chase refers to this hunt as the time she downed her "mud buck."

Hunting and fishing were how Chase got to really know her dad, and that means everything to her.

A BOW HUNTER'S TALE

CAROL MAUCH

Quebec-Labrador Caribou, White-tailed Deer

Fred Bear, famous archery-equipment manufacturer and big-game hunter, made sure Dick and Carol Mauch were properly married on 8 March 1982. He volunteered his office and his secretary, a company notary public, for the event. In Florida, notaries are allowed to perform marriage ceremonies. But this story begins long before that day.

Dick hunted often with Fred Bear and was a stockholder in Bear Archery in the 1960s before Fred sold the company. Dick and Carol met when she was teaching art in his Nebraska town of Bassett. He ran a bowstring manufacturing business he founded called Cornhusker Archery and had interests in farming and ranching. Carol and Dick were friends for years before they fell in love. Early in their friendship, Dick helped spearhead an effort to stop construction of a U.S. Bureau of Reclamation dam that would have flooded the beautiful Niobrara River valley near their community in the Sandhills. Carol, a local art teacher with a talent for sculpture, donated one of her pieces as a raffle item to raise money for the grassroots effort. The Fred Bear Sports Club and the Nature Conservancy also assisted the Save the Niobrara group, and the area is now under National Parks Scenic River protection.

Carol was attracted to this rabble-rouser and fanatical bow hunter, so she asked if he would teach her to hunt. At the time, Carol had a Hungarian Vizsla pointer and had always wanted to take him hunting. Carol took and passed a hunter-safety course and headed to the field. The rest is history.

Fred Bear once asked Dick how this romance came about. Dick answered that when Carol's Vizsla found a crippled turkey for them, he thought he might be falling in love. When the dog started pointing quail, he was sure, and decided to marry Carol to get that dog.

Fast forward to 1982. Carol and Dick sent a clever wedding announcement to friends and family and eloped. The announcement, with photographs of the couple and the Vizsla, Mouton, plastered across the front, read:

> The male and female pictured below have escaped from solitary confinement. They were recently seen in the company of close friends (accomplices) and Pastor Ellen Peterson leaving First Methodist Chapel at Columbus, Nebraska. They appeared to be shackled, handcuffed, or somehow tied to one another. Missiles

in the form of rice were being hurled at them, and the old shoes, cans, and trash tied to their escape vehicle did not deter their getaway. Both have visible arrow wounds, possibly inflicted by Mr. Cupid, notable ancient bow hunter.

The fugitives have known "hideouts" in the vicinity of Plum Creek, north Brown County, Nebraska, called Horse Thief Canyon, Dead Man's Draw, Deep Crick, and Bill White Canyon.

This pair may be extremely dangerous. They have vowed not to be separated until death.

REWARD: None should be sent. Couple needs only blessings for a continued free and happy life as they are already set with everything they need from their previous shady dealings and former crimes.

Dick and Carol waited until the evening before the big day to pick up their license because they wanted to keep the marriage a surprise. But neither had wed before and they didn't know there was a three-day waiting period before a couple could legally marry. They decided to proceed with the ceremony in the Methodist chapel and later left for Florida to attend Fred Bear's surprise eightieth birthday party. Fred learned about their dilemma and immediately made arrangements for them to be married in his office after the three-day waiting period in Florida. Following the short wedding ceremony, Fred and Henrietta Bear treated them to lunch.

Carol had never hunted, let along carried a gun, as a child growing up in New Jersey. Her grandfather let her shoot an air pistol in the basement, but her mother feared guns, although she never objected to hunting. Her father never hunted after he married. Carol majored in art education at Hastings College in Nebraska and in 1974 was hired as the art teacher in Rock County High School. Later she moved to Bassett, where she worked first at Farmers Union Cooperative and then for Dick at Cornhusker Archery.

"I married the boss and retired," laughed Carol.

Throughout their life together, Dick has organized a variety of grassroots efforts, and Carol supports him. Recently, they joined a committee of community leaders and successfully fought to keep the local rural hospital open, raising money to bring a doctor to the area.

In 2000 the Mauchs and other area volunteers successfully fought against a mega hog farm planned for their bucolic Sandhills area. The Sandhills Care Committee educated the public about the potential pollution problems and organized strategies to testify against the hog-farm proposal before the county commissioners. Carol created a hot-pink sign that read, "No Mega Hog Factories: Support Your Family Farm." The sign was ripped down the first night. Dick paid for an advertisement in the local newspaper describing the misdeeds and offering a $500 reward for information that led to the arrest of the vandals. The advertisement generated great press coverage. Tom Osborne, longtime head coach of the University of Nebraska football team and current U.S. Representative for Nebraska District 3, spoke in favor of the Sandhills Care Committee. Eventually, a state law restricting pollution of trout streams was the key to defeating the hog-farm development. Carol gives full credit to her husband for his willingness to step forward and be counted.

Dick and Carol love to bowhunt, bird hunt, and fish, and enjoy entertaining hunting friends at their cabin. A highlight of Carol's hunting career was using a bow and arrow to shoot the reigning world-record Quebec-Labrador caribou as recognized by the Pope and Young Club. The bull also is ranked ninth largest in the world by the Boone and Crockett Club. It was the second day of Dick and Carol's 1984 caribou hunt with Arctic Adventures on the Tunulik River in northern Quebec. They were with the camp's senior guide, Elijah, and an eleven-year-old apprentice guide and interpreter, Edward

Carol in the field with her world-record caribou.

Snowball. Elijah spoke only Inuit. The couple had met Edward two years previously and requested he be allowed to hunt with them.

The foursome headed upriver in a large outboard canoe to a peninsula Dick remembered as a good place to scout. He liked the lay of the land with its rutted migration trails leading to a single caribou "highway" and river crossing, and had killed a caribou in the area two years earlier. Dick hiked up the shoreline to glass and still-hunt on his own. Elijah sat on a high point to glass while Carol and Edward started a fire for tea. Shortly, Elijah motioned to them to come quickly to see three bulls entering the river on their way to the far shore. The crossing site was a mile or more wide, and a long, narrow, rocky island was one-third of the way across. Edward and Carol ran for the canoe, which Elijah had ready to go, and they headed for the island.

"Caribou have thick, hollow hair that makes them very buoyant," Carol said. "We could see the bulls swimming high in the water; even their tails poked above the surface." She said swimming caribou reminded her of old sailing ships gliding along. The caribou reached the island, crossed it, and reentered the water. The guides dropped Carol on the backside of the island and went on to the far shoreline. Earlier in camp, Glenn St. Charles, founder of the Pope and Young Club and a dear friend of the Mauchs, and Dick had discussed with the guides what constituted fair chase and the need to avoid herding caribou with boats. Edward listened carefully and understood the discussion.

The two Inuit guided the boat past the caribou and near the far shore. Elijah stopped the outboard and sat "dead in the water," as Carol remembers. The caribou spotted the boat and began a large circle, changing direction. Carol positioned herself in brush and rocks on the island's high middle so she could shoot left or right in case the bulls came ashore near her. They did exactly that, moving to her right, their feet clicking on the stony beach. Carol pulled her bow once to loosen her arms and thought, *Keep calm and wait for the big one.*

The two smaller bulls passed first; then the big one walked broadside to Carol. She released an arrow, hitting the neck just in front of the shoulder, and the caribou broke into a run. Carol quickly lost sight of it in the rough terrain. The blood trail was easy to follow, but she reached the far end of the island without seeing caribou. Where were they? She ran back to where she'd made the shot and climbed over a crest. The three bulls stood together, the big one facing Carol. She released a second arrow and filled her caribou tag.

Dick had been sitting on a hill a mile away, watching the events through his binocular, not knowing that the hunter was his wife.

Elijah and Carol field-dressed the bull, took pictures, and prepared the cape. And that's how Carol became the first woman in Pope and Young Club history to take a world-record animal. The caribou scored 434 in the Pope and Young record book and 431⁶/₈ in the Boone and Crockett Club.

Another Pope & Young trophy resulted from a deer hunt in 2001. The week before, Carol had spotted bucks near one of her Nebraska tree stands and placed a three-dimensional deer decoy in the brush underneath tagging it with red tape so she could find it in the predawn dark. The weather was ideal—frost and a slight south wind—when she left the cabin and walked to the stand in bright moonlight. She repositioned the deer decoy facing east, the direction from which the deer usually came to the alfalfa field. She climbed her tree, fastened her safety belt, pulled up her bow, and waited.

Soon the dark shapes of does began moving through the alfalfa toward the stand. One sniffed the decoy, but eventually left. Carol remained silent, her heart pounding, hoping. . . . Movement in sumac brush materialized into a big deer, but she didn't know if it was a doe or buck. When it stepped into the field, Carol thought, *Wow!* and told herself to calm down. The decoy was only ten or twelve yards from Carol, and the buck walked right up to it. She

Carol Mauch's 1982 Quebec-Labrador caribou, which has not been entered in the Pope and Young Club.

141

Carol Mauch in October 2001 with her P&Y trophy buck that field-dressed at 220 pounds. The typical whitetail scores 134⅛ points.

had never seen such massive, broad antlers. His head and face seemed to bulge where the antlers were attached.

The buck was facing Carol head on, and she needed to wait for a broadside shot. He lowered his head, eyed the decoy, and pawed the ground. Carol thought he would charge the decoy any minute, but instead the buck repositioned himself, apparently to get a reaction from the decoy, and stood broadside. Carol drew her Bill Stewart compound bow with a Bear Razorhead-tipped arrow and hit her mark. The buck ran a short distance into the alfalfa and started to circle. Branches blocked her view, but she knew he was going down.

Carol, gulping to regain composure, waited to stop shaking before she climbed down from the tree stand. She called Dick on her cell phone and told him to "Bring up some onions, we'll have fresh deer liver—I just shot a buck." From the ground she scanned the field with her binocular and saw where the buck had crashed about a hundred yards to the north. Carol picked up two cedar boughs to honor her trophy in the European way, placing one across the buck's side and the other in his mouth to represent the last meal. The buck field-dressed at 220 pounds and required a come-along winch to hoist it into the pickup.

The typical white-tailed buck scores 134⅛ points and sports a right main beam of 24⅞ inches and a left main beam of 24⅞ inches. The inside spread is 22⅜. The rack has four points on one side and five on the other—one large point was broken and not measurable.

A few years ago Carol began using her artistic talents to create one-of-a-kind necklaces, bolo ties, bracelets, pendants, earrings, and pins featuring western, wildlife, and Indian motif. Her clients are mostly friends and family, and her orders come via word of mouth. She fabricates silver and adds such unique items as fossil mammoth ivory, polished deer horn, fossil sand dollars, polished turquoise, fossil and petrified wood, and carved coral. Wildlife carvings are a special interest to her. Her pieces range in price from $38 for earrings upward to $600 and more, depending upon the complexity and materials.

Carol is a regular member of the Pope and Young Club and Dick is an honorary life senior member, a former records chairman, director, and executive secretary, and one of the originals at the time the club was founded in 1960. At national conventions of Pope and Young, Dick and Carol wear "unique" hunting outfits, made by Carol, which stand out in a crowd, to put it mildly. Dick has sports and tuxedo jackets tailored by Carol from at least six different camo patterns. "My latest creation," she said, "is a jacket with hunter's-orange camouflage highlighted with black velveteen lapels. It's a little outrageous!" she laughs. At the 2001 P&Y convention, Dick wore this particular jacket and a young man walked up and asked if he could borrow it for his upcoming wedding. His fiancée immediately piped up, "NO WAY!"

Carol wishes more women could experience what she and Dick find together in the field. She has one world record, but hunting is not about that. It's about nature, personal experiences with wildlife, and companionship with the man she loves.

KNOWING WHEN TO SHOOT
LINDA J. MCBRIDE
Pronghorn

No woman in the world has more pronghorns in the record book than Linda J. McBride. And only one male hunter can make that claim.

Hunting has always been a way of life for this petite, shy lady who grew up on a ranch outside Llano, Texas with a gun in her hand. She tracked squirrels, raccoons, white-tailed deer, and a variety of varmints. Linda was the youngest child of three but her half-sister and half-brother were more than twelve years older, so she was raised alone. She was born in Dallas but as a toddler moved to the ranch, so all her childhood memories revolve around rural Texas. They include riding off on a favorite horse and exploring by herself. As a teen she graduated to hunting white-tailed deer with her father.

She met her future husband, Dan, as a teenager, but they were reintroduced as adults when she went to work for Dan in his veterinary clinic. When she divorced her first husband in 1982, Linda and Dan began hunting together and eventually married in 1987. From the start of their relationship, hunting was their perfect time to get away from the hubbub of the office and savor the peace and quiet of the wilds. Dan taught Linda to become selective with the animals she takes.

"Dan always lets me shoot first, so I give him all the credit for my success in the field," Linda explained. Dan piped up and said the reason Linda is so good at hunting is that she has an uncanny ability to locate and judge trophy pronghorns. "Her stalking and scouting skills are as good as those of just about anyone I know," he said.

Dan says that when his friends come to hunt with them on leased land, they want Linda to be their guide because she has the knack for finding the best bucks. Linda says she always wants Dan around before she makes a final decision about an animal because he is the best judge. Together they make an unbeatable team.

Linda McBride adores pronghorn hunting. "People call them goats and don't take them seriously, but I love the way they act," she said. Linda especially enjoys walking the open range and glassing for herds of pronghorns. Crawling through the dirt and grass as she stalks the biggest buck really makes the adrenaline rush.

Linda's first B&C pronghorn came on a memorable hunt in 1991 in Mora County, New Mexico. Dan had studied where the largest pronghorns were being harvested in that state, using record-book listings and interviews with other hunters. He was the first to spot the buck Linda eventually downed. She remembers crawling toward a herd on her belly like a caterpillar for a long time, since there was no place to hide. One buck stood out among the rest, and Linda and Dan walked and crawled after him for forty-five minutes. Finally, as they lay watching two bucks bedded down facing each other, Dan suggested Linda shoot the one on the left. A single shot from three hundred yards, and the buck belonged to Linda. Its final score was 84⅝ points, almost three points above the minimum for entrance into the B&C all-time record book. This buck's right horn measures 16⅛ inches and the left horn 15⅞ inches, an extremely symmetrical trophy.

Two years later, Linda and Dan again traveled to Mora County, but decided to hunt with a guide on a different ranch. New Mexico offers three-day pronghorn hunts, and it was the afternoon of the third day when Dan spotted a good buck bedded down about a mile away. To avoid alerting the animal, they drove three to four miles away, then got out on foot for the stalk. The hunters

Pronghorn buck Number 1 for Linda McBride scores 84⅝ points and was dropped on a private ranch in New Mexico.

This B&C pronghorn scores 89⅝ points.

maneuvered to a low ridge, knowing the buck was lying down on the other side. Using a white-faced black range cow as a reference point, they crept as close as they dared, and a single shot by Linda downed the buck. Its final score was 82⅝ points, with both horns measuring 16⅜ inches.

Linda's sixth and largest B&C pronghorn was taken on 2 October 2000. She and Dan joined Dan's veterinary partner, Dr. William Kyle, Mike Stewart of Munday, Texas, and Keith Eason of West Palm Beach, Florida. William, Mike, and Linda had permits for one ranch, and Dan and Keith would hunt a neighboring ranch. Before they all gathered for dinner the first night, Mike called on his cell phone to say he had sighted a massive buck and suggested they drive to that area to check out its size. They all hopped into Mike's red pickup truck and drove along a dirt road. Near some power lines, Dan saw a buck at one thousand yards chasing a doe and oblivious to humans or danger of any kind. Keith dubbed it the "downrigger" for its odd forward-curving horns. They watched the buck chase the doe into the sunset.

"Somebody better get over here tomorrow and take a better look at that one," Dan commented.

"I just like how he looks," Linda said. "If no one kills him, I want him."

Mike wanted his guests to down a trophy buck, so he unselfishly elected to hunt a different place and encouraged Linda or William to take "downrigger."

William began hunting in that vicinity but saw another nice buck and filled his tag shortly after the season opened on Saturday. Linda, Dan, and Keith worked another ranch for a couple of days, but were itching to search again for "downrigger." They returned to where they'd first seen him, and unbelievably, along the same dirt road near the power lines stood the heavy-horned buck, grazing with three does. Linda wanted a better look. They drove within six hundred yards, but the does began to trot off with the buck following. Linda got out, worked her way closer, and fired at a range of 433 yards. Dan and Keith were sure she'd missed, but Linda knew it was a clean hit. The buck stepped forward a few steps and dropped. Its score: 89⅞ points. The right horn measured 18⅜ inches and the left 18⅜ inches.

In addition to six Boone and Crockett pronghorn bucks, Linda took a B&C barren-ground caribou near Alaska's Lake Becharof in late October of 1988. That experience was so positive that she and

Pointing straight forward are the odd horns of Linda's 1994 buck.

Dan returned to Alaska in 1996 and collected caribou that scored in the high 380s.

Caribou reminded Linda of pronghorns—both animals can see and smell a human long before the human sees them. Both animals make you doubt whether you'll ever sneak close enough for a clear shot. The stark land that caribou roam is reminiscent of the pronghorn's western plains. Neither habitat offers trees or brush to hide the hunter as she sneaks toward the prey.

Both Dan and Linda have children from earlier marriages, and all love to hunt with their parents. The products of their own marriage—sons Kyle (born in 1995) and Kelton (born in 1996)—both anticipate hunting with Dan and Linda in the years to come. In 2002 Linda took her young grandsons for their first target-practice experience.

Why hunt? Linda's answers are simple and to the point. What other pastime offers sights like a bull elk herding his harem down a Wyoming mountain, pawing the ground and flipping dirt over its head? Hunting brings a person closer to nature and life itself. Linda has no problem shooting an animal and finds exhilaration when it drops. "An even bigger thrill for me is taking a trophy animal," she said.

Linda McBride's next goals are to collect a trophy bull elk and a Rocky Mountain goat. She knows she will hunt as long as she can hike, carry a gun, camp, and climb a mountain. And she knows she will always hunt for pronghorns.

THE BONUS BULL
JAN OPAL
Quebec-Labrador Caribou

Fabulous animal "headgear" can stir the heart of even the most jaded hunter. Imagine what seeing a quartet of monstrous caribou bulls, which sport some of the continent's most spectacular antlers, would do to a woman accustomed to seeing mainly white-tailed deer.

Jan Opal, a resident of upstate New York, was on her first caribou hunt in 1994 with her husband, Jeffery. "We were so excited," Jan said. "But we arrived in camp with seventeen other hunters and seven guides to discover that the caribou hadn't yet started migrating. Jeffery and I were lucky that year to each take a cow."

But that ill-fated Quebec hunt sowed the seed of determination, and the couple booked another hunt for two years later.

"Two weeks before we were due to depart, we received a call from Henri Poupart, owner of Safari Nordik, our outfitting company. He suggested that we consider rescheduling our trip for 1997 because the caribou again were slow to migrate. Instead, we decided to delay our trip for several weeks, rebooking our flight so that we'd arrive in Fort Chimo in northern Quebec in late September. Surely, we thought, by then the herd would have begun its migration."

The couple flew to Chimo, a thousand miles north of Montreal, and then sixty miles by floatplane to Camp Gerido on the shore of Lake Gerido, one of the province's thousands of lakes. "We were the last two hunters of the season," Jan said.

That afternoon, Jan and Jeffery climbed into a boat with their guide, Jerry McDonald. "In this area caribou are hunted by boat," Jan explained. "You cover as much water as possible, always looking for movement along the shoreline or in the lake." Caribou are excellent swimmers and will readily take to the water.

That evening they spotted a good bull caribou swimming across the lake. When the animal clambered out on shore, the hunters beached their boat and started tracking it. After an exciting stalk, Jeff shot the animal. This hunt was off to a far better start than the preceding one.

The next morning it was Jan's turn to shoot. Later that day, she dropped a good bull, and the hunters spent the remainder of the day caping, skinning, quartering, and packing out Jan's caribou.

Jan and Jeffery had purchased two bull tags apiece. But their hunt was already an unqualified success, and any additional bull they might shoot would be a bonus, pure and simple.

The next day guide and hunters were back in the boat. As they searched the shoreline, they became aware of several "somethings" poking above the horizon and moving. Caribou antlers! Antlers so large that a good portion of their length was visible even though the animals bearing them could not yet be seen.

"We landed the boat and headed in their general direction," Jan said. "We hid in some boulders that seemed to be in their path, and the enormous bulls eventually approached to within fifty yards of us. Trying to decide which one to shoot wasn't easy, but the guide helped me. I shot, and my bull dropped."

The three had been hunkered down behind a huge boulder. Once Jan knew her bull was down, she yelled to Jeff. He emerged from the boulder's other side to shoot another giant bull. The Opals could scarcely believe their good fortune. Not only had they each filled both tags, but their bonus bulls were beyond belief.

Their guide suspected that Jan's trophy might be a viable candidate for the Boone and Crockett record book. He told them, though, that inches would be lost during the required sixty-day drying period. At the moment, neither Jan nor Jeff was worried about scores. They were still in a daze. "Jeff was extremely excited, about my bull in particular," Jan said.

Jeff, after all, was the impetus that had propelled his registered-nurse wife into hunting. "I'd never even wanted to hunt while I was growing up," she said, "even though my father and three brothers hunted. Hunting wasn't something a girl did, at least not in my family."

Jan and Jeff both work in health care, she as a nurse and clinical coordinator for an upstate New York medical center and Jeff as a pharmacist. Jeff probably had harbored secret hopes that Jan might someday join him afield as his hunting buddy.

"I learned when I was dating Jeff that if I wanted to spend time with him, I'd have to join him in the woods," Jan said. "At first I brought along a book to read or a camera. But Jeff would go to a hunting spot, check the wind, and then ask me to start walking in a particular direction, stopping occasionally. Several times he shot deer as a direct result of these 'drives'."

In 1976 Jan and Jeff were married. He continued hunting, and she started carrying a gun. As she walked through the woods, Jan realized that she was seeing quite a few deer—and field mice, chipmunks, and many species of birds. A partridge once flew into Jan's blind, and several times she was thrilled to see a chickadee briefly alight on her gun's barrel. A whole new world was opening up for her.

Jan grew to better understand nature's intricacies. "When you enter the animals' world, to succeed as either an observer or a hunter, you must assume certain animal behavioral characteristics," she said. "A hunter is merely another link in the chain of life."

Though she carried a gun, she didn't use it. "Perhaps I just wasn't ready yet," she said.

On the day she finally was ready, she was hunting a tract of land favored for years by the hunting members of her family. "On this property there is a tall, old tree that I like to think of as the 'Family Tree'," she explained. "Its base is large enough to conceal a hunter, and a branch grows out at the perfect height for steadying a gun.

"On this particular day, Jim was at that spot, and I was about two hundred yards distant, near a low stone wall. At noon I walked over to ask if he'd seen anything. He hadn't, and said he was going back to the truck for lunch and asked if I'd like to take his stand. Not ten minutes after he'd left, a doe ran up and stopped twenty

Jan Opal and her "bonus bull" with an estimated B&C score of more than 366 points.

Jan Opal and one of her dogs.

yards away. The moment must have been right. When the doe started to walk away, I shot her.

"Jim heard the shot and came back to tell me that now the work would really start. I was shaking as I field-dressed my doe. I think Jim really doubted that I wanted to hunt. I think he was truly surprised when he found out that I'd actually killed a deer."

On that autumn day Jan graduated to full-blown hunting-buddy status, and Jeff couldn't have been happier. The gun she used, a 20-gauge Remington 1100, had been bought by Jeff for his wife some months earlier with money received as gifts when he graduated from pharmacy college. Jan says this gun is still her favorite.

Jan often had contemplated how she would feel if she ever actually killed an animal. The hunting itself didn't bother her. She had grown up in a hunting household where wild game was often on the menu. Over time she decided that becoming a good shot was important to her, and reconciled herself to the possibility of having to finish the job if she wounded an animal. "That's a commitment all hunters have to make," she said. Her aim always is a one-shot kill, and Jan will pass up shots she feels are too risky.

She is extremely patient and sometimes allows deer to approach within twenty feet before she fires.

"One day I had a doe facing me only twenty feet away and decided to shoot her as soon as she turned to the side," Jan said. "She would rub her hind legs together and appear to be urinating. Suddenly, a buck appeared, walking up to sniff the ground where she'd urinated, and I shot him." That nine-pointer had a very respectable twenty-inch-wide rack.

Does she feel remorse when she shoots an animal? "Not if it has been treated with respect, the meat has been put to good use, and the kill is quick and humane."

Most people who choose nursing as a profession are caring individuals. Degreed nurses, however, soon discover that each person is his or her own best primary caregiver and largely responsible for his or her own health and well-being. Personal responsibility is important to Jan—one reason she wears full hunter orange whenever she deer hunts. "In my experience, the bright color doesn't spook them," she is quick to add.

Jan's parents were not exactly supportive when she shot her first deer. "My father may have believed that hunting was a man's sport. My mother was very opposed. When I told her I'd shot my

Thanks to bucks like this dandy whitetail, Jan Opal has gained an enviable reputation in New York as an excellent deer hunter.

deer, she said, 'Shame on you.' But I think they've become accustomed to it. Both my parents enjoy the venison we give them."

Jan enjoys sharing her many hunting adventures. "I once watched a buck and a doe moving through the woods," she said. "The buck disappeared, and the doe bedded down. Forty-five minutes later I heard a noise to my left, and there was a buck. As he started to approach me, I glanced downhill to see another buck, probably the one that had been accompanying the doe. The two stared at each other, then the first buck started toward me but stopped to rub his rack on a sapling. I lined up on the larger buck, but it suddenly dashed off. So I did what any other deer hunter would do: I shot the smaller buck, a seven-pointer. I believe this was my favorite hunting experience."

Jan so far has harvested three caribou, about thirty whitetails, and a bear. The Opals' home is decorated with many beautiful mounted animal heads, each displayed in its own place of honor and each bearing a name meaning something special to the couple.

Although Jan would enjoy the company of other female hunters, the only hunting woman of her acquaintance is a niece who pursues deer and waterfowl near her Arkansas home. "I admire her so," Jan said. "She is hearing-impaired, so what a challenge hunting must be!"

Coworkers have not exactly warmed to Jan's tales of hunting. "I've tried to change their perceptions of hunting and hunters, but many of them are just so adamantly opposed to the very idea of hunting that nothing I say makes a difference," she said.

On the homefront, though, things couldn't be better. "Jeff takes his share of razzing because it seems like I often bag larger animals," she said. "He doesn't mind. There truly is no competition between us. Besides, anything I take is due to him. He taught me everything I know about hunting."

One thing high on Jan's list of things to do would be to bag another black bear. Her first one created a memorable—and somewhat dangerous—moment. "Toward late afternoon one day during New York's early muzzleloading season, "I sat down in a nice ground blind in the midst of some fallen trees. I was snacking on cheese and pepperoni when I noticed a bear two hundred yards away that disappeared into the trees. Soon it came running out into an opening behind my stand, then headed straight for me." Jan didn't know if the tantalizing food odors had attracted the bear, nor did she care. "It was ten feet away and closing fast when I shot. It turned and raced away. I heard this truly awful sound, and thought I might only have wounded it." But she found it lying dead twenty-five yards from where she had shot it.

Jan Opal smoothly made the transition from nonhunter to hunter. Hunting is important not only to her but also to her marriage. She doesn't hesitate to advise other outdoor-oriented women to check out this wholesome activity. "I truly believe that many women would enjoy hunting, and it's an activity that most of them can master. Women hunters are less competitive than men. They also are more perceptive and infinitely more patient.

"Hunting can be very rewarding, especially if you learn from an ethical teacher. Above all else, remember that hunting is a privilege, and behave accordingly."

There may be no better role model than Jan Opal, health-care professional, conservationist, hunter, and Jeff Opal's favorite outdoor companion.

DANGER GIRL
LISA PASCADLO
Mule Deer, Shiras Moose

Danger Girl. The nickname has a certain ring to it. But is it mere hype? Or well-deserved? And would Lisa even want to be called Danger Girl?

The answer to the last question is yes—as readers will soon find out. Lisa hunts alone. She researches hunting areas, applies for permits, prepares for her hunts, and drives to her destinations a-l-o-n-e! She hikes—on her own—into remote backcountry areas, even in the dead of winter. And then she hunts alone unless she's required to hire a guide. She is responsible for every nickel doled out for her various and sundry hunts. When luck is good and she draws several coveted but pricey tags, she'll juggle the household budget to eliminate a few necessities rather than turn down tags. "I've gone on some really expensive hunts, thanks to creative financing," she says.

Lisa's go-it-alone lifestyle suits her for now, although she someday would like to find a guy as enthusiastic as she is about hunting. That, unfortunately, may prove to be difficult. Lisa believes that the mounting number of grueling adventures she's undertaken, together with her never-quit mentality, might be off-putting should she actually meet Mr. Right.

"I once came close to getting married," she said. "But my hunting killed that relationship. Since then, I've dated several guys. If they're OK with my hunting, the relationship takes a beating when they learn that I'm a police officer."

Lisa is a cute, smart blonde who knows far more about guns, bows, hunting, and self-defense than 99 percent of the available males, one reason her quest for a soulmate might not be an easy one. Moreover, she is wild about the two rottweiler-shepherd mixes—Toko and Timmy—with which she shares her home.

Lisa earned a degree in criminal law with a minor in linguistics from Utah's Weaver State University. "I would someday like to become a game warden or a biologist," she said. "They already call me the 'game warden' at work because they think I want to shoot any injured deer that's reported. Putting down injured deer is part of my job, but I don't like doing it. Only a psychopath would enjoy killing injured or starving animals."

During periods of heavy snow, Lisa, the police officer, has found herself face to nose with some of the huge mule deer bucks she likes to hunt in the mountains around Salt Lake City. "I could never kill any animal struggling just to survive," she said. "When I hunt, it must be done fairly or not at all."

Lisa so far has bagged turkey, Coues whitetail, mule deer, elk, pronghorn, Shiras moose, and one of New Mexico's highly elusive and coveted gemsbok, otherwise known as oryx. She dreams of hunting a Marco Polo sheep in Tajikistan, although she would settle for either a Stone-sheep hunt in British Columbia or a roaring-stag hunt in Scotland.

Lisa also enjoys football, skiing, hiking, and any other outdoor activity. She haunts www.monstermuleys.com, and she belongs to numerous organizations dedicated to gun rights, wildlife, and the environment, including the National Rifle Association, Rocky Mountain Elk Foundation, Mule Deer Foundation, Foundation for North American Wild Sheep, Ducks Unlimited, and the North American Hunting Club. Lisa is a volunteer at her Presbyterian church, and she also works with the Karl Malone Foundation, which aims to get kids involved with hunting.

"My earliest memories are of going deer hunting with my dad," Lisa said. "I think at the beginning I was gung-ho because hunting gave me a way to prove myself. I wanted to fill every tag simply because it was a goal I'd set for myself. Then there was a subtle shift. No longer am I frustrated if I don't fill every tag. Hunting has become more spiritual to me. I believe I now understand how Native Americans regarded hunting—as a gift, not only a means to survive. Hunting's aesthetics appeal to me. Every moment has its memory— the way snow drifts into a valley, or the way a sunset colors and patterns the sky."

For Lisa Pascadlo, the old nursery rhyme about "Sugar and spice and everything nice" would have to be reworded to "GI Joe and a dirt bike to go." "I grew up playing with boys," she said. "I didn't know I was different until I was eight or nine. The competitive spirit was rampant in my friends, so I guess that's where I got mine. Whenever the boys went deer hunting with their fathers, I'd want to go with mine."

It's quite a leap from riding dirt bikes to police officer. "I was an engineering major when I was hired to work with campus security to earn extra money for my tuition. Riding with the campus police hooked me on that kind of work. I think it's because a lot of police work is simply hunting people. It requires all my skills, even tracking. Of course, there's more frustration in police work."

But Lisa has experienced frustration in hunting matters, too. "I went to a sporting-goods shop to buy ammo," she recalled. "The sales clerk said, 'Did your husband send you down here to buy this?' I said, 'No, I figured it out all by my little blonde self.'

"You can't really blame him, I guess," she continued. "But it gets old after a while."

Lisa Pascadlo lets nothing stand in the way of hunting. "I was hunting the Paunsaugant here in Utah for a particular mule deer buck. I'd been chasing him for two or three days, but he'd travel to this one point in the rimrock and just vanish. I couldn't figure out where he would go from there.

"One night walking out, I stepped on a rattlesnake," she continued. "I felt it strike my leg. My pants legs were tucked into my boots and then bloused out military-style, and the snake's fangs got stuck in the fabric and wouldn't come out. I panicked. I briefly

Lisa and the Big 5, her Boone and Crockett mule deer that was really a 6x7.

considered shooting at the snake, but that could have blown my leg off. I calmed myself down, hooked my gun's barrel under the rattler's chin, and then pulled him up and out of the fabric and tossed him away. I was lucky to escape with just a venom-soaked sock."

But the "trip from hell" was far from over. "During the next several days, an itchy spot developed on the back of one leg," Lisa continued. "I didn't think much about it, but the spot grew larger and became hard as a rock and very painful. And it itched like crazy. When I could no longer endure the pain, I hiked out to Kanab and went to the hospital's emergency room."

Diagnosis: scorpion bite. "The scorpion must have crawled into my sleeping bag," Lisa said. Doctor's orders called for a shot of steroids, Benadryl, and a slathering of hydrocortisone cream, all to combat the bite's pain and itchiness. "As frustrating as that trip was, I still remember more good about it than bad."

The ability to focus on a trip's high points while ignoring its bad ones is a trait of successful hunters. Hunting can mess with your mind and body in ways the couch potato can't even imagine, but any hunter who concentrates on only the perilous or the miserable moments she's endured will not go hunting again.

Lisa deserves plenty of credit for being able to laugh at some of the hair-raising escapades in which she's been an unwilling participant. Which brings up her 2001 Mexican Coues deer hunt.

"Coues deer present an incredible challenge," she said. "They can spot hunters from two miles away and then they stand there like statues, staring at you.

"My guide's name was Manuelito. We were riding along when I heard him saying, "I'm sorry, I'm sorry!" I looked at him, and his face was alive with bees. Then the bees attacked me. We bailed off our horses and ran. I took off my hat to swat at the bees, but that was a big mistake. They flew into my hair and stung me seventeen times.

"Manuelito led me to a water hole, where I packed mud all over my face. When we returned to camp, the *vaqueros* laughed at us. Manuelito asked, 'Are you OK?'

"'No,' I said, and that's the last thing I can recall. I fell off my horse, unconscious."

Lisa is terribly allergic to bee stings So was the other American hunter in camp, and he had the camp's only epinephrine pen. Even worse, they were sixty miles from the nearest clinic.

The bees that attacked Lisa were Africanized or "killer" bees. "The reaction wasn't caused so much by my allergy but because I'd been stung so many times," she said. "The outfitter and guides were convinced that without the epinephrine, I would have died."

Did Lisa stay in camp after that? Not when there were Coues deer to be hunted. She found a hat that would stay on her severely swollen head, took some Benadryl, and went back out. She bagged a dandy Coues deer, too. "You might say I'm a 'vermin magnet'," she joked.

Lisa historically has had bad luck drawing mule deer tags in her home state of Utah. In 2000 it was more of the same. In dismay, she contacted Rich LaRocco, a hunting consultant from Logan, to see if he had any last-minute, affordable landowner tags available. The answer was yes and no. Yes, he had some available, but no, they weren't affordable by Lisa's standards.

Rich called back in July to tell Lisa that he'd acquired several Cooperative Wildlife Management Unit (CWMU) deer tags from a landowner. They were in a good big-buck area, but the hunt would be unguided and the price for the tag alone was what she'd normally pay for a fully guided hunt. Another negative factor was that the area had been declared a federal disaster area due to a prolonged drought.

Lisa's hunting friends advised her not to buy the tag. But she did a "background check": "Paging through the record books revealed that many book bucks had been killed in this area. I bought the tag."

In late August she drove to the CWMU and met with the area's manager, offering to help him post signs around the unit's borders. That way, she could get acquainted with at least a portion of the boundary and would rack up points with the manager.

It proved to be a good idea—the manager provided some clues to deer movements and showed Lisa a video of some of the area's outstanding mule deer. For several mornings running she posted boundary markers. Each afternoon she drove the area's road system and searched for sign.

The video revealed an amazing buck that everyone called the Big Five. "My goal now had a name," she said. The buck reportedly liked to hang out in Conservation Reserve Program (CRP) land next to some uranium mines. When heavy equipment had been brought in to reclaim the land around the mines, the buck had moved out. Lisa nevertheless continued to haunt the mine area, even through torrential rains, hail, and lightning that ended the drought.

She saw neither hide nor hair of the Big Five until the evening before the season opener. "I found him on BLM land," Lisa said. "I'd heard that big bucks tend to stay in a particular area, and I believed he would eventually return to the mines. I just hoped it would be in the next five days."

When Lisa returned to camp, the manager told her that the area's other three permittees had arrived. Without checking to see what plans she had made, the newcomers had decided to hunt near the uranium mine, too, based mainly upon conversations they'd had with miners. "To say I was mad would be an understatement," Lisa said.

Lisa harvested two monster bull elk in the same Wyoming meadow.

"I felt I had put in the time to claim my own little piece of ground out of the more than 22,000 acres in the CWMU."

Lisa visited the men's camp to discuss the matter. "I was friendly, but somewhat perturbed. They wouldn't back down, and neither would I. No compromise was amenable to them, except they agreed that everyone could meet and walk in together to a predetermined spot, then separate so everyone would know where the others would be hunting."

The next morning, Lisa discovered she was the only person in the party wearing Scent-Lok, the odor-absorbing clothing. "Anything downwind of us as we walked in could be spooked by human odor," she said. At the split-up spot, one hunter said he would post near the mine about a thousand yards from Lisa, another would walk out the sage flats to the north, and the third clammed up completely, so Lisa had no idea what his plans entailed.

"I planned to walk the perimeter of the CRP, then cross out to a lone patch of pinyon pine in the middle of the field, where I would hunker down and wait." When she reached the pinyon cover, she sat down and started scoping out the CRP. Directly ahead of her was a buck. "He was a twenty-six-inch four-point," Lisa said. "A second four-point appeared next, and I remembered that when I'd seen the Big Five, he had been with two smaller four-points." It seemed unlikely that the trio had traveled several miles in one night, but just as Lisa looked again, the Big Five stood up in full view.

A rangefinder revealed that the buck was only 206 yards away—perfect, since she's sighted-in her .280 Remington at 200 yards. "The Big Five was facing away from me," Lisa said. "I didn't like that shot. I got out a pair of shooting sticks and set them up. The buck turned so that he was quartering away, and I squeezed the trigger. The Big Five dropped."

The buck's rack had appeared awesome, but as she walked closer, Lisa feared "ground shrinkage." She needn't have worried. "The Big Five was everything I ever dreamed of," she said. "His rack

Lisa's Idaho Shiras bull moose netted 147⅞ Boone and Crockett points and qualified for the club's annual awards program.

measured 28 inches wide and 22 inches high and was a 6x7 rather than a Big Five. His Boone and Crockett green score was 214⅞. After drying, the rack netted 194⅜ Boone and Crockett points."

Lisa didn't hesitate when asked which of her many hunting experiences was the most memorable. "My big Wyoming bull elk," she said. "I'd been hunting elk in the same area for seven years, but had never been in the right place at the right time. In 1999, the weather turned bitterly cold and tremendous drifts piled up. Someone had stolen my clothes out of the dryer at the laundromat, so I had to hunt wearing just jeans and other clothing that hadn't been stolen. After the seventh day, I was physically exhausted— this was developing into one of my typical hard-luck hunts.

"The next day was foggy. I hiked in to a meadow, picked a spot, and sat down. *This is it*, I told myself. *I'm not moving*.

"I then saw two dim shapes walking through the meadow," Lisa said. "I thought they were hunters on horseback, but my binocular showed two big branch-antlered bulls. I put my scope on the second bull and shot. The animal went into the timber. After twenty minutes I walked into the trees, and the biggest bull elk I'd ever seen was lying there. I started to cry—that's how overwhelmed I was by my good fortune."

The sounds of Lisa's weeping alerted another hunter, who came over expecting to find someone in trouble. "I was leaning against the bull's belly, trying to pull one leg out from beneath the animal," she said. "I had no idea how big a mature bull elk would be." Together Lisa and the man gutted the bull, then Lisa went to a nearby camp to ask if she might borrow a sled.

"One hunter offered to pull my elk out with his horse, but when he saw the bull he said, 'That weighs more than my horse.' He showed me how to cape, quarter, and sled the elk out, though.

"I returned the next year and shot a big 5x5 bull in the exact same meadow."

Lisa has no children, at least not yet, but she's looking forward to teaching her best friend's daughter, perhaps prophetically named Hunter, how to hunt. "I'm her godmother," she said. "It's my duty. I've already taught her how to fish."

Lisa shows great promise as a writer. She wrote an article about her giant mule deer buck for *Trophy Hunter* magazine. Further proof is the following excerpt from one of her submissions, titled "The Stuff of Dreams." In it, Lisa has fictionalized what her bull elk—the King, as she calls him—was doing in the moments before she shot him:

> The King is left to find his own way, his companion the same arrogant [younger bull] who had sought his crown. Noses scarred

and torn hides healed, the two bulls follow a path as old as time itself through the maze of canyons, creeks, and cliffs humans call Greater Yellowstone. It was during this phenomenal migration that the King and I crossed paths. He, casually making his way toward the Refuge in a fog so thick that sound was swallowed as surely as his shape, and I, a miserably wet and sore hunter trying to fulfill a lifelong dream. . . .

Every time I lie on the couch, the King looms over me, a moment in our lives caught in perpetuity, and I can picture the valley, where the pine scent wafts on gentle mountain breezes, and the mist lies still on the meadow floor at first light.

It is for such moments that people like Lisa Pascadlo hunt.

πr² & TROPHY GOATS R WARY
JULIE PLY
Pronghorn

It's not that Julie Et.ing Ply hasn't worked hard for the game animals she's taken during her young life as a hunter—she has. Still, she has been fortunate to see—and harvest—several great trophies.

Julie was only three when she started traveling with her mother and father on their various western hunting expeditions. Each September, the three would depart their Missouri home and point the vehicle's nose toward the Shining Mountains, known now as the Rockies. The usual destination was Wyoming, where people were scarce and game and public land abounded. The family would hunt remote tracts of BLM or Forest Service ground from either their tent or a converted van. They befriended jade prospectors, cowboys, and other Wyomingites, including several employees of the state game and fish department. The little girl soon was intrigued by hunting, nature, and the outdoors. She could barely wait until she was old enough to hunt on her own. That day arrived in Missouri, where, at age eleven, she took her first white-tailed deer with her mother's .30-06. At thirteen she shot her first wild turkey, a jake, while her sleep-deprived parents snored after enduring nearly two weeks of 4 A.M. wakeup calls as they each bagged a Missouri gobbler.

But Julie's real red-letter day arrived not long after she turned fourteen, old enough to apply for a Wyoming nonresident big-game permit.

Late September, when many pronghorn seasons take place, and early October, wher. mule deer season opens in Wyoming's Region D, are often balmy and mild. People acquainted only with the state's reputation for treacherous high winds and severe blizzards are usually amazed when they experience one of Wyoming's pleasant "Cheyenne autumns." In Julie's first year of hunting muleys, though, the weather got lousy early and stayed that way. Lowering skies of steelwool clouds spit sleet and rain, while a howling wind bore down from the north.

During previous seasons, Julie's parents had met and become friends with Rawlins game warden Dennis Smith and his family. Dennis, whose teenage son Scott had recently bagged his own first big-game animals, was eager to help Julie. Late that first afternoon, the party watched a herd of big muleys boil up out of a dry wash, then line out for a ridgetop more than a mile to the west. Mom,

Julie Ply's big Wyoming pronghorn netted 83⅝ Boone and Crockett points.

Dad, Dennis, and Julie began to trudge after them across the rolling sagebrush plain. The slope to the skyline looked gentle, but the 8,400-foot altitude soon put a major hurt on the parents' flatlander lungs. Within a mere five hundred yards, Mom and Dad started lagging behind. Their stamina was no match for that of an excited teenager or a game warden notorious for his relentless pursuit of wildlife violators. Dennis and Julie ran and climbed, higher and higher, until they were specks on the horizon. It was nearly forty-five minutes before the parents eased out onto a rimrock slab to witness the climactic scene unfolding on the hillside below. Julie was belly-crawling through the sage, her rifle cradled in her arms. Dennis had halted so he could spot Julie's shots. As her audience watched, the teenager slowly settled down and steadied her rifle. Moments later, a single shot rang out. Ten minutes later, the parents joined their ecstatic daughter and one proud game warden-guide to help field-dress a superb 5x5 mule deer buck.

Kids grew up too quickly then, as they do now. Julie chose engineering as her college major, and it was many years before she once again put in for Wyoming tags. In 1988, after graduating from the University of Missouri's Rolla campus as a metallurgical engineer, Julie went to work at a steel mill outside Chicago. The following year she accepted another job in southern Illinois, closer to home. She became engaged, and about a year later woke up in the dead of night to hear the phone ringing. The news was devastating. Her fiancé was hovering near death after being injured in a motorcycle accident on a secluded country road. After spending thirty-seven days in a coma, he finally awoke, but with severe brain damage. Julie was determined to see things through, but after nearly a year she came to realize that the young man would improve no further. In one of the most heartbreaking and difficult decisions she would ever have to make, Julie decided to move on alone.

As the date neared for submitting Wyoming mule deer and antelope applications for 1992, Julie's parents asked if she would like to go hunting with them again, as much to speed the process of healing as for her companionship. Would she ever, she replied. Applications were completed and checks mailed. The three had applied as a party, and all received both antelope and mule deer tags.

Knowing she had licenses to fill was exactly what Julie needed to get her life back on track. She filled the time until the family left for Wyoming poring over catalogs for hunting clothes, outfitting her .243 Winchester with a bipod, and working it out at the shooting range.

The Etlings drove almost nonstop the eleven hundred miles to their south-central Wyoming hunting camp, and were still so wired

Julie poses with a fine Wyoming mule deer that has an outside spread of almost 28 inches.

upon arrival that it was all but impossible to sleep. They decided to concentrate first on their "goats," as pronghorns are widely known. Kathy spotted a couple of good bucks and devised a new strategy: She would lie in wait in a ditch and hope that one of the pronghorns would be fool enough to wander close enough for a shot.

Bob wanted to try to kill a goat with a Remington XP-100, a powerful handgun, but instead decided to help Julie bag her first pronghorn. They set their sights on a bona-fide "hummer"—a really fine goat—but after a day and a half had located no such buck.

Enter Kenny Funk, pronghorn guide extraordinaire. Kenny, at the time a guide for Bolten Ranch Outfitters, told the two about a big antelope he'd seen far out in Area 56. "Kenny said the buck's horns were at least sixteen inches high and retained their mass clear up to the almost eight-inch prongs. That sounded good to me," said Julie.

Kenny gave them complex directions involving a pond ringed with aspens, an eagle's nest, and an artesian well. "Dad had never seen any of those things, though he'd hunted that territory for many years, so we were lost right from the start," Julie said.

Our pair of stalwart hunters wound their way in and out of cuts and washes, but no matter where they went, the landscape looked the same. The clues they'd received were not panning out. As they sat in their vehicle, wondering what to do next, "A big herd of antelope ran out on a flat about a mile in front of us," Julie said. "We parked our truck, climbed down into a dry wash, and sneaked toward the herd until we were close enough to glass them. We saw a good buck, but his horns didn't look like they'd measure sixteen inches. Anyway, he was moving away from us."

They continued down the arroyo until it petered out and they had to stop. "Try a shot," Bob said.

Julie tried to settle in but couldn't get steady in the sitting position, the only one from which she was able to see the buck above the sagebrush. Finally the two gave up for the day.

That evening, they again cornered Kenny, who corrected each navigational error in turn. The next morning, the golden sunshine was gone, replaced by low, fast-moving clouds that threatened rain. And rain in that country is bad news. Bentonite in the soil becomes slick as snot with even a dollop of moisture, and the resulting morass is hell to drive in. "If it rains," Bob said, "we're out of here. No antelope is worth spending the night in our truck." But the farther the truck traveled into the ranch's interior, the hollower his threats sounded.

When the vehicle approached a pond surrounded by aspens, the hunters perked up. There in the treetops was an eagle's nest, exactly where Kenny had said it would be. Not far off was an artesian well whose cold, clear water streamed from a long, sloping pipe and into the pond. Bob and Julie scoured the landscape, and on the crest of a ridge she noticed a good buck antelope standing at full attention, staring brazenly at her. "I yelled, 'If I can get a shot at that one, I'll take it for sure!'"

Bob parked the truck, and Julie pulled out and loaded her rifle. Father and daughter climbed the steep hillside and walked across the ridgetop plateau to peer down into the remote canyon on the other side. A sizable herd of antelope straggled out through the sagebrush. Some animals were feeding; others had bedded down. Right below the two hunters, a nice buck ambled along. "I'd shoot him if I were you," Bob said. But Julie knew it was not the buck she'd spotted earlier and passed on the opportunity.

Julie then spotted a smaller herd milling about in a nondescript side canyon. She glassed them and saw a big buck bedded down in their midst. "That looks like a huge animal," she said. "Let's see how close we can get." Bob agreed.

The two closed the distance to about 150 yards. The problem with antelope is that most seasons are open during the rut's peak. Pronghorn bucks spend every waking moment chasing after does or running off other bucks intent on horning in on the mating action. Big herd bucks, especially, become extremely unpredictable. One might be resting easily one minute, then stampeding off the next. This one did just that: he lurched from his bed and raced toward his herd of does. When he did, he barreled below Julie's line of sight. Responding quickly, she hurried forward up the hill, extending her gun's bipod legs as she went so she would be ready to shoot from the sitting position. Then her father stood up. Bob could now see the buck, but the herd could also see Bob. Chaos erupted as antelope charged in every direction.

"Shoot, shoot!" yelled Bob.

"I can't see him!" Julie yelled back. But just then the buck attained enough height on the opposite hillside so that Julie could see him. He was running full speed at about a hundred yards, gaining distance on the shooter with each long, fluid stride. *Boom, boom, boom!* Julie knew that if she didn't drop the buck now, he would be far spookier the next time she tried to stalk close. Missourians don't get many chances to practice shooting at running targets at extreme ranges. But Julie calmed herself and adjusted her shooting to match the yardage as well as the pronghorn's angle and speed. Her next shot toppled the buck, but she didn't know it. The instant she shot, the buck disappeared over the ridgeline.

When the hunters topped out, the buck tried to get up. One final shot and the animal was down for good.

"Dad shouted, 'Wow! What a goat! You have to get him mounted.' He was right. I'm not sure I'd ever seen an antelope that big before, or have seen one since."

The gray skies had vanished, and a vast arc of cobalt blue extended as far as the eye could see. Back at the ranch house, Bob "Buff" Terrill, the Bolten's manager at the time, green-scored Julie's buck's horns at over 86 Boone and Crockett points. When the pronghorn was scored later back in Missouri after more than sixty days of drying time, it tallied 83⅝ points, making Julie's first pronghorn one for the books.

Julie gradually had fallen in love with the West. When a northern Colorado company, impressed with her resume, offered a job, she accepted. As soon as she was a legal Colorado resident, she began applying for plains mule deer rifle tags. After four long years, she drew one.

She had permission to hunt a vast spread in the state's northern agricultural belt. While scouting that summer, Julie located a number

Julie, shown here with her mother, accompanied her parents on most of their Wyoming hunting adventures until she was a junior in high school.

171

of huge bucks. She knew that once the shooting started, the bucks would make themselves scarce. Nonetheless, she volunteered to take the ranch owner's wife hunting for *her* first deer. The woman, who had never before hunted, came through like a champ with Julie's coaching, tagging a mule deer doe.

The next morning, the big bucks were nowhere to be found. But Julie persevered, eventually spotting a big old mossyhorns bedded down in a milo field. Unfortunately, the buck was about fifty yards across the line on a neighbor's property. Her heart sank as she glassed those high, curving antlers. "I'd already requested hunting permission from this farmer and had been turned down," she said. "I didn't think my chances now would be any better."

But she drove to a phone to ask again. The farmer, who lived a hundred miles away from his cropland, probably never would have known had she simply shot the deer and dragged it under the fence to where she had permission. But that wasn't how Julie had been raised. She called, told the farmer what she had seen, and asked once more. This time the farmer said, "Yes. Go get him."

And that's just what Julie did. Her big Colorado muley doesn't make Boone and Crockett, but that's not what matters to this young wife, mother, engineer, and hunter.

Julie has returned to Missouri, where she and her hunting husband, Rick, live on their own land. They are the proud parents of Shelby Leigh, born six days before the 2000 Missouri deer season opened. Shelby takes after her mother. Her first word was "buck."

ON TOP OF THE WORLD
TIFFANY PROFANT
White-tailed Deer

Delta Airlines had a memorable slogan in "We love to fly, and it shows." Tiffany Profant, a blonde beauty who is a flight attendant for Northwest Airlines, could easily give that slogan her own slant: I love to bowhunt, and it shows.

Tiffany is riding a wave that each year crests higher. That wave consists of an ever-increasing number of distaff bow hunters who aren't afraid to let the world know about their chosen sport. Some take up archery hunting on their own. Others, like Tiffany, are influenced by the men in their lives. It hardly matters. Tiffany Profant is sold on bowhunting.

One look at Tiffany's photo, and you might think she's part of her high school's "in" crowd. Yet as young as she still is, Tiffany has outgrown the need to hang out with school chums with whom she no longer has much in common. Tiffany said, "I'm always tuning my bow or heading somewhere for a 3-D shoot or preparing for a bowhunt. My old friends no longer fit into my world."

That world has changed dramatically for Tiffany over the past three years. She still works both domestic and international flights for Northwest, as she has for seven years. But she became enthralled with bowhunting almost overnight. That's what happens when, on your first bowhunt, you make a solid and accurate shot on a six-point white-tailed buck, as Tiffany did.

Tiffany is good for bowhunting, too. No shrinking violet, this woman takes to the aisles of jumbo jets to share with passengers and crew the photos and tales of her bowhunting adventures. "I've been able to get people excited about my hunting, even to the point where they say they want to try it themselves," she said. "I tell them how great it is to find deer tracks and big rubs or scrapes, and how excited we get when we spot a big buck before the season or find his shed antlers after the season."

Yes, Tiffany is good for bowhunting. She suffers badly anyone who is Bambi-delusional, yet she is never less than gracious even as she begs to disagree with their assessment of an activity that has become such an intrinsic part of her life

She said, "A passenger sometimes will ask, 'Do you shoot Bambi?' "

"I'll say, 'You have no idea how many deer I *pass up* each season, including many Bambis. And you have no idea how many deer are roaming this country in habitat that can't support them all, and what kind of horrible death awaits them.'"

We must travel into the past to pick up the threads that mark the beginning of this young woman's story. "Several years ago I was chosen to be a princess of Columbia Heights, Minnesota," Tiffany explained. "The chaperone assigned to me had an older brother. That's how I met my boyfriend, Lee Lakosky, a chemical engineer."

Love didn't bloom all at once. Nearly seven years passed before things began to click between the two. "Lee, I discovered, was a dedicated archer and bow hunter," Tiffany said. "When we started dating, he asked if I'd like to try shooting a bow. I said OK, but I had reservations about hunting. My dad used to take me fishing, but hunting seemed so foreign. I wasn't sure I'd be able to shoot any animal, or how I'd feel about it afterward."

Tiffany practiced with Lee until he felt she was ready for a real hunt from a tree stand. Not wanting to risk putting out Tiffany's spark of interest, he climbed into the tree stand with her. When the six-point appeared later that evening, Lee's presence bolstered her confidence.

"After I made a good shot on that buck, I was totally surprised," Tiffany said. "All my fears melted away. What I felt was joy, elation, and just the greatest feeling of accomplishment. Rather than feeling bad about killing an animal, I felt pride that I'd been able to put the buck down quickly so it didn't suffer.

Tiffany downed her biggest whitetail to date on her own Kansas farmland.

"I think some of Lee's excitement was communicated to me. That wasn't a bad thing. It helped me to better understand what I was feeling. He told me afterward that there are plenty of men who can't stay focused enough to make a good, killing shot on a deer. Being with Lee on my first bowhunt brought us even closer together.

"When my father came back from the war in Vietnam, he never went hunting again because he'd seen so much pain and killing. My father died at about the time I became a flight attendant seven years ago, but I think he would have taken to archery just like I did.

"My mom had no photos of Lee and me together, so I gave her one of the two of us with my first buck. She couldn't bring herself to frame it until she'd cut the deer out of the picture."

There's no way a cute, bright, gregarious blonde bow hunter with a one-shot kill to her credit would escape the notice of other archers. Tiffany began traveling with Lee, who besides being a chemical engineer is also a noted outdoor writer and photographer. The pair began to haunt industry shows such as the Archery Manufacturers Organization (AMO) and the Shooting, Hunting, and Outdoor Trade (SHOT) expositions. In no time Tiffany found herself an integral part of an entirely different social set. "Where I once loved going out to lunch or to shop with my girlfriends, I now had people with whom I could share my hunting experiences," she said. Tiffany met many other women hunters, too, including Kandi Kisky, featured in another chapter of this book. "Kandi and I hit it off immediately," Tiffany said. "She understands what I'm feeling. We aren't limited to chatter about clothes or hair. Having a female friend to share my bowhunting with makes it even more enjoyable."

Lee bagged his first Pope and Young whitetail in 1994. Since then, bowhunting trophy whitetails has become his near-obsession. That obsession gradually infected Tiffany. The two share something else: great latitude with their work schedules. "Lee works only fourteen days each month for a petrochemical company," Tiffany said. "I have a lot of freedom with my flight schedule, so we have a lot of time to scout and travel to bowhunting spots and hunting shows."

The two plan to marry someday, and, as a testament to their increasing bond, they purchased a Kansas farm that other whitetail fanatics would kill for. Tiffany said, "Some people think Kansas is flat and ugly, but our Flint Hills farm is beautiful. It was there that I first saw a buck in velvet, and Lee and I really love to scout for deer there. Kansas is where everything about deer hunting finally came together for me in one neat package."

Tiffany's biggest whitetail was taken on the Kansas place. "I'd placed my stand in a cedar tree," she said. "Lee was set up nearby so he could video my bowhunt. It was warm that day, about 70

Tiffany Profant makes scouting pay by paying close attention to large rub trees like this one.

degrees. A real nice buck with six points on one side and five on the other came in, but my rangefinder revealed that he was forty-six yards away, too far to risk a bow shot. We estimated he would have scored about 160 Pope and Young points.

"The big buck eventually wandered off, and soon afterward another good buck came by. He was walking purposefully, as if on a mission, but I couldn't shoot because too many limbs were in the way.

"Two days later we returned to the same stand," Tiffany continued. "The fog was extremely heavy, and it was after 7 a.m. by the time there was enough light for filming. Almost at that instant, the second buck we'd seen on our previous outing appeared out of the fog. He had dandy antlers, not as large as the first buck, but definitely a shooter. When he was within range, I shot. The buck ran off, hit through both lungs."

Tiffany shoots a Mathews Ultra 2 set for a twenty-four-inch draw length, and Red Line arrows. This setup did its job. They found her buck piled up in a heap not far from where she had hit it. Tiffany said, "Our farm seems to be a very good place for large bucks. Lee shot one there that scored 196." Tiffany's buck's rack tallied 145⅞ Pope and Young points. "His basic eight-point rack is nineteen inches wide, and it has character—the one G-2 point is split, and there's a sticker point off one brow tine."

Tiffany Profant has been hunting for only three years, but she has made those three years count. To date she's taken her Kansas buck, another Pope and Young buck from Wisconsin that scored 126, four additional white-tailed bucks, a Minnesota black bear, and an Osceola gobbler that weighed twenty-two pounds and sported a nine-inch beard, which she took with a shotgun.

Tiffany is a woman of influence, perhaps because she shatters the stereotypical mold of how a female hunter should look and act (as do all the women featured in this book). "Our local DARE antidrug program's police liaison just called me," Tiffany said. "He wants me to address the DARE graduates and tell them what hunting means to me."

Tiffany's high spirits, vivacious personality, and love for bowhunting have inspired others. "My friend Ashley Black, who works for Realtree, had never hunted," she said. "In 2001, though, Ashley went on a Texas bowhunt and shot her first Pope and Young buck. She told me, 'I only tried it because you enjoyed bowhunting so much, and I wanted to see what you were talking about.'

"To get the most out of it, though, women need a good support group, and they must have equipment that fits *them*, not their husbands or boyfriends. You can't use hand-me-down equipment. If your hunting trip isn't fun for you—and it won't be with the wrong gear—you won't want to stick with it. When I started hunting, Lee

Tiffany resorted to her 12-gauge Benelli shotgun to bag this big Osceola tom.

bought me my first bow and my first gun. He made sure they were right for me. He's a one-of-a-kind guy."

Remember the mother who once cut Tiffany's buck out of a photo? Tiffany prevailed there, too: "My mom really came around. Today she's just as excited about hunting and what we do as I am. Mom's even going to hunt turkeys with us in Kansas this year.

"Before I became a hunter, each November my mom and I would vacation in Maui, where I'd lie out on the beach and work on my tan. Now, though, we'd rather travel to Alaska to view wildlife. That's our new getaway spot. And this year I think we'll stay a few days longer so we can search for moose sheds."

WHINING PAYS!
JAMIE REMMERS
White-tailed Deer

Jamie Remmers, an attractive young mother of three, has been hunting since 1982. "My husband was a big hunter, and it was either go hunting with him or see him rarely, if ever," Jamie said. "It's sort of funny, actually. We divorced, so now I don't see him at all and yet I'm more involved with hunting than ever."

Jamie and her family live in a small agricultural community that reminds the casual observer of a Norman Rockwell heartland setting. The attractive brunette melds life as the mother of Torey, age fourteen, Katlin, twelve, and McKenzee, three, with owning a preschool and teaching there. Jamie can scarcely decide where work stops and home life begins, so busy are her days, yet she finds the time to indulge in her personal passions of outdoor photography, gardening, and deer hunting.

This young conservationist has set her sights on improving wildlife habitat on her thirty acres of fertile Kansas soil so it will provide better shelter for the birds and other animals. "Forage isn't the problem around here," Jamie explained. "I live in an intensively farmed area where fields are planted each spring in crops of milo or corn. Cover is what's lacking, so I'm allowing cedars to grow into dense thickets that will provide shelter to all types of wildlife during severe wind, rain, or snow.

"My father was a bird hunter," she said. "He'd take me out hunting, but only so I could be his 'bird dog.' It didn't sit too well with him that I actually wanted to hunt; in fact, the mere idea eventually developed into a major battle between us. My father believed hunting was a man's activity, while I always thought it would be challenging, enjoyable, and fun for anybody, including me."

Jamie longed to do more than merely trudge through the countryside for someone else. But she remained stuck in the same unfortunate rut until she married. "I'd never been around deer hunters before," she said, referring to her ex-husband and his friends. "It was so different from bird hunting As soon as I tried deer hunting for myself, I loved it."

Hunting appealed to the lively Kansan for many reasons. "The act of hunting isn't simply about getting a deer. It's taking the time to sit out in nature, enjoying whatever creatures may grace you with their presence, and pausing to enjoy the gifts all around you. You can embrace solitude and regroup so you can get on with an often hectic life. Hunting lets you gather your wits about you."

Some women travel to the far corners of the earth to hunt, but Jamie has found her own hunting paradise close at hand. "Rather than pay to travel elsewhere, my dream is to buy more land right here."

Jamie's phenomenal hunting record has sealed her place as one of the century's most successful whitetail hunters, male or female, one who to date has garnered acclaim from every corner of the hunting world.

Jamie ascended into hunting's stratosphere during December of 1997. That deer season began as innocuously as the previous fifteen, but that autumn she was busier than usual. She was working in the afternoons at her parents' lumberyard in town in addition to a full morning schedule at her preschool. Driving from home to town and back again each day gave the young woman plenty of chances to spot deer feeding or moving through nearby fields. "I'd already seen several trophy-class bucks that fall," she said, "including a tremendous nontypical. But other hunters had seen him, too."

Hunters talk, and those from small towns seem to talk more than most. Everywhere Jamie went, she heard this hunter or that one hoping he'd bag the big deer.

Her job responsibilities prevented the young mother from hunting the first three days of the firearms season. On 7 December 1977, though, the opportunity she'd been waiting for arrived. It was Sunday; so there was no work that day. "I'm a hard hunter," Jamie said. "In years past I've put in some long, grueling days of deer hunting. But that morning I just wasn't up to it."

Four months pregnant, Jamie felt fatigued more often than not. A long stretch of early mornings had so drained her strength that, as she put it, "The only thing I was hunting that morning was a few more blankets."

Since first she donned an orange vest, loaded her gun, and headed out to see what hunting deer was all about, Jamie had become a seasoned pro. Although she didn't always draw a deer permit—the Kansas deer population was still rebounding from historic lows, so permits were sometimes hard to come by—she always applied. When she drew, she almost always made the tag count. "I'd taken several bucks," she said, "but nothing huge." And yet over time—and without even realizing it—Jamie Remmers had evolved into a big-buck hunter. She was in an ideal place for giant whitetails. Kansas farmland bucks grow racks of prodigious size, and their body weights are pretty incredible, too.

"We have a small herd of cattle and my husband hunted," she said, "so we really didn't need the meat. So before that particular season even started, I decided I wasn't going to shoot at a buck unless it was nice enough to hang on the wall."

Kent, Jamie's husband, knew how tired his wife was that morning. He also realized how badly she wanted to get away for at least part of the day to hunt. So Kent asked her to take part in a drive that afternoon. His plan went like this: He and friend Jeff would stroll quietly through the dense cover along a small stream bisecting the Remmerses' property, allowing their scent to blow ahead of them. Any buck that dawdled too long before moving out ahead of the men might give one of them a shot, but it was more likely that they might push a decent buck or two toward Jamie.

Whitetails are smart, sneaky creatures. Sometimes they can be spotted out in the wide open spaces, seemingly without a care in the world. Let them hear a few shots or catch too much human scent on the wind, though, and they'll strike out for the nearest cover

Jamie Remmers killed this Kansas bobcat in 1986. The big tom weighed 31 pounds.

and bed down there until dark. This creek-bottom drive was intended to capitalize on this whitetail tendency. The season had been in full swing for more than three days. Rifle shots and hunters slogging through fields and woodlots had given the local deer all the clues needed to know they were being hunted. Streambeds allow deer to get out of a blow, and the sometimes severely undercut banks cast welcome shade during the heat of the day. Creek-bottom forage is sweeter, too, especially during droughty years. And bottomland areas are sometimes too boggy to plow during planting seasons, which means heavier cover.

All three hunters were aware of these facts. Jamie realized that she probably would see deer, but would she see the trophy of her dreams? The preceding evening, Jamie had whined to anyone who would listen that she still had no big rack to show for fifteen years of hunting. Maybe that's why Kent and Jeff were being exceptionally gallant this day. Jamie didn't know and didn't care. She was deer hunting after three and a half days of wishing, and that was all that mattered.

Jamie took her stand while the men checked the wind and then cautiously headed toward the portion of creekbed they intended to drive. If Kent and Jeff were to walk briskly and noisily, the deer would most likely race from their hiding spots and present a difficult running shot. During a silent drive like this one, though, the animals would be less frightened. They would move out, but at a more leisurely pace and probably along favored travel routes—routes known to Jamie, who had for years been absorbing details of the animals' daily routines. Two main trails merged at a point just beyond where Jamie was waiting.

Jamie felt exhilarated at simply doing what she loved, and was excited about the possibility of soon seeing deer. Little did she know that the excitement had scarcely begun.

Her every sense was alert for the flick of an ear, the twitch of a white tail, or the horizontal lines seen through vertical brush that signal to the seasoned hunter that an animal is nearby. The two men had barely started driving when a couple of does and a small buck emerged from the trees to Jamie's right but a quarter-mile distant. They were in no real danger from Jamie as they threaded their way back into the trees. Then two or three larger bucks ventured out into the open. Jamie pressed the .270 Winchester hard against her shoulder, trying to decide if one of them might be the trophy she was searching for. None was. Jamie reluctantly lowered her rifle.

At that same moment, another buck stepped out from the trees. "I remember thinking, *Who needs a scope to know this is the ONE?* He seemed to be nothing but rack, and he was headed my way. I could only hope and pray that I'd set up in a spot where I would get a shot."

Diana, the Greek goddess of hunting, must have been smiling down upon Jamie that afternoon. As the mighty buck fled back into the cover of the trees, the hunter momentarily panicked at the thought that he might escape. "But even in that dense brush I could easily follow his movements by watching that massive rack," Jamie said.

She kept her cross hairs on the buck. "The other deer kind of moved in and out of the trees, but the big one stayed near the edge," Jamie said. When the distance between hunter and hunted had

Jamie's giant nontypical whitetail in the place where he fell.

narrowed to one hundred yards, the big buck broke away from the rest of the group, carefully picking its way beneath an old abandoned tree stand. A few steps farther, and the monster would be just where Jamie wanted him. *Now,* she thought, *if I can just stop trembling!*

"I knew this might be my only chance ever at a buck of this size. I kept repeating, *You can do it, Jamie, you can do it*, even though I was shaking like a leaf. I had to get a grip or my bullet would fly wild. I willed myself to calm down, then aimed behind the buck's front leg." When the buck was just fifty yards from the hunter, Jamie slowly squeezed the trigger.

At the shot, the buck spun around and raced back the way it had come. Jamie didn't panic. "I've taken most of my bucks with one shot," she said. "I thought I'd probably done OK."

The two men heard the rifle's report. In a newspaper article written soon afterward, Kent Remmers said he honestly believed his wife had a buck down as soon as he heard her shoot. "I've seen Jamie shoot," he said.

Jamie watched the buck retreat a few yards and then crumple to the ground. She hurried closer, intent on the spot where he'd fallen. Getting high-centered on a pesky barbed-wire fence was the only thing separating the excited hunter from the trophy of a lifetime. As Jamie rushed to her huge buck, a little voice was nagging, "Whining pays!"

And how! The big whitetail had thirty-four scorable points. Its mass yielded a net typical frame of 194 inches as well as 63⅛ inches of nontypical antler growth. The nontypical Boone and Crockett score of 257⅛ inches ranked fourth at the time in the Kansas record book, and had Jamie entered the rack, it would have been listed as No. 33 in Boone and Crockett's all-time records of nontypical white-tailed deer.

Word travels fast about a buck as big as Jamie's. Visitors from myriad places descended on the couple's home. The phone began to ring off the hook. Everybody had to know more about this fantastic creature.

Included among the well-wishers were the folks at *Buckmasters* whitetail magazine. When scored using the Buckmasters Trophy Record system (BTR), which allows a rack full credit for all points and mass, Jamie's buck scored 249⅛. Either way you score the tremendous rack, it was the largest whitetail taken anywhere during 1997. And it is the largest whitetail ever taken by a woman. In recognition, Buckmasters awarded Jamie its 1998 Golden Laurel Citation for the most significant rack entered into the BTR system from the previous season.

Jamie proudly fielded requests for interviews by reporters awed by the fact that a Kansas woman had scored on a once-in-a-lifetime

Jamie's buck is the largest whitetail ever shot by a woman. The rack scored 257⅛ under the Boone and Crockett system and 249⅛ using the Buckmasters Trophy Record system.

buck. She remains thrilled about the buck that everyone wanted—and she tagged.

Jamie discusses her family with similar pride: Katlin, who accompanies Mom on shed-hunting expeditions; McKenzee, who at age three put on Mom's camo face mask and stuck a scrap-paper "tag" on her plush horse to claim her own "deer," and Torey, fourteen as this is written, the manager of his high school's football team, who shot his first deer recently.

Jamie especially admires Torey for all that he's put up with and accomplished. "Torey was born with spina bifida," she said. "He's wheelchair-bound, but you know, he never lets it get to him. He can't participate in all the activities that other kids can, but he does what he can. I think that's another reason hunting means so much to me. When Torey hunts, he's not that much different from anyone else. He can travel to his stand in a six-wheeler, or we'll push him in his wheelchair. He's a good shot with both his rifle and his muzzleloader. He got a doe this past season while hunting with his dad." Jamie sounded as enthusiastic about Torey's first deer as she did about her own world-record-class buck.

And speaking of family, did her dad ever come around to Jamie's way of thinking in regard to hunting?

"Has he ever!" Jamie said. "I was using his gun when I took my big buck."

GIANT BROWN BEAR AND TINY LADY
CINDY RHODES
Brown Bear

Cindy Rhodes—all 4 feet, 11 inches of her—has the distinction of taking the world's twenty-third-largest Alaska brown bear and the largest brown bear ever taken by a woman. She has hunted for twenty-five years and has collected only one Alaska brown bear and one Colorado elk.

"I'm very selective and conservative when it comes to hunting," Cindy explained. Living in Alaska amid a wealth of wildlife, Cindy sees trophy animals almost every day but has collected only these two because she didn't feel the desire to take others. Hunting for Cindy is getting out in nature and becoming one with the cycle of life.

Cindy relishes the time she spends in Alaska's wilderness. It's a pause in her busy life as owner and operator of the Brown Bear Roadhouse in Glennallen, 180 miles east of Anchorage. She has worked in the restaurant industry for decades, so she can add special twists to the chicken, steak, and pizza dishes served each day. She and her husband, Doug, moved to Alaska from Michigan in 1980 after the children were grown. They arrived with twenty dollars in their pockets and no jobs. Soon Doug was working as a laborer and Cindy was working in various restaurants.

"Doug always dreamed of living in Alaska, so I followed his dream and went with him. I've never regretted that," Cindy explained.

Doug, an avid hunter since childhood, encouraged Cindy to consider hunting. She'd done a little whitetail hunting in Michigan but never filled her tags and was never serious about hunting until Doug entered her life.

"I never hunted as a child," Cindy said. "My family wasn't against hunting. They just never did it." Her six-foot husband more than made up for lost time, and now the couple hunts exclusively with each other each season.

New to Cindy's life is the effort to organize the Copper Basin Shooting Club. She and other founding members are working feverishly to secure property that can be used for the clubhouse and shooting ranges. They've applied to the National Rifle Association for grants and are talking to the Wells Fargo Bank about financing the purchase of land, which runs $3,000 to $5,000 per acre.

"Kids have nothing to do here, so I thought this would be a great activity for them as well as their parents," Cindy said. "This is going to be a fine facility for the whole community."

One of the hunting highlights of her life was the trip she and Doug shared in 1997 on the Aliulik Peninsula. They both had applied for a brown bear permit since the early 1990s. In 1997 they anxiously awaited the list of permit recipients to be published in the local newspaper, but were late in buying a copy. Besides, all their friends said they weren't listed as recipients of any permits that year.

"Over coffee the next morning, I scanned through the list, and there it was . . . my name under brown bear. I sat staring at the paper to make sure it was really me," Cindy remembered.

Doug walked in as Cindy was talking excitedly to friends about her luck in the draw. Together they rejoiced and began to plan for the hunt of a lifetime. Later that day a dear friend and master guide, Andy Runyan of Exclusive Alaskan Hunts, called to congratulate Cindy and offered to take her on a fourteen-day spring bear hunt. Now she was jumping out of her skin with excitement. She had six months to plan and wanted to do it right.

Cindy and Doug decided to fly to Kodiak a few days before the hunt was to begin. They arrived in camp on 14 April and were met by Andy and his assistant, Craig Rose. They spent the evening

Cindy Rhodes in the field moments after downing the twenty-third largest Alaska brown bear ever taken.

A display of Cindy Rhodes's massive Alaska brown bear and her outstanding Colorado elk can be seen at the Brown Bear Roadhouse in Glennallen, 180 miles east of Anchorage.

around the kitchen table in Andy's cozy cabin discussing the next day's events. Cindy remembers feeling anxious, excited, and so nervous she couldn't sleep.

The next morning dawned bright and a little windy. They climbed into a skiff and motored down a bay three miles to a lookout point, where they spent time glassing. Cindy quickly noticed a huge brown bear, which she pointed out to Andy. Andy directed her to another bear in the same vicinity that was even bigger. Moments later Doug called their attention to a third bear walking along the sand that Andy dubbed a "beach bunny" because of its small size. His exact quote was, "She looks like Abe Lincoln with leg warmers." It was obvious to Cindy and Doug that Andy knew his bears.

Doug and Cindy are in constant motion ten to twelve hours a day at their restaurant, so sitting for hours on end was really getting to Cindy. When she stood up to stretch, Doug called out, "What's the matter, Granny, you getting stove up?" From that moment, Cindy was "Granny" to Andy. She and Doug have six grandchildren, so Granny is an appropriate name. Andy laughingly called his adventure with the Rhodeses the "Granny and Andy Show." The hunters spent the next few days exploring various lookouts but finally decided to return to their original perch overlooking the ocean. They stayed near that lookout for several days, but finally Andy decided to explore another area.

Getting there required a three-mile ride in the skiff to a beach, where the three started walking. Boulders the size of pickups made for rough going. When they reached a freshwater stream, they stopped to fill their water jugs before climbing almost straight up to the top of a rugged mountain. To make progress, Cindy had to cling to clay, rocks, and stand on her hands and knees as brush

Cindy Rhodes stops for a photograph moments after downing a massive American elk in October 2000 outside Gunnison, Colorado.

slapped her face and body. Three-quarters of the way up, they reached an alder patch, where they stopped to catch their breath.

"I was wondering just where in the hell Andy was going," Cindy said. "I'm forty years old and Andy's sixty-eight, so if it was much farther, neither one of us was going to make it." But they soon reached the top, where they savored a breathtaking view of mountains, ocean, creeks, and gullies.

Andy and Cindy started glassing and soon spotted a nice-size bear meandering on the mountain straight ahead of them, then a second bear. But it was late in the day and the weather was disintegrating, so Cindy and Andy stood up to return to camp. They looked to their left, and there, across the valley, walked the largest bear Cindy had ever seen in her life.

"Let's go, Granny," shouted Andy and down the side of the mountain the pair ran, trying to keep the bear in their sights. At the base of the mountain, Cindy paused to catch her breath and shed some clothing. That accomplished, she and Andy crossed three creeks in the direction of the bruin.

"Do you see him?" Andy asked.

"No," Cindy replied.

Andy pointed to a little tuft of fur, and they quietly crept across the last creek and into tall grass. The grass obliterated Cindy's view, so they crept closer, then sat quietly for a few minutes and watched the bear wallow in a deep mud hole. It started walking toward them, and Andy hissed, "Do you plan to shoot that bear?"

Cindy had been waiting for just the right shot, but now she had no other choice than to aim her Ruger 7x57 between the bear's eyes. So close was the animal that all Cindy saw in her scope was fur. A single shot with a Barnes 160-grain bullet did the job at twenty-three yards, and the massive brown bear was hers.

"A whole bunch of things raced through my mind as the bear came toward me. *Stay calm, Cindy, stay calm,* I kept telling myself." She was a quivering wreck as Andy shouted, "Good God, Granny, he's HUGE!"

The bear was indeed huge. It received the second-place award for the Boone and Crockett Club's 23rd Big Game Awards Program (1995–1997). Its skull scored 29 14/16, only an inch below the world record's score of 30 12/16. The bear's skull is 18 inches long and 11 14/16 inches wide. The world-record brown bear's skull is 17 15/16 inches long and 12 15/16 inches wide.

Cindy's Colorado elk hunt was equally memorable. In October 2000, she and Doug flew into Grand Junction to hunt a private ranch in the Black Canyon of the Gunnison National Park with Gary Robertson of North Rim Trophy Hunters. She and Gary climbed to an elevation of close to 10,000 feet and witnessed two bulls doing battle for territory and a harem of cows and calves. Gary began calling, and the larger bull took the challenge, crashing through the brush as it charged toward Cindy. Just as the sun was rising, it dipped into a valley and then charged to the ridgetop and stood silhouetted against the blazing sky, looked around for its antagonist. Cindy raised her rifle and fired a single shot at a distance of sixty yards. The bull's teeth were well worn, and three of its tines were broken. The rack scored 376½ SCI points.

Visitors to Cindy and Doug's restaurant can see her giant brown bear, re-created as a full mount by Tony Loverchio of American Wildlife Taxidermy.

Z-MAX Q
BRENDA SAPP

Rocky Mountain Elk, Pronghorn, Mule Deer

Brenda Sapp's story is really the story of two dedicated archers. Together Brenda and her fiancé, Bob Bergquist, have set out to rewrite bowhunting history. What makes their story so compelling is that only rarely does this pair go bowhunting with outfitters. They prefer instead to do it on their own whenever possible.

The couple lives in Wyoming, where Brenda works for a bank and Bob for a petroleum refinery and sometimes as a hunting guide. He is known throughout the state as a fine and discriminating hunter and an excellent shot with either rifle or bow. Bob was scouted out to become a member of the U.S. Shooting Team in shotgun events, an opportunity he turned down.

Bob has hunted most of his life. Brenda, though, is a Janey-come-lately. "I was exposed to hunting while I was growing up," Brenda said. "I never hunted, though, until I met Bob. If you know Bob, you'd better know hunting."

Brenda eased into hunting. "I started out just going along with Bob," she said. "After a few times, I decided that I might enjoy it, so I bought a bow and shot until I finally felt capable enough to make a good shot on an animal. I attended local archery shoots, too. That's the very best practice you can get. Shooting 3-D targets forces you to judge distances and shows you where the vital areas of many different species of game animals are located. 3-D shoots also help a bow hunter ensure that equipment is in good working condition well before the season begins."

After a remarkably brief learning period, Brenda geared up for her first big-game trip, an antelope hunt in the sagebrush country near their southern Wyoming home. "I still wasn't sure how I'd feel about killing an animal," Brenda said. "And I had a real fear of wounding something. That fear was put to rest after I killed my first antelope. I saw how deadly an arrow could be when shot accurately. It still amazes me how quickly an animal will go down after being shot by a well-placed arrow."

The young woman doesn't mess around when it comes to gear. She purchased a Mathews Z-Max, one of today's top bows, and does her utmost to be worthy of such superb gear. And it helped her earn a nickname. When the St. Louis Rams football team made it to Super Bowl XXXVII, coach Mike Martz said he expected each player to approach every play at "Max Q" intensity. That's the way Brenda

Sapp bowhunts these days. Since she uses a Z-Max, the term Z-Max Q became the perfect label to affix to a young woman who will continue to shatter bowhunting's records for years to come.

Brenda only recently obtained her position with the bank, and she was aware that a shortage of accrued vacation time would put a serious crimp in her and Bob's bowhunting plans. "I'll be able to hunt only on weekends. In my old job I was able to take off during much of September, and there's no better time to be out in the forest. Bob works a lot of overtime at the refinery most of the year, and we really look forward to sharing our hunting time each fall. It's our quality time together."

Though this young Wyoming woman has one of the state's best guides in the state to help her, she also has become more adept at scouting and hunting on her own. She never forgets, though, that it was Bob's expertise that helped her develop so quickly into one of the continent's premier trophy bow hunters. So far she has taken four antelope, six deer, and four elk with her bow, and one

Wyoming's Brenda Sapp killed this 323⅞-point Pope and Young bull elk in 1998 with a bow.

antelope with a rifle. Almost all of the animals shot with a bow qualify for a listing well up in the Pope and Young record book. Included are Brenda's 2001 mule deer, which grossed 177⁶⁄₈ and netted 172⁴⁄₈; a 2000 mule deer in velvet that grossed 161⁷⁄₈ and netted 150⁶⁄₈; a bull elk in 1997 that grossed 283¹⁄₈ and netted 271³⁄₈; a 2001 pronghorn buck that grossed 83⁴⁄₈ and netted 81⁷⁄₈; a 2000 pronghorn that netted 78⁴⁄₈; and the 1998 bull elk that grossed 323⁷⁄₈ and netted 307⁶⁄₈. In addition, Brenda's 2002 Wyoming pronghorn will thunder into the record book with a gross score of nearly 86 points.

"My family wasn't shocked when I took up hunting," she said. "What shocked them was the size of the trophies I was bringing home." Brenda is quick to credit most of her success to her best friend, lover, and mentor, Bob Bergquist. But every bowbender knows that it takes great patience, steady nerves, and pinpoint accuracy to consistently score with a bow on animals old enough to have grown trophy antlers or horns.

She advises other women to try bowhunting for themselves before passing judgment on it. "I'm amazed that some men today still tell their wives that 'hunting is my time, and you're not welcome'," Brenda said. "I'm very lucky. My man wants me out there hunting with him, and I want to be there. We celebrate each other's successes and share each other's defeats."

Brenda's 1998 bowhunt for elk is her most memorable hunt to date. "Early that morning," she recalled, "Bob and I were sitting on top of a canyon rim, listening for bugling bulls. The trick to taking one would be seeing a good bull moving through the forest or hearing one bugle so we could pinpoint its location.

"Bob was glassing when I heard him say, 'There's a shooter.' I looked and had this sudden sinking feeling—the bull was in the bottom of a very deep and extremely steep canyon. All I could think about was getting down there and, worse, getting back out, especially if I succeeded in shooting the animal.

"I told myself that I was here to hunt elk," Brenda continued. "I wanted to kill the best bull I could, so I'd do whatever it took. Bob said, 'Let's go' and headed off into the canyon. Well down into it, I smelled the strong, musky odor of elk. Bob pointed straight ahead—we were right on top of the herd. I got set up, and then Bob began working his cow call. I could see and hear cows moving toward us. Then Bob began bugling like a bull.

"That bull started rushing around, rounding up his cows and trying to push them away from the 'intruder.' Suddenly I saw him whirl around and come racing back toward us. I looked all around, calculating yardages through the trees in my head and trying to determine which way he'd come in to me. I finally

Brenda's 2000 pronghorn buck scored 78⅝-net Pope and Young points.

selected one spot as the most likely place the bull would appear, and sure enough, a few moments later, he stepped through that very opening. Bob called one last time, and it stopped the bull broadside to me. I shot. The bull ran, but piled up in a heap after covering just thirty-five yards." Brenda's huge six-point bull grossed 323⅞ Pope and Young points.

Brenda and Bob scout during the evenings and weekends before hunting seasons open, sometimes beginning their quest in early summer. They'll hunt private land when it's available, but they don't neglect public land—in fact, most of their largest animals have been taken on public ground. The two are particularly high on Wyoming's new walk-in program. "Our Game and Fish Department is working to convince private landowners to take part in this program," Brenda explained. "Landowners open various lands for a fee, but only a designated number of hunters is allowed on those lands. Another facet of the program is opening designated roads so that hunters can travel through private property to reach landlocked public land."

Don't put anything past this dynamic duo. A few years ago, during a span of just two hunting seasons, Brenda and Bob each killed two Wyoming pronghorn bucks that green-scored over 80 Boone and Crockett points. One of Bob's bucks became Wyoming's

No. 1 pronghorn to be killed with a bow. All these bucks were taken on "checkerboard" land, a confusing mix of square-mile sections of private land and public land such as BLM or U.S. Forest Service holdings. Some hunters refuse to hunt checkerboard land. Others, like Brenda and Bob, seek out the most remote of these checkerboard areas because they often serve as trophy pronghorn factories.

In 1999 Brenda drew a resident bowhunting antelope tag for south-central Wyoming's checkerboard area. While scouting, she and Bob located two good bucks and erected a blind near a water hole the animals were using. On opening morning, they entered the area before sunup and climbed into their blind. An hour after

Brenda's 2001 muley buck scored 177⅞ Pope and Young points.

daylight the smaller of the bucks came in for a drink, and Brenda sent an 85-grain Thunderhead through both lungs at seventeen yards. The animal, which green-scored 80⅝ Pope and Young points, ran just thirty yards before piling up.

The following spring, Brenda and Bob made another pilgrimage to the windmill to check up on the bigger of the two bucks. He was still hanging tight.

Wyoming's antelope-tag drawing is far from a sure thing; only one in three applicants gets a tag. Luckily, both drew tags again. They traveled the faded jeep trail every week to keep themselves convinced that the big devil hadn't vacated the area. No problems developed until 1 August, when the water hole's windmill broke. With both wildlife and thirty head of cattle watering at this tank and no windmill to pump water, it didn't take a Los Alamos scientist to figure out that the pond would quickly go dry.

"If the water disappeared," Brenda said, "the buck would go someplace else. It was either let the buck go and hope we might find his new watering hole, or haul water in to this one."

They outfitted the back of Bob's pickup with a tote that could transport 250 gallons. Their first trips were made at night. But they soon determined that 250 gallons wasn't near enough. Too many critters were watering here.

Brenda had also drawn a tag for this area, so the pair had been scouting for a good buck for her. When bow season started, she was hunkered down inside their blind. Two hours past daybreak, the buck she was after nervously approached the water. The blind seemed to be making the animal extremely spooky, but at last it closed the distance to twenty-five yards. Brenda's shot angled through the animal's lung. This buck, which green-scored 81⅛ Boone and Crockett points, traveled a hundred yards before collapsing.

At one that afternoon, Bob slipped into the water-hole blind. He hunted until dark, but the big buck he was after never ventured anywhere near. It stood instead upon a ridgetop a half-mile away, never moving a muscle. Bob would time the animal. Sometimes it would stand like a statue for forty-five minutes, staring down at the water hole the entire time.

Meanwhile, Bob and Brenda continued to haul water, sometimes making two trips a day. Even this amount proved insufficient, so they upped the ante to three daily round-trips of 250 gallons each. This routine continued for eleven days. Bob had checked with the game department to see if hauling water could be construed as baiting and was given the green light to continue. Besides helping out wildlife, he was also watering the rancher's cows.

When Bob wasn't hauling water, he was hunting every moment of daylight. Finally, after many additional days of water-hauling and bowhunting, the big pronghorn finally came in. Bob's carbon arrow rocketed off his string, and the three-blade 100-grain mechanical broadhead took out the big antelope's heart and pierced a lung. It ran just fifty yards. The goat's horns were even bigger than Bob had estimated. After the required thirty-day drying period, the gross score was 88⅜ and the net score was 87⅔, good enough for Number 10 in Pope and Young's all-time archery record book.

Brenda Sapp and her fiancé and mentor, Bob Bergquist, really can conquer bowhunting's heights.

BIG MEDICINE
KIM SCHWANKY

Central Barren-Ground Caribou

It's a wonder Kim Schwanky finds any free time at all. For starters, she is a licensed veterinarian who owns and operates a thriving animal practice in Alberta. She's an avid long-distance runner, and prides herself on the quarterhorses she has shown successfully. Toss in the TV show—*The Outdoor Quest*—on which Kim regularly appears with her friend Sandi Mellon and the women's respective husbands, T. J. Schwanky and Richard Mellon. The women are known as the "Outdoor Chicks" and the guys as— what else—the "Outdoor Guys." Kim helps maintain the Chicks' Web site, contributing photos she's taken and articles she's written. It's enough to make the head spin.

Whenever Kim can find the time, she indulges in her love of the hunt. So far moose and wild sheep have provided her greatest thrills. "My first moose hunt really hooked me," Kim said. "Two days before we were to go, a cat bit me on the middle finger of my left hand, one of the perils of being a vet. My hand became swollen and sore. The doctor suggested I be admitted to the hospital since the infection was deep and spreading rapidly. I told him I'd rather not, so he prescribed megadoses of powerful antibiotics, but they made me extremely nauseous. T. J. said we'd simply go for a ride not far from our home and scout in an area where a friend had reported seeing some moose earlier in the week."

At 10 A.M. they parked near one of Alberta's wilderness areas at a special place T. J. called the Valley of the Grizzly. "I agreed to try to hike into this valley," Kim said. "If I continued feeling poorly, T. J. said we'd postpone our hunt until another day.

"As we walked in, a grizzly bear spooked from her bed not fifteen feet in front of us," Kim continued. "I honestly don't know why we're still here." It was almost as though Someone was protecting the couple because the grizzly dashed into the undergrowth with nary a backward glance. After the excitement had ebbed, T. J. decided to make a fire because Kim was getting chilled and large snowflakes had begun to sift down. "I was walking toward the fire pit when I suddenly smelled a strong odor of urine," Kim said. "Just a few yards from where we'd been resting, T. J. discovered a fresh moose wallow. He suggested that after I felt rested, he'd try to call in a moose."

Kim regained strength by the fire, and when finally the pair arose, they noticed fresh moose tracks right at the edge of the campsite. They followed them into the timber, where T. J. began uttering guttural grunts. After forty-five fruitless minutes, the couple prepared to leave.

"What's that?" Kim whispered. Her keen eyes had discerned a single moose paddle gleaming wanly against a backdrop of dark timber. Although she tried to get a better view, the bull merged with the darkening forest. T. J. grunted, and now the moose repeatedly grunted in reply. T. J. added the sound effects of antlers thrashing willow trees, and the moose responded by crashing around in the timber. "Suddenly, there he was, thirty yards to my left," Kim recalled. "I swung around and centered the cross hairs of my four-power Leupold scope on his chest. T. J. was yelling, 'Shoot—he's going to charge!' just as I fired. I was shaking so badly I could hardly grip my gun. After the shot the bull was still standing, but swaying badly. I shot once more, and he dropped to the ground.

"I stood there marveling at his size, his rank smell, and the unusual antlers," she said. "There was a reason I'd seen just one of his paddles. The left antler was formed perfectly, but the right one swept around like the horn of a Cape buffalo."

After hours of field-dressing and deboning—mostly by T. J., thanks to Kim's infected finger—they loaded the last of the meat into their packs. The skull and antlers were balanced and lashed

Kim Schwanky's huge Alaska-Yukon moose scores 210 Boone and Crockett points, and the rack measures 58 inches in width.

into place, and then the two hunters staggered to their feet under their ponderous loads. "I teetered and fell onto my back like a rolled-over turtle," Kim recalled.

The hike back out was four miles. Kim was burdened with a pack that weighed close to one hundred pounds; T. J. toted more than that. The path took them up small hills that seemed nearly insurmountable, and down long slopes only slightly less difficult. Halfway to their destination, they saw a huge boar grizzly perched imperiously on a boulder, watching the hunters. "His message was clear—'This is my domain'," Kim said. They safely skirted the bear and reached the trailhead.

With only one normal antler, Kim's moose did not score well, but the experience of taking her first big-game animal meant more to her than all the trophy moose in the world.

"I remember my father hunting when I was a kid," Kim said, "but I never had any desire to hunt. T. J. led me so gently toward hunting that I never felt forced."

Kim said that she had no moral or ethical qualms about hunting. "Neither issue ever crossed my mind," she said. "After all, most of us eat animals.

"I did, however, feel a surge of remorse after killing my moose, so I began doing things that would make hunting right and consistent in my mind. I went from being a nonhunter to becoming a trophy hunter. My goal now is to take the best animal I can wherever I'm allowed to hunt. I enjoy hunting for trophies, and yet the meat is also important. No matter how far I journey into the backcountry, once an animal is down, I won't leave an ounce of meat on the mountain, even if I must make many trips to retrieve it. To show proper respect for those animals I kill, I feel I must do everything legally and ethically."

Despite such integrity regarding her favorite sport, Kim is sometimes questioned by her clients. "As a veterinarian I must be cautious in discussing my hunting. If someone has seen photos of me in hunting magazines and asks me questions, I do my best to explain how I try to save animals on one hand and then go out and kill other animals on the other hand. I've never lost a client because of my hunting, so I think they appreciate what I say and how I say it. Whether that helps change their perceptions about hunting, I don't really know."

Kim has learned that many people truly cannot understand what makes a hunter tick. Many nonhunters remain incredulous that any woman would place herself in such physically demanding or life-threatening situations.

"For those very reasons," Kim said, "sheep trips are not only my favorite hunts but also my most memorable. It may sound odd, but I'm completely enthralled with sheep and sheep hunting. Maybe it's because the sheep mountains humble me so.

Kim wears a Boone and Crockett smile over her barren-ground caribou that scores 366 ⅞ points.

"Take the day I shot my bighorn ram, for instance. We started climbing and spotted five rams about three miles off in the distance. T. J. and I waded through waist-deep snow directly toward those sheep. It was a beautiful fall day; the skies were such a brilliant shade of blue. The snow made it interesting, but we were more wet than cold by the time I shot and killed my ram."

Kim bagged that bighorn in Alberta. She's also taken a Dall ram in the Yukon.

"I shot that beautiful twelve-year-old ram at the end of our third day of hunting," Kim said. "It's not a typical ram because his horns are so heavily broomed there are no lamb tips. The horn bases measure fourteen inches around—pretty incredible for a Dall.

"After I shot my Dall, T. J. asked, 'If you could go anywhere to hunt anything, where would you go and what would you hunt?' For the longest time I had no answer. Then I realized that if money wasn't an issue and I really could go anywhere, then I would want to get either a desert bighorn or a Stone sheep."

The Schwankys realize that the Holy Grail of hunting—the Grand Slam of North American sheep—might someday become a reality for one or perhaps both of them. "I finally started applying for desert sheep permits," Kim said. "Since I can hunt for the TV cameras, taking a Stone sheep and maybe a desert bighorn during the next few years has certainly become more feasible than it was in the past."

Any hunter who ventures into the high country will eventually run into trouble. It happened to Kim in 2001. "We were goat hunting during September in British Columbia, reining our horses up an extremely steep, narrow, and slippery trail," she said. I'd just turned in the saddle to ask T. J. if he thought I should dismount and lead my horse up the trail. On our right was a sheer sixty-foot dropoff.

"I suddenly realized that our guide and his horse, just ahead, seemed about to flip over on top of me. The same thought must have occurred to the guide, and he reined his horse up the slope so that we could pass him. I tried to do that, but my horse literally sat down so that his rear end was hanging off the trail on the right side; his front legs were extended, flat on the ground, across the trail. Before I could step out of the stirrups, my horse started sliding backward and sideways down the trail. My mount and I gathered momentum and slammed into T. J.'s horse, knocking him off his feet. The force of the blow catapulted me from my horse, and I went somersaulting down the hill, my horse rolling down after me. I remember opening my eyes at one point and seeing hoofs flying above me while people were screaming for me to get out of the way. I wasn't sure where 'out of the way' was, but I finally rolled in one

With a net score of 176⅜, Kim's Alberta bighorn ram barely missed qualifying for Boone and Crockett.

direction and the horse tumbled past in a different direction until he slammed into the ground at the bottom of the slope.

"Both the horse and I could have died As it was, my only injury was a sore rotator cuff. The horse wasn't hurt at all. My rifle scabbard was torn, but my gun was OK, and that was a miracle."

Kim Schwanky, Outdoor Chick, is one of hunting's best spokespeople. "I'll do everything in my power to encourage women to hunt," she said, "even if it's only to go out with someone whose company they enjoy for the experience of being along on a hunt. Don't hesitate—go! When I was younger, I never thought at all about hunting. Today I can't imagine my life without it.

BORN TO HUNT
PHYLLIS TUCKER

Brown Bear, Grizzly Bear, Dall Sheep,
Central Barren-Ground Caribou, Alaska-Yukon Moose

The woman never doubted the depths of her own resolve, despite the doubts of those around her. She set about earning money enough to make her dreams come true, no matter the setbacks. When an outfitter she'd booked dawdled before taking her into his high-country camp, then made her hike up a mountain to camp rather than flying her up in a plane like his other hunters, the woman gritted her teeth and continued climbing. Sixteen hours later, she made it to the top, where she wept for joy at the spectacular Alaskan landscape stretching miles in every direction.

"That was the most profound moment of my life," said Phyllis Tucker, the pretty, slim mother of two. "I couldn't help but think, *Why did I have to wait until I was forty years old to experience this moment?* Moments like this should have been my life. This is why I'd been born."

Some people spend a lifetime searching for true inspiration. Most go to their graves failing to find it. Phyllis Tucker, though, knew as a small child what she wanted more than anything else in life: She wanted to hunt! "I grew up in Tennessee and Indiana, and if someone needed me, they had to look for me in the woods," Phyllis said. "I'd pretend to be hunting as I sneaked up on animals. I didn't have a gun then, and it would be a long time before I got one.

"At that time girls were raised to get married and have a family. I was no different. Although I attended both Ball State University and Anderson University, I married when I was in my late teens. My children started arriving by the time I was twenty-one, first my son Todd and then my daughter Nikki.

"My husband, Roger, and I became partners in a residential construction business. All this time I longed to learn about hunting, but Roger wasn't buying into that at all. He'd say, 'I don't hunt, and women don't hunt. I'd be ashamed to take a woman into hunting camp.' He was sure the other men would laugh at me.

"More than twenty-five years elapsed before I started hunting. During that time I taught myself to shoot and read everything I could lay my hands on about hunting. I studied big-game animals and their habits and kept myself in shape with aerobics, hiking, and backpacking. I focused on becoming a big-game hunter."

Phyllis's Dall ram would score well up in any record book.

One and a half pounds of steel rod and more than 30 screws inserted to hold her leg bone together didn't slow Phyllis down in her quest for this huge brown bear with its 27-inch head and almost 10-foot pelt.

Before she bought her first rifle, Phyllis experienced her first moment of doubt. "I'd never fired a gun of any kind," she said. "I knew no one who hunted, including my father, three brothers, and my husband. Nevertheless, I walked into a gun store and saw the most beautiful rifle on display. I had to have it. It was a .300 Weatherby Magnum, quite powerful for someone who had never shot a gun of any kind. The recoil didn't bother me. "I thought all rifles were alike, so I just got used to it."

The rifle posed no problem, but the husband did. "When my children both left home, I decided it was time to do what I wanted for a change," she said. "I'd worked in the business for years and had saved a lot of money for the hunts I planned to take one day. My kids were gone, and besides that, my husband had started another business in commercial construction and hadn't asked me to be his partner. For the first time in my life, nothing was holding me down."

Phyllis wanted to hunt Dall sheep more than any other animal, so she booked an Alaska hunt. "About nineteen years earlier, I'd begun writing to outfitters and requesting information. I'd sign my name P. A. Tucker because I was afraid that if they knew I was a woman who would be hunting alone, no one would contact me. Several replies came addressed to 'Mr. Tucker,' but none sounded interesting enough to pursue further.

"Then one day an outfitter called asking for 'Mr. Tucker.' I told him he wasn't there, but that I could probably answer his questions. After several minutes, the outfitter said, 'You're the hunter, aren't you?' I asked why he thought that. He said, 'Because I've talked to very few men—and no women—who know as much about hunting as you do'."

Phyllis asked if being a woman would be a problem. He said, "I've never hunted with a woman before, but you can come up if you want to."

"The next year passed quickly," Phyllis said. "I didn't dare tell my husband that I'd booked this hunt because I knew he'd berate me the entire time. He hadn't changed his ideas about female hunters, and neither had I. I finally told him about my plans a week before I was due to fly to Alaska. He was appalled. He tried to frighten me by saying the other hunters would laugh me right out of camp. I was excited to be going hunting, but worried that my husband might be right."

The outfitter hadn't been wholly convinced of Phyllis's grasp of hunting and wildlife. To test her, he made her trek to the top of a mountain, as mentioned earlier. "He was so sure I wouldn't 'make the grade' that he'd arranged for a male hunter to hike up solo to take my place. The joke was on the outfitter, though, because the other hunter never made it up the mountain. He abandoned his gear along the trail and took the next flight home.

"The outfitter was stuck with me. Each day we backpacked to a new camp in the Talkeetnas. We never spotted a single ram. When my hunt was over, the outfitter apologized and said, 'I wasn't really looking for sheep. I just wanted to see how much punishment you could take.'

"That was my introduction to hunting," Phyllis recalled. "But the outfitter now was convinced that I was tough enough, so he offered to take me on the same hunt the following year at no charge. I accepted, and I've never been mad for a moment at this man or what he put me through."

When she returned to civilization, Phyllis called home. "Well," said her husband, "I guess you finally got hunting out of your system." I replied, 'Far from it.' When he found out I hadn't taken anything, he laughed his head off. That just made me more determined."

The family owned a remote cabin in the Tennessee hills, and Phyllis told her husband that she wanted to unwind there after the rigors of her hunting trip. But instead—and without telling him— she traveled to Newfoundland, where she'd just booked a hunt for moose and caribou.

Phyllis shot both caribou and moose in Newfoundland, returning to her Indiana home with four hundred pounds of moose meat, four hundred pounds of caribou meat, and a huge caribou head, cape, and antlers. "I didn't know what to do with it all," she said. "Remember, my husband had no idea where I'd been or what I'd been doing. I carried everything into my bathroom and put it in the bathtub. Then I went out and bought a lot of bagged ice and just about filled the tub.

"Never in my life had I known my husband to use the bathroom where my venison and trophies were hidden in the tub, but I closed the shower curtain just the same. Wouldn't you know? For the first time ever, he went into that john to use it."

Suddenly a terrified scream came from the bathroom. "What's the matter?" she yelled back.

"The biggest deer in the world is in our bathtub!" he shrieked.

When she began hanging trophy heads in their living room, the marriage bonds frayed irrevocably. Although she regretted the breakup of her marriage, it finally freed Phyllis to do what she'd always wanted: hunt.

Phyllis started construction on a large trophy-room addition to her home. "My ex thought that was a waste of money," she commented. Perhaps. But today the trophy room is stocked with more than seventy-five big-game species, including a huge Alaskan brown bear, grizzlies, several black bears squaring over eight feet, two Dall rams (one a real hummer), a Stone sheep, a caribou slam, mountain lion, mule deer, bison, and many others. World sheep species she's taken include the hippa sheep, aoudad, Armenian sheep, Hawaiian black sheep, Tibetan blue sheep, Gobi argali, and Siberian snow sheep. In Africa Phyllis has taken an African lion and lioness, Cape buffalo, hippo, leopard, and sable.

"Many of my animals are record-book quality," Phyllis said. "Some would score extremely high. But I hunt for myself, not for the record books."

Phyllis's favorite place to hunt is Alaska. "I recently built my own cabin there. That, too, has been a dream come true. Alaska is one of the last of the world's truly wild places. I could hunt the state's various mountain ranges for the rest of my life and be perfectly content. Everything I'd see would be new and different and wild."

A person who hunts as often as Phyllis will have her share of dangerous moments. "I once was hunting moose in dense forest near my cabin in the Alaska Range," she recalled. "I was walking along when a grizzly charged me at full speed. It happened so quickly that I reacted rather than acted. I fired my .300 Weatherby Magnum from

Phyllis Tucker, hunter extraordinaire, and her British Columbia Stone sheep.

the hip when the bear was just five yards away. The bullet missed to the left, and the animal wheeled and raced away. It was almost dark, and I can tell you I wasted no time getting out of there.

"Another time I was hunting the Zambezi Valley in Africa," Phyllis said. "My PH and tracker and I had been eight long days in thick undergrowth, searching for a huge lion many other hunters had been pursuing. We cut a fresh, large track and knew he must be nearby. Large boulders surrounded us, and I knew the lion could be crouched behind any of them, waiting to spring.

"We suddenly heard a loud roar that was much too close for comfort. 'There,' said the PH, 'I see his foot.'

"'No, there!' I said. 'I see his eye.' There were three lions, as it turned out. They were all around us!

"My PH, our main tracker, and I trained our rifles on the lions. 'That one's tail is waving,' the PH said. 'He's going to charge!'

"The three lions false-charged several times from a distance of about ten yards. *This could be the day I die*, I thought. I thought about my children, said the Lord's Prayer, and promised to be a better person if I survived. The lions came even closer. My PH determined which was largest, then said, 'Shoot now!' I nailed the big guy in the nick of time with a single shot to the neck. The rest of the lions ran away."

Changing the subject, Phyllis said, "I tried to get my kids interested in hunting, but neither of them has taken to it the way I have. That's OK. My son-in-law thinks it's fantastic that I've hunted all over the world and taken so many animals. He lives in Alaska and has become interested in hunting partly through me. I can't wait to go brown bear hunting with him this fall.

"My grandsons call me Grand Bear and really enjoy my trophy room. I live for the day when I can share with them my love for wildlife and wild places and that great feeling of freedom that comes from hunting. I believe my life's great passion will be teaching my grandchildren to hunt."

Phyllis Tucker truly was born to hunt. "For me," she says, "hunting is life!"

GRAND SLAM FOR A GRAND DAME
CAROLYN WILLIAMS
Desert Bighorn, Muskox, Mule Deer, Cougar,
Shiras Moose, White-tailed Deer

Carolyn Williams thrives on adversity. And the word "can't" isn't in her vocabulary. Her husband, Max, and most of her many friends have seen firsthand what Carolyn is capable of once she makes up her mind. In short, Carolyn Williams is one small, determined dynamo, complete with a Texas drawl that's just about guaranteed to melt the hearts of the toughest hunters, outfitters, and guides in the business.

So once Carolyn set her sights on becoming the second woman in history to complete a firearms Grand Slam of North American Game—dubbed the Super Slam by some and the Twenty-Nine Slam by others—she used every outdoor skill at her disposal and a few feminine wiles, too. She had to do that to convince a few of those hard-nosed fellows mentioned above that she was dead serious about accomplishing her goal. And she would do it in spectacular fashion, too.

Not that anyone who knows her would ever doubt Carolyn's grit and resolve. No one would be so foolish. Still, all twenty-nine species of legal North American big game?

Carolyn today remains fairly blasé about the scope of her accomplishment. Comprehend the trials and tribulations endured by this woman to get the last several animals needed for her Slam, though, and you realize there was nothing blasé in her determination to finish what she'd started. With grace and courage, Carolyn overcame each obstacle in turn to ultimately prevail.

But let's start the story at its beginning.

Although Carolyn Cooper Williams was raised in the country, neither her father nor her mother was a hunter. The young woman attended Southern Methodist University, where she met Max. They soon became engaged, and married in 1960. From the start, Max was eager for Carolyn to become his hunting companion. He badgered her to accompany him on bird hunts. "I wasn't much of a hunter," Carolyn admitted. "But Max took time to show me how to handle and shoot shotguns and rifles." Soon she had acquired skill enough to harvest her fair share of doves and quail.

Max still wasn't satisfied. "One day he said, 'In the morning, join me while I deer hunt for a few hours. You've really never watched the sun come up. I think you'll enjoy it.' I went along, and later that morning, I was there when Max shot a doe.

Carolyn shot one of the best desert sheep taken during 1982, a great ram from Baja California that qualified for the Boone and Crockett record book.

"But I wasn't hooked yet. I remember warning Max, 'Don't you be bringing any mounted heads into our home'."

Max, a star athlete in college, liked to stay busy mentally as well as active physically. He counted golf, tennis, and hunting among his hobbies. Carolyn played some tennis, but no golf. As she pondered hunting's possibilities, she began to warm to the notion.

"We traveled to Africa for a safari in 1974," Carolyn said. "I thought being out in the bush for several weeks while Max was hunting would be a great way to see for myself what hunting would entail. Being with him while he bagged several animals convinced me that hunting looked like fun. I told him I had to try it for myself, so he bought me a few permits." This safari— on which Carolyn shot a nyala, springbok, and impala—served as her initiation into hunting and an auspicious beginning for the drama that would follow.

Carolyn and Max returned to the States, but the die had been cast and things would never again be the same. She soon was hunting white-tailed deer in the south-Texas brush country, then heading west for mule deer, elk, and black bear. In 1980 Carolyn traveled north to Alaska for Dall sheep and Alaskan moose.

"By then I'd decided I'd like a Grand Slam of sheep," Carolyn said. "Sheep seemed like such beautiful and fascinating animals, and fewer than ten women at the time had completed a Grand Slam." Carolyn took her Rocky Mountain goat in 1981, and during the following extremely intense year of hunting, she bagged a Stone sheep, a Rocky Mountain bighorn, and one of the best desert sheep of the year, a great ram from Baja California, that qualified for the Boone and Crockett record book. Carolyn had indeed become one of the first ten women to complete the Grand Slam of sheep, as well as the 336th hunter, male or female, to do so. Don Corley, a friend from Fort Worth, suggested that her next goal should be the even more difficult Twenty-Nine Slam.

"What an adventure!" Carolyn said. "That period of planning and travel was just such great fun. Max and I went everywhere together in search of big-game animals. Nothing can compare with the rapture of sitting alone at the top of a mountain, far above timberline, looking over that endless and beautiful country. It's just a fabulous feeling."

Max and Carolyn had planned to become the first two hunters to complete the Twenty-Nine Slam, but early in their quest the U.S. economy suddenly tanked. "Land prices were plummeting, and banks were failing," Carolyn explained. Max's petrochemical business—he owns U.S. Companies, Inc.—required that he remain close to headquarters during this time of crisis. "I may not be able to go," Max said to his wife. "But I can pay for you to go. Go on without me. Complete your slam."

The bar had been raised. With her husband so solidly supportive of her endeavor, Carolyn dug deep and discovered an inner reserve of fortitude that would help her through the months

Another record-book qualifier, this whitetail sported a rack with 26 scorable points.

and years to come. She would travel alone to the far reaches of the continent in search of those North American game animals she had not yet taken.

"I felt like quitting many times," this petite mother of two admitted. "I remember being out on a dogsled with an Eskimo guide, chasing after caribou and thinking, *I must be nuts!* For all I knew, my guide could have been crazy. He didn't speak a word of English, and I didn't speak Inuit."

216

Despite numerous hardships, Carolyn prevailed. After bagging her muskox, the weather soured and she had to return home rather than continue on after polar bear. Six weeks later she was back. "There's nothing like bouncing along through the Arctic in subzero conditions," she said. "The ocean's waves have frozen into humps and ridges, so the sled ride is anything but smooth. While we were searching for a good muskox, a whiteout suddenly developed. Within minutes neither the guide nor I had any idea where we were or what was around us. The only thing we could do was stop, pitch our tent out on the ice, crawl inside, and go to sleep." The frozen escapade paid off a few days later when Carolyn connected with a muskox that scored high enough to be listed in Boone and Crockett.

Any traditional hunt with the Inuit requires lots of preparation. "You first send your measurements to the Inuit women so they have enough time to cut and sew raw caribou skins into the clothing you'll wear while you're hunting. It's bulky but very warm. The Inuit tan caribou skins the old way: by urinating on them. Above the Arctic Circle, it's so cold that skin clothing rarely thaws. "I grew so attached to this cozy outfit I wanted to bring it back home," Carolyn said. "When I got back and the skins warmed up in this Texas heat, the smell was simply dreadful."

In 1983, the year she bagged her muskox and polar bear, Carolyn also took a Columbian black-tailed deer in California, an Alaskan brown bear, a pronghorn antelope in New Mexico, and one of the largest jaguars ever killed in Mexico. At that time, the U.S. banned imports of both jaguar and polar bear into this country, so she reluctantly left her trophies behind. "I have my photos, though," she said.

In fact, the coveted Twenty-Nine Slam would really be a Thirty Slam were it not for worldwide restrictions against hunting the Pacific walrus. A few years after Carolyn killed her polar bear, restrictions were relaxed and it once again became legal to bring a hunter-harvested polar bear into the United States.

Little by little, Carolyn was closing in on the Twenty-Nine Slam. She allowed herself to be sidetracked only on those occasions when she traveled outside North America to hunt.

Was she ever frightened? "Oh, yes," she said. "One of the worst times occurred in Rhodesia. I'd been hunting Cape buffalo but had not yet taken one. Max and I were returning to the Land Rover and unloading our guns as we walked along. When one of our professional hunters stepped out of the bush, I decided I'd just duck in at that same spot to relieve myself. I did, then walked into an opening and went toward a tree. As I neared the tree I heard a loud roar. A lion was less than thirty yards away and rushing toward me. I backpedaled, yelling, 'He's coming after me!' The men, who

Carolyn's tremendous woodland caribou helped her close in on the Twenty-Nine Slam.

were still back at the vehicle, loaded their guns. As I tried to stay ahead of the lion, I started worrying that the men would come after me, see the lion, and attempt to shoot it with me in the bullet's path. When it was just seven yards from me, it paused, then turned and ran away. We later discovered it was a female protecting her cub."

The year 1984 was shaping up to be a busy and fulfilling one. Carolyn had booked a full schedule of autumn hunts, in addition to agreeing to chair several Dallas charity functions. It was August. Max had planned a trip to the East Coast to play golf, and Carolyn would be traveling with him. On the day they were to leave, Carolyn woke with a terrible headache. "Go on without me," she told her husband. "It's a migraine. I'll be fine by the time you return."

But Carolyn wasn't fine. When she awoke a few mornings later, she immediately realized that something was terribly wrong. A massive cerebral hemorrhage—stroke—had paralyzed her entire right side despite no family history of stroke and Carolyn's excellent physical and cardiovascular condition.

She was raced in an ambulance to a hospital, where she found herself confined to intensive care for two weeks. Then she endured months of painful physical therapy. "The paralysis affected both my tennis playing and my fishing. I could no longer cast with any strength. I was extremely lucky it didn't affect my ability to shoot accurately."

By late October, Carolyn had recovered enough to hunt mule deer on her own in Colorado. The strength in her right leg would never fully return, but her will spurred her onward to continue chasing her dream. Never a word of complaint did she utter. She simply bore down and, as the Texas rangers say, "Just kept on a-comin'." She soon was well enough to travel with Max to south Texas, where she hunted whitetails, javelina, wild boar, and several exotic species. The near-fatal stroke had registered barely a blip on this brave woman's determination meter.

Carolyn now was closing in hard on the Twenty-Nine Slam. In 1985 she bagged Canada moose, mountain caribou, and a tremendous woodland caribou.

She completed a slam of bears in 1986, adding a grizzly to her trophy room after several unsuccessful hunts for this mighty animal. She completed her Deer Slam, too, with the addition of a Sitka blacktail and a Coues whitetail.

The blacktail caused the woman a few anxious minutes when a guide doubted that her 250-yard shot had been true. "I hit that deer," Carolyn said, certain that they'd find the buck close-by. When the two almost stumbled over it after the doubting Thomas had again expressed his feelings, Carolyn was vindicated.

Carolyn that same year closed out the caribou species with a barren-ground, a central barren-ground, and a Quebec-Labrador caribou. One of her most elusive trophies became a possibility in 1986 when she finally secured a Wyoming Shiras moose tag. After stalking for many hours through thigh-deep snowdrifts, Carolyn connected on a Boone and Crockett bull moose.

During 1987 she took a free-ranging bison in the Dakotas and a Roosevelt elk along the California coast. The last animal she needed to complete the Twenty-Nine Slam was the cougar. Carolyn finished off her amazing accomplishment in fine fashion, taking a Boone and Crockett tom on her third hunt for the animal.

When Carolyn Williams looks back at that feat, she takes special pride in knowing that five of the twenty-nine species scored high enough to qualify for Boone and Crockett's *Record Book of North American Big Game*. These trophies include muskox, desert bighorn, Colorado mule deer, whitetail, and Shiras moose. What's more, twenty-three of the twenty-nine are listed in Safari Club International's record book.

When asked about her favorite big-game animals, she replied, "I love to hunt the bears and the big cats. I think they are regal. Leopards were legal the last time we were in Africa. I wouldn't mind returning there to get a leopard and a lion.

"But hunting with Max has been the best thing," she said. "He has always been so proud of me, even though he wasn't able to go with me while I went after the Twenty-Nine Slam."

Maybe that's why the greatest hunting story she could relate took place on the Williams's northwestern Colorado ranch with Max acting as her guide.

Carolyn got up close and personal with this huge Alaskan brown bear.

"We had worked our way to a ridgetop overlooking a huge sagebrush valley," she said. "After I got into position, Max dropped down into the valley to see if he could spot any good bucks while I remained on top. I watched him through my binocular. Before long, he was pointing up my way and frantically motioning me downward. He was holding his arms well above his head to indicate that he could see a big buck somewhere beneath me on the slope. I moved downward until I reached a rock ledge where I would be able to rest my rifle. Finally, I could see the deer below me. I hastily selected a rest for my gun, found the deer in the scope, and squeezed off a shot. When the gun recoiled, I lost the buck.

"Due to circumstances too involved to explain here, I was shooting Max's gun, a Weatherby .270 Magnum, left-handed version," Carolyn explained. "I'm not left-handed, though, so shooting at this buck consisted of making the best of a bad situation. When I looked up, I could see deer bounding off in every direction. The big buck, though, was nowhere in sight. I was devastated! I couldn't understand how I had missed such a large-bodied deer, even shooting left-handed."

Carolyn looked down the slope. Max was motioning for her to stay where she was. "He later told me he'd blinked at the moment I'd shot, so he had also lost track of the deer," she said. "Max began climbing toward me after he'd made certain that none of the fleeing deer was mine. At the same time, I started downward. As I slowly made my way down, I noticed something in a deep ravine that looked like a deer. It was!"

When Carolyn reached her giant muley she discovered that she'd taken the buck of a lifetime: more than 32 inches wide, with ten long tines. The rack would later gross-score 211 and net 198 Boone and Crockett points as a typical.

This outdoor trouper has made the Ten Best-Dressed Dallas Women list numerous times. The list of other honors she has won includes the 1988 Outstanding Hunting Achievement Award of the Dallas Safari Club. She is a member of many hunting and conservation organizations, including the Dallas Safari Club, Safari Club International, Grand Slam Club, and Foundation for North American Wild Sheep. She is a past board member of the Dallas Museum of Natural History, the Susan G. Komen Foundation, and the Kidney Foundation. When she first got involved with the Susan G. Komen Breast Cancer Foundation, Carolyn helped plan the very first breast cancer benefit, which raised nearly one million dollars for research.

On the homefront, Carolyn enjoys cooking for her extended family of husband, children, their spouses, and her two grandsons. She is also a talented interior designer who makes rooms come alive with her excellent taste in fabrics, wallcoverings, furniture, and artwork.

"Neither my daddy nor my mother hunted," Carolyn said. "If Max and I hadn't hunted, our children probably would not have hunted. But both Wayne, our son, and Laura, our daughter, are hunters. My daughter went on one African safari where she had eleven tags and bagged eleven animals, ten of which were one-shot kills. My son's two children, ages fifteen and twelve, are fantastic hunters, too. And while Laura's fiancé had never hunted before meeting her, he's now totally gung-ho for it."

At one time the Williamses owned five ranches, one of them a focal point for wildlife research. "Owning so much land and being so involved with wildlife kept the entire family interested in the outdoors," Carolyn said. "Hunting is a wonderful pastime to pass on to your children and your grandchildren.

"I have always enjoyed the challenge of going up against an animal's incredible instincts. You might see an animal from a great distance and do everything right to get into position to take it, and yet you fail more often than not. Whenever I was able to outwit a wild animal's well-honed instincts, I found it very satisfying. I still love hunting after all these years."

SLAM DUNK
MODESTA WILLIAMS
Rocky Mountain Elk, Canadian Moose, Shiras Moose,
Mountain Caribou, Pronghorn

You could say that Modesta Williams never met a sheep species she didn't want to hunt, assuming it was legal somewhere in the world.

Yes, Modesta Williams is crazy about sheep and sheep hunting. The list of the exotic and desolate places to which she's traveled, combined with the twenty different species of sheep she's taken there, is simply incredible. Only a few men have taken a North American Grand Slam of wild sheep, a World Slam of wild sheep, and a Super Slam of sheep; even fewer women have done so. Modesta is just the second woman in the world to accomplish this grueling task. Micheline Henrijean, a Belgian, beat the beautiful Texan to the punch by completing her Super Slam six months before Modesta, mainly because Micheline was able to hunt in Iran while Americans, like Modesta and her husband, Clayton, can not legally do so. Modesta had nothing but praise for Henrijean. "She's my friend," Modesta said. "I was very happy for Micheline."

Hunting sheep, even under the best of circumstances, can be brutal. "Far from the beaten path" doesn't even begin to describe the high, lonely country where most wild sheep are found. A quest for a Super Slam or an Ovis World Slam means that a hunter must travel to countries as far-flung as Afghanistan, China, Russia, Mongolia, and Nepal. She must be ready, willing, and able to bear the brunt of the fiercest mountain storms, subsist on unfamiliar foods for extended periods at almost incomprehensible altitudes, and attempt to communicate with native guides who don't understand a word of English. Some who have scampered along the rooftops of the world after sheep have perished after lungs or heart gave out. The dedicated sheep hunter defies danger on a regular basis.

Modesta is a woman who willingly traverses glacier fields, skirts the gaping maws of icy crevasses, and contends with unwilling yaks and stubborn asses—not always of the animal variety. And she braves Third World countries where armed conflicts break out with alarming frequency. But only once does she mention feeling dread or uncertainty while in pursuit of the animals that fascinate her so.

"The date was September 11, 2001," she said. "We were in Turkmenistan, where we'd hunted both the Trans-Caspian and Afghan urials. When we came out of the mountains, the driver's first words to us were ominous—there was a lot of news, and none of it was good."

Modesta and Clayton were shocked by the startling images flickering from local TV screens. The terrorist attacks had so adversely affected the political climate that returning to the U.S. would present serious problems. The volatile international situation made the couple rethink their plans to fly directly to Moscow from Turkmenistan and then on to the United States.

Staff members with Clayton Williams Energy, her husband's company, made contact with the couple through the U.S. State Department. Their advice was: "Get out of the Middle East now." Modesta said, "They found us airline tickets from Turkmenistan to Frankfurt, Germany, but before we were able to board, an airline representative halted us, saying, 'The plane is grounded. The Frankfurt airport is completely overloaded, and no flights are taking off.' We boarded anyway, and the plane eventually took off. After thirty-six uncertain hours in Frankfurt, two seats on a Lufthansa flight to Dallas became available, and we bought them. Even Dallas seemed more like a ghost town than a thriving metropolis."

Modesta's 7x7, 1985 bull elk scored over 370 points and just missed making the Boone and Crockett record book.

Modesta's life has been full of spectacular adventure, and yet her family remains her first love and priority. There is Clayton, the husband she married in 1965 and whom she adores. There are the couple's five children: two sons, Clayton and Jeff, and three daughters, Kelvie Muhlbauer, Allyson Groner, and the youngest, Chicora Modesta, affectionately called Chim. There are three grandsons, all avid hunters, and one granddaughter.

Knowing how to shoot various firearms is important to this family, whose roots penetrate deeply into the Texas hardpan. As important is abiding by gun-safety rules. Modesta said, "So much of our life is centered around hunting that we raised our children—boys and girls—to accept guns and hunting but to always be safe. We're gratified that even our daughters-in-law now embrace the sport.

"I started hunting big game in 1966, back when few women hunted anything," Modesta said. "I was born and raised on a ranch just north of Big Spring, Texas. We didn't have deer back then, but I spent many enjoyable hours hunting birds and rabbits. Moving on to bigger game seemed like a natural progression.

"Ever since my first trip to Clayton's deer camp, I've been a proponent of hunt camps open to both men and women. Spending time in a camp where wives and kids are welcome is just such a joy. At our own family deer camp, we reserve the week of Thanksgiving for the kids. Since the youngsters are hunting, many of their mothers visit to see what this sport is all about. You can tell that most of these women have never experienced anything like deer camp. Once they finally allow themselves to be swept up by the sheer fun of the occasion—the big evening campfire, the western music, the chuckwagon meals—they truly enjoy the experience. It's just another small step to where the moms want to try hunting, too."

Modesta attended Texas Christian University in Fort Worth while Clayton went to Texas A&M. A recent one-million-dollar bequest to Texas A&M by Modesta and Clayton was earmarked for improvements to athletic facilities because family members are such diehard Aggie sports fans. Clayton made the pledge at a time when oil prices hovered at a solid twenty-eight dollars a barrel. When the time to donate arrived, however, prices had plunged to ten dollars a barrel. Clayton had to sell one of his companies to make good on his promise.

Modesta first hunted mule deer and then began accompanying her husband in pursuit of species to add to their collections. By the end of the 1970s, Modesta was well on her way to obtaining the four species of wild sheep that comprise the North American Grand Slam: Dall, bighorn, Stone, and desert bighorn. She completed the feat by harvesting a Rocky Mountain bighorn ram

This magnificent mountain caribou scored 405⅞ points SCI and won for Modesta Williams the club's coveted First Place Award in 1980.

in Wyoming. "I've never been what you'd call a lucky hunter," she commented. "I always put in a lot of effort to bag my game."

So far Modesta Williams has taken twenty-six total sheep of twenty different species. "Soon we will return to Russia's Khabarovsk region to try for another snow sheep," she said. "These animals are found at extremely high altitudes, but the country and scenery are truly breathtaking."

Why this fascination with sheep? "It's hard to explain," she said. "Sheep have always been our passion. Our first international hunt took place in 1974 in Afghanistan. Clayton and I started out on Arabian horses and then switched to yaks when the going got rough. We traveled up the Wakhan Corridor, then followed the Marco Polo trail to one of the very places our troops were fighting after September 11. Back then, though, we first spent a week in Afghanistan to get accustomed to the altitude, the people, and their culture while trying to decide if we really wanted to tackle such forbidding mountains. I was familiar with the horror stories about women being beaten and petty criminals being stoned to death in that country. But slowly we came to know and understand the people around us and realized that they were simply good, kind, country people—the kind who were our neighbors back home in Texas, the kind you find wherever people live close to the land."

Modesta paused for a moment, then said, "It's so sad. The people who helped us out back then are probably all dead today. The Russians invaded not long after we left in 1974."

Modesta has climbed to more than 17,000 feet in pursuit of various sheep. "My Marco Polo ram came to rest right at 17,000," she said. "Our camp on that trip was pitched at 14,000."

How can she endure altitudes extreme enough to have killed some sheep hunters? "We were advised never to ride in vehicles or on animals when we got into the mountains," Modesta said. "If you ride, your body and lungs have no chance to acclimate to altitude changes. If you walk everywhere, as tough as the going may seem, your body gradually adjusts. We've taken oxygen bottles along, but thank goodness we've never had to use them."

Modesta cited several adventures that were particularly noteworthy. "Nepal was just breathtaking," she said. "We hunted on foot for twenty-two days at altitudes of 15,500 feet. Afghanistan was wonderful. Another unbelievable trip took place in Mongolia, where we bagged *Ammon ammon* in the Altai."

Wild sheep aren't the only fabulous trophies taken by this stalwart hunter. "Clayton and I were the first to hunt polar bears from traditional dogsleds once outfitters were no longer allowed to hunt the animals with airplanes."

Modesta's Boone and Crockett Canada moose garnered SCI's Gold Award in 1983.

Modesta also bagged a Rocky Mountain bull elk that missed qualifying for Boone and Crockett by one point. And she was charged by a leopard in Africa's Kalahari Desert. "I was lucky," she said. "I came out of that leopard attack with nothing more serious than blood blisters and a tattered tennis shoe."

Her most dangerous experience took place at home. "We raised a few mule deer," she said. "We even let some of them into our house. One day one of our bucks was in a nasty mood. He'd bang the front door with his antlers, then bang the back door. I went out to feed him some cookies to calm him down, but he charged me. He eventually knocked me over and started hitting me with his rack and striking at me with his hoofs." Modesta escaped, but the muley chased her, pinned her against a rock wall, and started raking her with its antlers. When Modesta was finally able to get away for good, she was dripping blood, and the skin hanging from her arm was loose and bloody. "It took the doctors two and a half hours to stitch up my wounds," she said.

Modesta has also taken a huge nontypical pronghorn, a Boone and Crockett Canada moose that scored 195⅛ B&C (206⅝ SCI), and a Shiras moose that also missed making the Boone and Crockett minimum by a single point. One super pronghorn taken on the Williams Ranch in Texas received SCI's 1983 Bronze Award.

The Williamses have hunted extensively in British Columbia, partly because they had the foresight in 1973 to invest in one of the province's premier hunting outfits. "If I were to describe a perfect day of hunting, that would be it," Modesta said. "All our gear stuffed into panniers for the trek into the mountains. Sleeping in tents and breathing in that crisp, clean mountain air. Then riding horseback higher up to search the slopes for sheep. I like the fact that you must get into fantastic physical shape to conquer those mountains. It seems so much easier to communicate with your Maker when you're so close to the clouds."

Modesta collected this 40-inch Dall sheep in 1989 in the Northwest Territories.

Did competition ever rear its ugly head? "Whenever we hunt together, Clayton is a perfect gentleman," Modesta said. "He always insists that I shoot first. When we strike out solo, though, he with his guide and me with mine, the competition increases. He hunts his heart out, and so do I. If I take a bigger animal, he doesn't take it too well."

Modesta Williams is never too busy to serve the less fortunate. She volunteers for the United Way and with Midland Soup Kitchen Ministries, her pet project. She does this even though she runs several large trusts and breeds and raises quarterhorses.

Conservation issues also interest her. "I've just joined the Texas Parks and Wildlife's Trans-Pecos Task Force, which is investigating declines in mule deer and pronghorn populations."

The Williamses are members of the International Sheep Hunters Organization (ISHA) and also of Shikar Safari International, an organization founded in 1952 to advance scientific knowledge about the world's wildlife. They became active in the fight to preserve both the Iranian red sheep (Kermanshah) and the Armenian red sheep. When an opportunity arose in 1983 to buy perhaps the only free-ranging herds of these animals outside Iran, a country closed to American hunters, and China, which had not yet opened to hunters, the Williamses jumped at the chance. Their small herd was kept in a pen at the Williamses' sixty-square-mile High Lonesome Ranch in the rugged Davis Mountains. Embryo transfer allowed wildlife veterinarians to implant eggs from a donor Kermanshah ewe into recipient ewes of other sheep species. In this manner the endangered sheep herds slowly became repopulated until, in 1993, numbers finally reached four-hundred-plus individuals. The sheep then were released to roam free on the ranch. Each year from November through February, a few lucky hunters are allowed to pursue one of these magnificent creatures.

The couple's efforts with red sheep were so successful that they have agreed to work with Texas A&M researchers to help struggling desert bighorns with a similar program.

"We visit our ranch two or three times each month, and I always take the time to climb up into those mountains and simply stare off into the distance. When I do this, I really feel that I know where I came from and why I'm here. It's a spiritual thing, and difficult to explain to anyone who isn't connected to the land. I could never be a city girl. I need the country and its wild creatures to make me feel good. This is who I am. And it's who I always want to be."

A TRUE CONSERVATION LEADER
PEGGY ANNE VALLERY
Desert Sheep

Turkeys gobble in the background when a caller reaches the National Wild Turkey Federation switchboard in South Carolina. One of the leaders of this dynamic conservation group is Peggy Anne Vallery, a true modern conservationist and big-game hunter, not to mention a fanatical wild turkey hunter.

Rob Keck, chief executive officer of the NWTF, without hesitation points to Peggy as a superb volunteer during this, one of the most dynamic times in the organization's history. Since its founding in 1973, NWTF members and affiliate organizations have raised in excess of $150 million and sponsored more than 20,000 projects to benefit wild turkey populations, restore habitat, and promote hunting activities. Thanks to volunteers like Peggy, the wild turkey population has grown from 1.3 million birds in 1973 to more than 5.6 million birds today. NWTF's membership, which started at 1,300, has blossomed to more than 450,000 today, making it one of the most influential and powerful pro-hunting and wildlife conservation organizations in the world. Peggy is one of a handful of NWTF's national leaders.

Her journey began in rural Maryland, where her parents raised champion race and trotting horses. Peggy observed nature and human–animal interactions daily and came to love the outdoors. Meeting her future husband, Clyde, fanned her interest in hunting and conservation work and introduced her to Safari Club International. Clyde, a bird hunter, never shared Peggy's dream of traveling to faraway places to seek big game, but he always encouraged her to participate to the fullest. He readily volunteered to care for their four children while balancing his busy career as partner of an aeronautical engineering and manufacturing company when she left for a trek to some exotic place.

"I made up my mind that I wanted to be the Number 1 woman hunter in the world, so I set a goal of taking all twenty-seven species of North American big game," Peggy explained. She did just that, beginning in 1978 with an Arizona javelina and following up in 1980 with a Dall sheep in Alaska and a Quebec-Labrador caribou in Quebec. The beat continued in the years to follow. Ten of her North American trophies (black bear, bison, Quebec-Labrador caribou, elk, cougar, Canada moose, muskox, desert sheep, Stone sheep, and javelina) are entered in the SCI record book, and her Quebec-

Peggy Anne Vallery with her 161-point desert bighorn sheep.

Labrador caribou is listed in the Boone and Crockett Club's all-time record book.

Her list of African, Asian, European, New Zealand, and Australian big game is equally comprehensive, and includes seventeen specimens taken in 1979, twenty-five in 1980, twenty-two in 1981, and nineteen in 1982. She completed fifteen African safaris and bagged a total of seventy animals over a short period of time, including the Big Five—leopard, lion, Cape buffalo, elephant, and white rhino—and a sable antelope. In Spain Peggy took the world-record Spanish ibex, and she was the first American woman to hunt in Bulgaria, where she took a roe deer as a guest of General Christo Rouskor in 1981. Peggy was the first western woman to hunt in the People's Republic of China, where she took a Himalayan black bear in Upper Manchuria near the Russian border in 1981.

Somehow, during that same time period, Peggy spent countless hours as a volunteer, serving as the first administrative director for SCI's International Wildlife Museum. Her specialty is writing policy and procedure manuals, and this she did for the museum in its various stages of planning. She organized a film festival in Reno that attracted celebrities such as George Peppard and Cheryl Tiegs and raised much money to benefit the new museum.

For a decade Peggy served as president of the Fan Kane Research Fund, which raises money for brain-injured children. From 1994 through 2000, Peggy was chairman of the Off-Road-Vehicle Advisory Board, appointed by Arizona's governor to spend money raised by the state gasoline tax to benefit Arizona trails for outdoor use. She was the only hunter on the seven-member board and knows that her leadership serves as a positive example to others who do not hunt.

Peggy's involvement today reads like a who's-who of those organizations that work to improve wildlife habitat and promote hunting activities. She founded the Southern Arizona Chapter of Quail Unlimited in 1994 and served as its chairman. She was

Her western bongo was killed in Sudan.

233

Peggy Anne Vallery surrounds herself with mounts that remind her of her hundreds of adventures around the world.

involved in hosting one of the first Women in the Outdoors workshops in the United States. And her commitment to NWTF is shown by her Diamond Life Membership.

"Peggy is an incredible resource and asset to our Board of Directors, both personally and professionally," said Keck.

Peggy's professional career spanned stints at *Encyclopaedia Americana* in the accounting department, R. E. Darling Company as an office manager, and efficiency expert and writer of policies and procedures for numerous corporations.

Among her favorite hunts was a quest for a desert bighorn in Baja California. Her guide, Ramon Arce Agundes, met Peggy at the plane and they traveled by pickup truck over a dusty road for two and a half hours. In camp she slept on a cot in a small tent, and was glad she'd brought along a sleeping bag.

"This was one of the most physically and mentally exhausting trips I've ever had, especially toward the end. In Mexico the hunt ends on the tenth day, whether or not you bring out a sheep, and the cost is still $10,000," Peggy explained.

During her ten days, Peggy returned to camp and her sleeping bag for only three nights. The rest of the time was spent hiking farther and farther from camp, climbing mountains, sleeping wherever they were at dark, and eating Spam and tortillas with a few cans of tuna fish and fruit cocktail mixed in for good measure. On the last day, Ramon spotted a legal ram on a distant mountain and motioned for Peggy to run closer since the sun was setting and time was running out.

"For about thirty-five minutes I found myself running across rocks. The rocks were sliding, and I could look down several hundred feet," she remembered.

They lost track of the ram, and Peggy was frantically searching with her binocular when Ramon pushed her down and pointed to where the ram stood 190 yards away. Peggy trusted Ramon's judgment that it was a legal ram, raised her 7mm Weatherby, and fired. A second shot put it down for good. The green score of the horns was 161 points—a ram for the record book.

Peggy's memories also are vivid of a cougar hunt in New Mexico with guide Orvel Fletcher of Santa Fe and his famous dogs. For four days they worked three teams of dogs so that each animal received two days of rest after a full working day. Peggy was introduced to a mule that insisted upon brushing her body against prickly trees she was certain could have been avoided.

At the end of the fifth day, Orvel announced they would relocate to another area, but he added that she would have to collect her cougar with bow and arrow as no gun was allowed there. Peggy was game, so off they went into higher mountains where snow and ice remained on the trail. About 10 A.M. they located a lion kill, and the hounds raced off on a fresh cougar trail. Peggy strained her ears to hear the distant wail of the dogs. Eventually the female cougar ran up a small scrub pine. Old Brandy, one of the lead dogs, stood on a boulder below the cat with blood running from where the cougar had slashed him.

Peggy got off her mule, walked within fifteen feet of the cougar, pulled the bow back, and lined up on its shoulder. A single shot and the cougar dropped.

"Not a really big lion," Orvel remarked, "but a good fighter."

That was about the highest compliment Orvel Fletcher would likely pay to anyone or anything.

Peggy Anne Vallery remains an inspiration to current and future hunters and to anyone who wishes to become involved with the modern wildlife conservation movement.

A PHOTO GALLERY

Marnett Love-Hamrick

Marnett Love-Hamrick had to act fast to get a shot at her Kodiak brown bear.

Marnett Love-Hamrick has hunted both in North America and in Africa. She has taken nine trophy animals by Safari Club International standards. A Limpopo bushbuck and klipspringer both rated Gold Awards, while Marnie's common nyala rated a Silver Award. She garnered Bronze Awards for her Livingston eland, southern impala, leopard, southern greater kudu, and blesbok.

Marnett Love-Hamrick lives in Alaska, home to a place where the williwaw gusts violently (which is a Native American word for "a very strong wind," and the *permafrost heaves and buckles. She has climbed the banks of pingos—the upheavals in the tundra that catch snowmelt to form small ponds or lakes—and she has gazed from great heights upon this Land of the Midnight Sun that she has made her own.*

"When I was hunting Kodiak brown bear, Michael and I climbed a small mountain behind camp to glass," Marnie said. "After climbing for an hour and a half, we settled down to rest while we glassed the mountain slope opposite. I looked down the slope and saw a bear walking along the river just a hundred yards from our tent. His pelt was thick and beautiful, its color dark brown with reddish highlights. I asked Michael to check him out for size while I gathered my gear. When Michael said 'He's a keeper!' I raced back down the slope in seven minutes that had taken me an hour and a half to conquer. At the bottom of the hill we shed our packs and took off after the bear. We slipped up behind the animal, but he moved off after spotting us. Rather than chasing after him, we followed the riverbank. I reached one sharp bend where a clean shot from a hundred yards presented itself. My first shot with the .375 magnum Bearclaw bullet hit him solidly, but I had to shoot twice more before he was down for good."

Marnett Love-Hamrick's common nyala was recognized with SCI's Silver Award.

Janice L. Hemingson

Janice Hemingson, surrounded by her hunting companions, sits beside her B&C Rocky Mountain billy goat in 1988 when she became one of only three hunters in Colorado to collect a trophy mountain goat. The goat scored 51 points. Her hunting buddies include, left to right: Larry Lindholm, Steve Pickett, and her husband, Jim. (Photograph courtesy of Janice L. Hemingson)

Janice Hemingson never intended to take a Boone and Crockett Club billy goat when she left for her long-awaited hunt with husband, Jim, and friends Steve Pickett and Larry Lindholm on 24 September 1988, but she did anyway. Janice hunts because she loves spending time in the wilderness far away from the grind of everyday life. She has discovered that half the fun of hunting is finding wildlife in its natural habitat. She hunts whenever she has free time from her normal duties as a high school principal. To date, though, she has never yet seen anything quite as impressive as her B&C goat.

Janice was merely trying to get a clean shot when she collected this outstanding trophy. She will forever remember the moment as the hunt of her lifetime. After putting her goat down for good, Janice de-boned the meat for the pack trip back out to civilization. She then carried the rifle and day packs, while Jim packed out the heavy cape, and their two friends transported the meat.

Janice, a teacher at the time, asked Greg Brown, a former student as well as an accomplished taxidermist, to mount the animal's head. It was Greg who arranged to have the magnificent set of horns officially scored. Janice's billy is one of only nine Rocky Mountain goats taken in Colorado to qualify for listing in the B&C record book. It currently ranks as the second largest goat ever taken in Colorado.

Carolyn Zanoni

Hunting has been her life, a fact illustrated by the span of forty years in which legendary bow hunter, Carolyn Zanoni, broke new ground for female hunters while also putting big-game animals in the record book. Carolyn now is content to ponder the many happy memories she made while bowhunting throughout North America with her husband, George.

Carolyn grew up in Quincy, Illinois. Although she admits to having been a tomboy, she had no experience with hunting at all until the fateful day she joined her high school's archery club. One auspicious day in 1957, the young woman headed out with her bow to later collect her first game animals: several cottontail rabbits, which were then abundant near her prairie home. Carolyn, whose maiden name was Siebrasse, completed her education to become a registered nurse. She collected her first trophy white-tailed buck in 1961. The big 12-pointer stood not only as the largest buck killed to date during a modern Illinois bowhunting season, but it also placed second in the National Field Archery Association's (NFAA) Prize Buck Contest. The buck's rack can still be found gracing the records of the Pope and Young Club with a still impressive score of 131⅝ points.

Carolyn Zanoni's was the first Pope and Young Club white-tailed buck taken in Illinois. It was shot near Quincy, Illinois, in November 1961.

Linda Peters

Hunting in bare feet has become Linda's trademark. For her Boone and Crockett white-tailed deer hunt, Linda concentrated her efforts on a thirty-acre thicket of briars and honeysuckle located on her own Midwestern farm. Neighbors had told her that they'd seen a huge buck traveling back and forth among their various farms. Linda decided that the overgrown thicket, crisscrossed with winding paths and narrow logging roads, would be an ideal hideout for a wise, old trophy-class white-tailed deer.

Linda spotted the buck twice in 1997 before she got down to the serious business of actually hunting the animal in 1998. The rut was underway when Linda decided to use the tactic of grunting like a white-tailed buck to attract deer. As she completed her calls, she looked behind her just as, against all odds, "her buck" stepped from the thicket only two hundred feet distant. The buck was savvy enough to remain partially hidden behind several white oaks that grew near the thicket's edge. Linda hurriedly plotted her strategy. Thinking that the buck probably would re-enter the thicket to travel along a nearby woodland road, the woman carefully removed her shoes so that she could move more quietly. The thick woolen socks she wore not only protected her feet from pebbles and sharp sticks jutting from the ground, they muffled the sound as she crept quietly to the place where she thought she might intercept the mighty buck. The date was 18 November, so the socks also protected Linda's feet from the bitter Midwestern weather.

Linda hurried up the hill in the opposite direction taken by the buck. She reached another faint road where she stopped to catch her breath. After waiting a full minute, the hunter started following this second wooded road. She soon began to glimpse flashes of the buck through the brush. The game of cat and mouse continued as Linda trailed the buck and the buck kept a wary eye upon Linda. Although the wind was in the woman's favor, she was unable to see the buck's antlers clearly through the dense undergrowth. She finally halted altogether, hoping the buck would mistakenly continue to walk through one of the small openings in the brush. As she waited, one tine (G-1) almost magically appeared through the brushy maze. It was BIG! Then, in the blink of an eye, the buck's neck could be seen within a small, five-inch square hole in the tangle of brambles and brush. The animal had turned! Breathing deeply, Linda squeezed the trigger as she chanced a close, offhand shot with her Remington rifle, chambered for .270 Winchester. Linda's perseverance and extraordinary woodsmanship were rewarded when the huge Boone and Crockett buck dropped in its tracks. The tremendous rack later scored an impressive 205⅝ points.

"Giant!" was the simple statement scrawled across the official score sheet of Linda Peters's 1998 nontypical white-tailed buck. It measured 205⅝ points, with a right main beam antler of 26⅝ inches and a left main beam of 27⅝ inches. To Linda, this massive buck represented three generations of sound farm practices begun by her grandparents during the Great Depression.

Elisha G. Hugen

NASCAR racing, white-tailed deer hunting, and sharing the outdoors with son, Eric, are Elisha Hugen's three passions in life.

Elisha began hunting with her father, Don, and two older brothers, Tim and Terry, while she was still a girl growing up in rural Iowa. She is grateful to her parents because they never discouraged her from hunting, fishing, or trapping. Elisha was a tomboy from the start. Playing with dolls or engaging in "dress up" simply never appealed to this young, outdoors girl. Elisha remembers driving her brothers crazy when the three were youngsters. No matter where the two boys wanted to go, exploring deep into the timber or hanging out down by the creek, Elisha did her best to tag along with them. Her parents didn't mind. Neither seemed to find anything unusual about a daughter who preferred outdoors activities like hunting over other, more traditional feminine pastimes. The active young tomboy has grown up to become a lovely young wife and mother who hones her bowhunting, trapping, and angling skills with her favorite companions, her husband and son.

When Elisha downed the mighty whitetail whose image graces these pages, she knew at once that the animal's rack was big. She had no idea, though, that it was big enough to qualify for listing in Boone and Crockett until one visitor after another, and then her taxidermist, insisted that the huge whitetail was something special. Elisha previously had taken other, average-sized white-tailed bucks. When the big one finally showed up, it took her by surprise.

The minimum scores required for entry into Boone and Crockett's two awards programs are 160 points for the awards book, and 170 points for hunting's Holy Grail, the all-time record book. Elisha's buck qualified easily for the all-time record book with a score of 182⅜ points. The rack's greatest spread measures 26⅝ inches, while the two main beams tallied an impressive 27⅞ inches on the right side and 26⅝ inches on the left. Before the meager 3⅜ inches of deductions for irregularities, Elisha's buck's rack had attained a whopping 188⅞-point gross score.

Elisha Hugen stands beside her B&C buck that was mounted by Marlin Hoch of Hoch's Taxidermy in Dallas, Iowa. The buck has been on display at various sports shows and featured in numerous publications.